# Pictures at an Execution

WENDY LESSER

HARVARD UNIVERSITY PRESS

Cambridge, Massachusetts
London, England

Copyright © 1993 by Wendy Lesser
All rights reserved
*Printed in the United States of America*
Second printing, 1995


First Harvard University Press paperback edition, 1995

Library of Congress Cataloging-in-Publication Data
Lesser, Wendy.
    Pictures at an execution / Wendy Lesser.
        p.      cm.
    Includes bibliographical references.
    ISBN 0-674-66735-2 (cloth)
    ISBN 0-674-66736-0 (pbk.)
    1. Murder in mass media. I. Title.
    P96.M85L47    1993
    302.23—dc20                                                                93-7336
                                                                               CIP

# FOR ARTHUR LUBOW
*the reporter who doesn't look away*

# Acknowledgments

Several initiating factors made this book possible. One was a course I taught at the University of California, Santa Cruz, which gave me a number of the central ideas; for these, I am grateful to my students in American Literature 140N, alias "Murder." Second, I owe an unrepayable debt to William Bennett Turner, who alerted me to the issues involved in the legal case *KQED v. Vasquez,* generously put his office and his staff at my disposal, and kindly checked the manuscript for legal inanities. Third, I wish to thank the National Endowment for the Humanities, which supported me with a Senior Fellowship during the year it took me to write the book.

I have been collecting some of this information for so long, and have come across other bits so casually, that it would be impossible to thank everyone who helped with the book. Of those who stand out at this end of the process, I would like to mention James Billings, Michael Covino, Nancy Goldman, Thom Gunn, Thomas Laqueur, Lisa Mann, Leonard Michaels, Errol Morris, Irene Oppenheim, Robert Post, Joanne Sutro, Deborah Treisman, and Steve Vineberg. For help in the actual writing, I particularly want to single out Phillip Lopate, Arthur Lubow, Christopher Ricks, and Erik Tarloff, each of whom kindly, thoroughly, and intelligently went through a draft of the manuscript and offered invaluable suggestions. My agent, Gloria Loomis, read *every* draft and remained a stalwart friend throughout. My editor, Lindsay

Waters, and the wonderful staff at Harvard University Press—Lisa Clark, David Foss, Jean Heffernan, Alison Kent, Claire Silvers, and especially Camille Smith—have continued to earn my greatest respect and gratitude for their honorable dealings with the printed word and image. Howard Brodie, Susan Kismaric, Liz Portland, and JoAnne Seador all went beyond the call of duty to get me the pictures I needed. Finally, no acknowledgments would be complete without thanks to the Rizzos: my son, Nicholas, who learned more about the death penalty than any child of seven ought to know, and my husband, Richard, who came up with the title for the book. I know it has not been an easy book to live with, and I am enormously grateful to them for living through it with me.

# Contents

# Illustrations

# Pictures at an Execution

# 1

# What Draws Us

I am interested in our interest in murder. Specifically, I am drawn to the increasingly blurry borderline between real murder and fictional murder, between murder as news and murder as art, between event and story. I say "increasingly," but it is not clear that these categories were ever easily separable. Plato, in his complaint about the mimetic poets and tragedians, was convinced that their stories had a practical, often negative effect on the behavior of their audiences. His rationale for banning poets from the ideal republic—"the imitative poet produces a bad regime in the soul of each private man by making phantoms that are very far removed from the truth and by gratifying the soul's foolish part. . . . it succeeds in maiming even the decent men"—has been used ever since to object to violent or otherwise offensive art. One hears echoes of it in the anxieties that gave rise to the 1986 Meese Commission on Pornography or in the even more recent feminist denunciations of violently pornographic art. None of the high-minded commissions assigned to investigate the connection between spectatorship and violent behavior has been able to come up with a causal link, despite the fact that this was the one thing they all desperately wanted to demonstrate, but the question is constantly raised anew. It is not a question that seems likely either to be resolved or to disappear; we have always been worried that made-up stories might give rise to undesirable activities.

But there is something new, I think, in our increasing tendency to move in the opposite direction: to convert real-world murder into made-up stories, or into artworks that offer the same satisfactions as made-up stories. Works like Truman Capote's *In Cold Blood*, Norman Mailer's *The Executioner's Song*, Errol Morris's *The Thin Blue Line*, and Janet Malcolm's *The Journalist and the Murderer* characterize our era. In the course of drawing on real murders to feed our wish for narrative, they also comment on our preoccupation with murder stories. Even the movie *The Silence of the Lambs*, garishly and self-proclaimedly theatrical as it was, seemed eerily connected to reality, referring backward to the 1950s crimes of Ed Gein—a killer who skinned and stuffed his female victims—and, more surprisingly, forward to Jeffrey Dahmer, whose cannibalistic antics hit the little screens only a few months after Hannibal Lecter's reached the big ones.

My delight in Hannibal Lecter, or in Anthony Hopkins's portrayal of Hannibal Lecter, and my more guarded, more disgusted and perhaps self-disgusted, but still admissible curiosity about Jeffrey Dahmer, do not set me apart as an eccentric in late-twentieth-century America. On the contrary. We all seem to be interested in murderers these days. They are our truth and our fiction; they are our truth *as* fiction, and vice versa. I want to ask, in this book, why that should be so.

I don't intend to ask the question about what effect the witnessing of murder—in books, in movies, on television, in the newspapers, whether real or fictional or somewhere in between—has on our collective or individual behavior. I doubt that it can be answered, and in any case the tools for even attempting to answer it lie far beyond my reach, in realms where sociologists rush in. It seems to me that the kind of experiment needed to demonstrate a causal connection between spectatorship and violent behavior would, if accurately conducted, be so morally reprehensible as to invalidate the results.

But that particular question is not the only one worth asking about the connection between art and murder. There are questions about murder that can be asked and answered by a person sitting alone at a desk. This book is not a work of philosophy, nor is it a work of literary criticism; but it will be asking the kinds of questions that are asked, or used to be asked, by philosophers, and it will be using the techniques and materials of literary criticism in an attempt to answer them. Why are we drawn to murder, as an act and as a spectacle? Who in the murder story are we drawn to—the victim, the murderer, the detective? Why, in particular, are we so interested in *seeing* murder, either enacted or caught in the act? What are the sources of pleasure in a murder story, and how do those kinds of pleasure connect with any sense of the morally suspect or reprehensible? *Is* it morally reprehensible to take an interest in murder, and is it possible to talk about such things without sounding either self-righteous or sleazy?

I take the word "interest" to be the appropriate one here, signaling, in its opposition to "disinterest," our involvement in the subject, our complicity in its ethical implications. (This is not to disparage disinterestedness; we may need to bring to bear our best efforts at disinterested analysis if we are to uncover the nature of our interest.) I also view "interest" as appropriately understated: "fascination" or "obsession," while accurate for some, overstates the general case, while modifiers like "ghoulish" and "depraved" tilt the argument unfairly from the beginning. The question of whether there is indeed anything wrong with such an interest is part of what I hope to explore.

The answer to this question seems simple if we apply it to, say, mystery novels. Very few people would condemn the readers of murder mysteries as depraved or ghoulish or otherwise morally inadequate. But the question gains more pressure, more immediacy, the further we move away from the neatly contrived and the artificially resolvable. In particular, the question seems to alter as we move from the realm of fiction to the realm of the explicitly real. If it is acceptable to be interested in fictional murders, is it equally or similarly acceptable to be interested in real ones? Why does it matter that we be able to tell the difference between real and fictional murders? Ought our interest in seeing a murder enacted be allowed to extend to watching someone killed before our very eyes?

This is not a merely hypothetical question. In 1991, a trial held in San Francisco asked, and temporarily answered, the question of whether a television station should be allowed to record and broadcast the execution of a condemned man in the California gas chamber. That legal case, *KQED v. Daniel B. Vasquez*, will provide the central framework of my discussion in this book, for in the course of the trial there emerged all sorts of information and ideas about how we respond to murder as spectacle. At present, in America, any state-run execution will be that of a murderer, since murder, for at least the last two decades, has been the only crime for which civilians are put to death. An execution is itself the only kind of murder that is planned and publicly announced in advance, so that we know exactly who the victim will be and when he will die. It is thus the only form of murder that anyone but the murderer and the victim could count on attending. (Come to think of it, anyone but the murderer; the victim always has to be there too, but, except in the case of executions, he won't *count* on it in advance.) As a killing carried out in all our names, an act of the state in which we by proxy participate, it is also the only form of murder that directly implicates even the witnesses, the bystanders.

Supporters of capital punishment, and even some of its opponents, will want to argue at this point that execution is not equivalent to murder. I agree that they are not identical categories. Some kinds of murder, particularly those enacted in the heat of passion, bear no external resemblance to executions, which are by definition planned and coldblooded. Some executions—of Nazi concentration-camp directors, for instance, or professional torturers—might be viewed by most people as "justified"; but then, some private murders—those committed in self-defense, or in response to extreme abuse— are also described that way. We tend to say that if a killing is justified, it is not murder. But the definition of what is justifiable alters over time. The fact that the majority supports something, as eighty percent of Californians and more than half of all Americans are presently said to support capital punishment, does not mean that it can be justified in moral terms; the majority used to support slave-owning, vigilante lynching, hand-removal for stealing, and other forms of torture that we now consider barbaric. For my purposes, execution shares enough of the characteristics of murder to be counted as part of the general category: it includes a victim who does not want to die, and an agent that nonetheless kills him. And execution has special characteristics—in particular, that it can be watched, and *is* watched—which make it more accessible than most other kinds of murder.

Some may agree with me that an execution is murder, but may feel that the execution of a murderer (or, for that matter, the mob lynching or jailhouse stabbing of that same murderer) is a less reprehensible murder than a similar act committed against someone who is not a criminal. There is a tendency, that is, to take into account the relative innocence or goodness of the victim when measuring the seriousness of the crime of murder—a tendency that has recently been formalized in some American courtrooms, where a separate hearing on the *victim's* character is held before sentencing takes place in a murder case. This seems to me a wrong tack for jurisprudence, not to mention morality, to take. If someone murders a complete stranger, how can she be held accountable for whatever meritorious qualities her victim had? How can those qualities enter in any way into our judgments about motive or intention or responsibility, which should be central to our judgments about murder? Should the killer of a small child be punished more than the killer of a rambunctious teenager? Should the murderer of a United States president (surely one of the less innocent jobs a person can hold, since even the best presidents have to make hard, sacrificial choices) be less intensely condemned than the killer of a comparatively innocent, law-abiding, household-supporting factory worker? How are we defining innocence? Does Freud come in, for instance? (In which case we may even hold the small child responsible for such un-innocent qualities as perverse sexuality and homicidal wishes.)

Such questions sound ridiculous, but the jurisprudential trend toward taking into account the victim's character as a measure *in itself* of the crime's seriousness seems no less ridiculous to me. To link the severity of our judgments about murder to the murder victim's character is to perform the same theoretical operation that Raskolnikov did when he decided the old pawnbroker was an expendable person. As Dostoyevsky suggests, it is not up to us to make such judgments. Murder is a variable crime whose degree of criminality can be defined in part by the murderer's intentions and in part by her relation to her victim. (I want to stress that "in part," for motive, intention, and relation to the victim are not all that affect our judgment about murder. Luck, for instance, comes into the determination. If someone recklessly drives a car into someone else and the victim dies, the driver is guilty of murder in a way that she is not if, as a result of exactly the same actions and intentions on her part, the victim suffers only a broken leg.) But the seriousness of, and hence the just punishment for, a particular crime of murder can never be determined by the victim's character alone. So while the convicted murderer may not be an *innocent* victim, her murderousness in itself does not prevent her from being a victim of full-fledged murder.

As you may have gathered, I do not approve of the death penalty, and that attitude will naturally color my coverage of *KQED v. Vasquez*. It will not, however, determine my response to the central question in the case—whether executions should be televised or not—for there were critics of capital punishment on both sides. Some death-penalty opponents insisted that televising executions would cause people to vote against capital punishment, others that these broadcasts would only arouse the population's bloodlust. I don't know which, if either, of these predictions is the correct one; as I said, the effects of art and media on behavior are not my concern here. What I find useful in the legal case is the way it opens up and clarifies some of the other questions that concern me about our interest in murder.

Specifically, the case of *KQED v. Vasquez* points up the crucial connection between murder and theater—between death imposed on a human being by another human being, and dramatic spectacle. This connection is not limited to murder's inclusion as a plot device in theater, though that is importantly there, from Agamemnon's, Clytemnestra's, and Orestes' murders of their various family members, through Shakespeare's tragedies and the bloody Jacobean dramas, to that debased modern version, the murder-mystery play that runs for years if not decades on Broadway or in the West End. Nor am I referring only to the theoretical overlap between theater's way of working on its audience and the fascinations of violent spectacle, though that too is there, in Artaud's elaborations of his Theater of Cruelty, in Brecht's discussions of his "alienation effect," and in other analyses of drama's assaultive function. All these connections remind us that there is a profound and historical link between murder and theater. But what has especially struck me, in thinking about *KQED v.*

*Vasquez,* is the way the murderer takes on the role of the central performer in his plot, converting us by default into audience members. While this figure of speech can be applied to all chronicled or broadcast murders, it is actually true in the case of an execution, where the murderer himself is murdered before the eyes of assembled spectators — where the murderer, for once, becomes a victim as well as a killer. Thinking about execution and its real or potential witnesses can help us to understand why and how we identify with the various participants in a murder story. It instructs us about the ways in which murder plays on our desire for a story that will take us out of ourselves. It allows us to focus on our suspicions about the reliability of sense data and visual evidence. It also offers us new realizations about the link between pleasure and horror.

My questions and concerns about murder don't fit neatly into the subdisciplines — ethics, aesthetics, epistemology — that philosophers have devised for us. Rather, my investigations suggest that these areas overlap in important ways, so that some of our pressing ethical questions (for instance: How much should we be allowed to indulge our interest in and curiosity about murder in the face of another person's death? What harm, to the murdered person or to ourselves, do we do by using someone's murder as the occasion for our entertainment or instruction?) can be answered in part by exploring aesthetic questions (How does art work on us, and in what ways does fictional art differ from "true-life" art or unshaped life?) and epistemological questions (How do we take in and interpret information if we are present at an event, as opposed to seeing it on television or in a movie or reading about it in a novel or a newspaper? How is experience mediated, and how do different kinds of mediation make themselves felt to us?). Murder, as a subject, makes us especially aware that such questions, like their answers, do not fit into one philosophical division or another, but cut across divisions.

This is why a book like Joel Black's *The Aesthetics of Murder* announces its shortcomings as early as its title. From that unpromising beginning, Black goes on to assert that our "experience of murder and other forms of violence is primarily aesthetic, rather than moral, physical, natural, or whatever term we choose as a synonym for the word *real*"; that it can therefore "be subjected to the same kind of inquiry that literary historians and critics practice in the case of texts"; and thus that "murder can be studied in a relatively disinterested mode as a morally neutral phenomenon." As a summary of much contemporary criticism this can't be improved upon, and I hope it will explain, in part, why I have chosen to emphasize my use of the word "interest."

I have suggested that I too would be practicing the techniques of literary criticism, but I think I mean by this something very different from what Black means. I mean, first of all, that my "we" is really "I." My starting point in writing about murder will be my own visceral reactions, my own interpretations of language and image, as filtered through the reading and looking and thinking I've done on the subject. I also mean that the writing and images I examine will be scrutinized closely—more closely than we are accustomed to doing in everyday conversation. I will be applying this kind of scrutiny to a wide variety of forms not all of which are traditionally viewed as art, ranging from the legal case itself to novels about trials, from fictionalized versions of real murders to nonfiction documentaries, from theatrical renderings of stagy deaths to sketches, photographs, and eyewitness accounts of actual murders and executions, from beautifully crafted works of fiction to newspaper articles, true-crime books, and television shows. For a critic to be inclusive in material considered—unsigned press clippings as well as Dostoyevsky novels, "Columbo" as well as *Macbeth*—is not to deny the importance of hierarchies, of discriminations. On the contrary, inclusiveness requires us to sharpen the discriminating tool itself, applying it to whatever lies at hand, so that we can actually see why this newspaper article is better than that one, this TV episode superior to its predecessor. Criticism is not an airlessly secluded, primly aesthetic task; it is a part of daily life, and making such distinctions is an important aspect of that life. Here I side with T. S. Eliot, who said that one function of criticism was "to exhibit the relations of literature — not to 'life,' as something contrasted to literature, but to all the other activities, which, together with literature, are the components of life."

If I want to answer the question of why we are drawn to murder, I must begin by asking myself why I am drawn, or at any rate how. I'm not sure when I first got interested in the subject of murder and its renderings. I know I followed with great eagerness, as did hundreds of thousands of others, the serial publication of *In Cold Blood* in *The New Yorker* during the mid-1960s. At about the same time I read *Anatomy of a Murder* and decided on its basis that I was going to become a lawyer. (Luckily this decision was later rescinded.) But I was not yet a regular reader of murder mysteries, or a willing viewer of any movie on TV that featured a serious murder plot.

No, I think my intense, some might say obsessive interest in the topic came later, when I was in my early twenties and the century in its mid-seventies. Perhaps the initiating experience was an adult education literature course I taught on the campus of the University of California at Berkeley with my friend and fellow graduate student Katharine Ogden. Intended to attract university employees during their nonworking hours, the class also contained a range of other students, including back-to-school housewives, elderly immigrants, and one rather sullen young man (though he was probably older than Katharine and I were at the time) who announced that he was taking the course only because "my P.O. made me." In our innocence, we had no idea what he meant; only later did we determine that he was referring to his parole officer.

About four weeks into the class, this student—who used the nickname "Crip" for reasons that never became apparent to us; he signed his papers "Eugene 'Crip' Taylor," like a politician or a prizefighter—turned in the most remarkable document I've ever received from a student. In response to our assignment to write some kind of memoir or fictionalized memoir, Crip produced a thirty-page epic poem in free verse, consisting of nine views of the same story told by nine different people affiliated, either by blood, marriage, or friendship, with an Oakland ghetto family. The central plot involved an armed hold-up of a drugstore in which one brother—the most innocent of the gang, practically a bystander—was killed by the stray bullet of a friend, as a result of which another brother, rather than the guilty friend, took the rap and went to jail for the killing. It was an Oakland *Rashomon,* with one or two of the voices coming from beyond the grave; or it was an Oakland *The Sound and the Fury,* with a Jason-Compson-like stepfather who figured meanly in some of the teenaged children's early "chapters" and later came in to present his viewpoint more sympathetically in a chapter of his own.

Astounded by this epic, Katharine and I decided to have Crip read it aloud to the other students in the class. He read it well, and they too were stunned. After a moment of appreciative silence, they began raising their hands and asking him questions about what had happened "since then" to the various members of the family. There was no question in their minds that this was a real story, no doubt—despite the multiple viewpoints, the voices from beyond the grave, the poetic structure, the obvious *artistry* of the whole piece—that Crip could provide factual answers about each person's fate. Which he proceeded to do.

"And what happened to the brother that went to jail?"

"Still there."

"And what happened to the friend?"

Did Crip pause for a moment before answering, or do I only imagine that now? "I'm the friend," he replied.

This time the silence was deeper and more pronounced than before. It contained elements of shock, and embarrassment, and awe. In front of us, in our own classroom, sat a self-confessed murderer, if he could be believed (but none of us doubted him for a moment)—a murderer who was nonetheless, or therefore, an extremely talented writer. The silence lasted uncomfortably long, and then one of the students politely broke it with an obviously artificial question about literary technique. But it was Crip's final remark about life in Oakland that stayed with me. "You got to remember," he said, "that when you're out on the street there, it doesn't feel like real life. It's like you're in a movie all the time. That's how you think about it—like you're a character in a movie."

About fifteen years later, I offered a literature course called "Murder" to undergraduates at the University of California at Santa Cruz. Between my first teaching experience with Crip's class and this later venture, a number of developments had taken place in the murder industry, including the publication or presentation of at least a third of the works I was using in the course (Mailer's *The Executioner's Song,* Joan Didion's "The White Album," and Morris's film *The Thin Blue Line* among them). Following the 1976 lifting of the Supreme Court's ban on capital punishment, the death penalty had been re-adopted in the majority of states, including California. And, in general, interest in murder as both a terrifying social phenomenon and a source of grisly entertainment was burgeoning.

At my first meeting with the predictably oversubscribed class, I explained why I thought murder was a good way into the discussion of literature. "It raises all kinds of questions about sympathy and identification," I said to them. "After all, we're all here because we're interested in murder, and yet no one in this classroom is actually a murderer." Amid the polite laughter, I saw two of the students—well-dressed, suburban-looking young men—exchange a covert glance. Leopold and Loeb? I hardly think so. But it did make me think back to the time I'd taught a literature class that *did* contain a murderer, which in turn made me feel chastened about assuming who "we" in the class were.

Whodunit: even that murder-mystery moniker suggests the extent to which questions about murder are usually questions about identity. The issue is not just who committed the crime, and what kind of person one would have to be to do that; it is also who would be interested in such a crime, as either news or entertainment, and what that interest says about us.

At the end of my Santa Cruz course, one of the students said: "I've really enjoyed the course, but I'm worried that it's hardened me. I mean, I don't know how seriously I take murder any more."

"Yes," I agreed with her, "that's the risk. If you start looking at it as art, you move away from the thing itself."

But part of the problem, I have come to feel, is that one never *can* get at the thing itself. That is the fascination of murder as a subject, and why it lends itself to all kinds of renderings, from the true-life to the highly artful. It is also what makes murder so difficult to write about, as I've discovered in the course of putting together this book. Murder is an inherently frustrating subject because it keeps moving away from us, evading us. We want to ask big questions; more than anything else, we want to get the *answers* to big questions. Yet all we can get at, finally, are the details. That's why the enjoyment of murder (if enjoyment doesn't seem too heartless a word here) always consists of wallowing in the gory details. The details are all we can grasp.

Our interest in the details is not just an indication of our sleazy character. It also signals our admiration of craft, which can only be admired at the level of detail, where small signs and acute discriminations matter. An interest in murder crucially involves the admiration of craft—the craft of the murderer himself (this is why all "Columbo" episodes focus so lovingly on the initial design and execution of the murder plot) as well as the craft of the detective who exposes him. A recent newspaper article on the good new TV series "Law and Order" describes how one of the chief actors in the show, Chris Noth, followed around some Manhattan police detectives to observe their technique. Noth and the officers together visited a suspect's apartment, but the interrogation initially revealed nothing.

> Later, Mr. Noth recounts, on the way downstairs, one of the detectives said: "'I can't get over the fact that I smelled death up there. Let's go back.'" The punch line, of course, is that they found the body in the apartment.
> "The detective smelled death," Mr. Noth says, admiringly.

Noth admires the detective's craft, as we, watching the show, admire Noth's: both his craft as a detective, conveying what he learned from the real policemen, and his craft as an actor, embodying that knowledge and making it real to us. And whether watching or reading a murder story, we also admire the craft of the author who has shaped that story. This too, like our admiration for the actor-detective, manifests itself simultaneously on two levels: on the one hand in our involvement in the story, our immersion in its thrills; and on the other hand in our detached, critical admiration for the intellectual achievement of a tightly knit tale.

All representational art is, to a certain extent, about the difference between shaped art and unshaped reality. As readers or viewers of a fictional work, we are meant to be taken in, to be deluded into believing, and we are also meant to understand that what we are believing in is not real, is not life on the same order or under the same rules as we live it. Murder is a special instance of this general pattern, for whereas murder in real life is, for those directly involved in it, a tragedy, or at the very least a depressingly squalid event, murder in fiction is often a game, and always a drama.

One can reasonably argue that this distinction is true of all mimetic plots, or at any rate a large number of them. Rape, seduction, adultery, divorce, child abuse, con artistry, theft, unrequited infatuation, marital squabbling, death by old age, death by illness, death by suicide ... these events, sordid or tedious as they may be in real life, all provide fertile material for fictional plots. What, then, makes murder a special case? As a plot element, what differentiates murder from other kinds of events, and in particular from other kinds of crimes and other kinds of deaths?

Unlike marital squabbling, divorce, theft, or con artistry (to choose only from among those plots already listed), murder is irrevocable: the sundered pair can be reunited, the stolen booty can be returned, but a life, once taken, can never be restored. Like marriage or divorce or con artistry or theft, and *unlike* suicide, murder necessarily involves a relationship between at least two people. Yet it is a relationship that one of the people fails to survive. This offers the opportunity for a new relationship (for instance, between the detective and the murderer) to take the place of the old one, in terms of the audience's sympathy or interest. The murder plot thus offers us a chance to change horses in midstream, especially if the victim dies early in the plot, before we've become too attached. At the same time, the fact that *only* one person in the murderer-and-victim relationship survives means that the plot is likely to contain a stronger element of mystery than, say, a story about property crime or even violent assault. The usual primary witness, the victim of the crime, is in this case unavailable for testimony, and the only remaining witness has good reason to lie. (Here execution is unusual: it has many murderers, and it also has many witnesses, all of whom can testify to what took place. In this respect and others, it is execution's *difference* from other murder plots that makes it a useful point of entry.)

Despite its irrevocability, murder is potentially a less painful plot than the others. If the murder takes place early, the pain ends quickly—as it does not, say, in a hostage plot or a torture plot—and we can get on with the comparatively pleasurable working-out of the plot's solution. What may interfere with our enjoyment of a murder plot, of *any* plot, is our sympathy with the victim; that sympathetic pain is short-lived in most murder plots, which allow us to have our masochism and eat it too. (This is not true of all murder plots, however. The film *Henry: Portrait of a Serial Killer* actually verges on a torture plot because its violence is so extensive and unmitigated; and an execution story like *I Want to Live* or *Let Him Have It*, which converts the murderer into the victim, also has this quality of relentlessness.) Murder can be less anxiety-producing than other plots because, unlike death in general, it can sometimes be averted. This is even true of execution plots, where clemencies, successful appeals, and last-minute stays lend a strong element of suspense to what otherwise might seem a fixed conclusion. And, except for Americans who are young, black, and male, murder is a relatively rare form of death, and this too may lessen its anxiety quotient. We *know* we are going to die, but most of us think it unlikely we'll be murdered.

Yet the certainty that a murder will take place, a certainty that goes against all realistic principles, is what fuels the artful murder plot. The dramatic quality is initially produced by our expectation, by our foreknowledge of the murder itself. When we pick up a murder mystery or watch a murder movie on TV, the genre contains a promise that must in some way or other be fulfilled; whereas murder in real life—again, with the exception of an execution—is almost always unexpected, and its dramatic possibilities are therefore limited. Events can become a "story"—news, in that sense, can become art—only when the case is closed and the pattern is viewed in retrospect. In general, only the shaped or completed murder story has dramatic interest. "The novel is significant ...," Walter Benjamin once wrote, "not because it presents someone else's fate to us, perhaps didactically, but because this stranger's fate by virtue of the flame which consumes it yields us the warmth which we never draw from our own fate. What draws the reader to the novel is the hope of warming his shivering life with a death he reads about." The murders rendered in art—in books, in film, on television—are reassuringly not our own: we can't experience our own murder, and don't wish to. But the possibility that it *could* be our own must be there for the work of art to produce the heat, the flame, that warms our "shivering life." The game of art won't work, the theatricality won't come to life, if we don't at least partially believe in the reality of the fictional deaths being described to us.

Still, the nature of that belief is tricky. The actuality of the murder, the fact that historically it *did* happen, is no guarantee of our belief, if belief is taken to include a degree of emotional investment and even fear. Millions of people were scared to take showers after seeing *Psycho*, and continued to be frightened, in some conquerable but nonetheless tangible way, for years afterward; but very few people will avoid the streetcorner where a murder took place the week before. We may be least likely to believe in, in the sense of caring about and being frightened by, those murders which are the most newsworthy. For the newsworthy, the real, is quite often the unexplainable.

This problem of belief means that a story about murder, whether real or fictional, is also, obliquely, a story about the existence or absence of God. This is partly what Benjamin means by our "shivering life." We who inhabit reality are out in the cold because we have no author shaping our fate, no murderous artist planning from the beginning to bump us off.

So art about murder tends to be art about the search for structure and meaning in an apparently random existence. This is true even of nonfictional reconstructions of real-life murders, like Capote's *In Cold Blood* or Ann Rule's *The Stranger Beside Me*, in which notions of fate, coincidence, irony, near-miss, and there-but-for-the-grace-of-God loom large. It also explains why formula is so important to the genre, and why the murder plot lends itself so neatly to the enforced closure of the one-hour television show. "Twin Peaks" was an instant failure with murder fanatics like myself because we sensed from the beginning that this show had no interest in solving its mysteries, that it preferred its own red herrings and false leads. Even trashy TV murder shows can offer us the reassuring presence of an author; but "Twin Peaks" had no Author, only a Camera, and the "solutions" were unabashedly perfunctory.

An author need not show herself overtly in order to govern the plot. She may, for instance, choose to delegate the search for structure and meaning to a detective, whose responsibility it is to seek out the guilty murderer. This works best when there is some acknowledged connection between the detective and the murderer, some explicit or implicit nod to the fact that they are each other's opposite faces. In a whole range of mysteries and thrillers, including Kenneth Fearing's *The Big Clock*, Patricia Highsmith's Ripley novels, Jim Thompson's *The Killer Inside Me*, the movies *Manhunter* and *The Silence of the Lambs*, and the Thomas Harris novels from which these films derive, the central point is that the detective *is* in some way the murderer. Not only must one imagine oneself to be the murderer in order to find him (much more often *him* than *her*, in art as in life); one must also admit to the existence of one's own core of unknown and generally inaccessible violence. This goes for the reader as well as the detective—for the reader *as* detective, since the strategy of detective fiction is for us to stay one jump ahead of the plot.

Yet the murder story needn't depend on a detective to be about the search for self: the murderer alone can play the game. Raskolnikov murders the old woman at least in part to determine who, or what, he is; and Bigger Thomas finds out who he is only after killing a white girl, by accident, and then a black girl, on purpose. The detectives in *Crime and Punishment* and *Native Son* are, in that sense, mere addenda. They set in motion the mechanism of socially enforced justice, but they do not bring about the killers' pursuits of their own identities, which are central to these plots. Richard Wright makes this idea explicit when he says about Bigger: "And yet, out of it all, over and above all that had happened, impalpable but real, there remained to him a queer sense of power. *He* had done this. *He* had brought all this about. In all of his life these two murders were the most meaningful things that had ever happened to him ... Never had he had the chance to live out the consequences of his actions; never had his will been so free as in this night and day of fear and murder and flight." Ann Rule makes a similar point about the real-life murderer Ted Bundy in *The Stranger Beside Me,* where she shows him going off to New England to search out his birth records. "He had to know who he was," she says of this man whose shamefully hidden illegitimate birth she elsewhere connects to his serial killings. Bundy's discovery of his identity is in some ways the opposite of Bigger Thomas's: a discovery of predeterminism rather than will, as if, like Oedipus, he needed to submit to his fate as a murderer in order to resolve the mystery of his birth. "It's like some incredible Greek tragedy," Bundy said about his own life toward the end of his series of trials—though, given the unrelenting fury of the anti-Bundy forces, he may have been referring to *The Eumenides* rather than *Oedipus Rex*.

The mystery in such cases is oddly one-sided: Ted Bundy may have to discover who he is, but we in the audience already know, for his name has become synonymous with serial killing. Part of the point of these works about real-life killers like Bundy or Gary Gilmore is that their reputation precedes them. So, as with Oedipus, the story is actually closed before it even opens. The killer thinks he's a free agent, but *we* know exactly where he's headed. This is true even of fictional murder stories, where the genre forecasts the main event and portentous clue-dropping is a crucial technique. In some works about murder, this sense of genre determinism conspires with other shaping factors, such as sociological or psychological determinism, to make the murderer's fate, and hence that of his victim, seem unavoidable. In *Native Son*, for instance, Richard Wright presents Bigger Thomas's crime as intimately linked to, if not directly caused by, his role as a black man in a white-run society; this is part of what gives the power and poignance to Bigger's own sense of murder as his one "free" action. And in Paul Theroux's *Chicago Loop*, the protagonist's skewed vision of women—not to mention of life in general—is what produces our sense of foreboding; the killer's psychological makeup, his "loopiness," seals his fate as surely as does the author who weaves the plot into its circular loop. Such works are satisfying because inner and outer determinism merge in them. We don't feel that the authorial hand is too heavy, because it takes us in the direction already dictated by the material.

Murder stories interestingly combine a feeling of suspense with a preexisting knowledge of how the story comes out. I am always amazed by the number of mystery readers who turn to the last page to find out the end before they start, or the number of people who are anxious to see the movie of a murder novel they've already read, or vice versa. They want to be scared, but not too much; they want certainty amidst their dislocation. They don't at all mind, as the ancient Greek audiences of *Oedipus Rex* didn't mind, watching a central character enact a plot that has already been fixed in advance. This is not necessarily because they are sadists, enjoying the prospect of a rat caught in a wheel. They—or, to drop the pose of distance, we—find other ways than the ending to break the rigidly deterministic cycle. We are not only asking "What happened?" but also "How?" (which needs to be answered in detail, over the course of the work) and "Why?" (which can be answered only insufficiently, if at all). The murder story is in this sense a strong version of all novels, where we grant the characters some integrity and openness even though we know their fates have long been fixed on the page.

Art retains its meaning for us over time, over historical time and over our own lifetimes, because it continues to bear on the life we know outside art. Art about murder would be of only anthropological interest in a nonviolent society; but then, there is no such society and probably never was. Murder as a plot device defines both the initiation of the social order (as in *The Oresteia*, the first courtroom drama) and its dissolution (as in *Henry: Portrait of a Serial Killer*, where Law is so absent that no cops even make an appearance). Whichever way it is used, such material gains its meaning from its relation—indirect, self-conscious, distanced, but also pointed—to the level of violence in our normal lives. Normality now includes violence to such a degree that Ann Rule, a crime reporter by profession, could remark of the usual sixty-homicide-per-year, pre–Ted Bundy murder rate in Seattle: "Not a bad percentage for areas highly populated, and things appeared to be normal. Tragic, but normal." There's something wrong with that final phrase, which in its effort to convey a moral response defeats its own point. Routine murders cannot, for the uninvolved majority, be tragic; we are not capable of supplying individual emotions for all the murders we hear or read about. Such violence is an expected if deplored part of our daily experience.

Yet "experience" is an odd word to use here, because we don't actually undergo the murders in our morning newspapers or our nightly TV news any more directly than the ones we read about in novels or see in films. Unless we know the people involved—and most of us, in each case, don't—we may not even feel as much personal connection with the real-life murderers and victims as we do with well-drawn characters in fiction. In any event, our response is conditioned by the skill of the drawing: actual murderers and victims become real to us to the extent that their depictors, whether newsmen or novelists, succeed in presenting them to us as if they had the fullness of literary characters. This is why the Ted Bundy of *The Stranger Beside Me*, whom Ann Rule knew for years, is so much less persuasive than the Gary Gilmore of *The Executioner's Song*, whom Mailer never met. It is not just that Mailer is the superior artist, though he is, but that Rule is the more responsible journalist. She refrains from going beyond the facts and gives us a partial portrait of Bundy, the equivalent of an extremely thorough police file. Mailer makes Gilmore up wholesale, and thus satisfies our desire for a level of knowledge that only fiction can provide.

Fictional murder seems more credible because more can be known about it. The author, the artist, can create facts and explanations to fill the gaping hole of our curiosity. Yet fictional murders must also give us some sense of unknowability—some acknowledgment that causes don't lead inevitably to effects, that certain dark corners remain permanently obscure—if they are to be persuasive. Murder is mysterious; even if we know all the who-what-when facts (as we do when the murder is an execution), the distance between our own lives and the act of murder leaves a space where mystery creeps in. We seem able, though, to accept the full subtlety, the full complexity of the mystery only in a work of fiction, which can give us other satisfactions than The Definite Answer.

If fiction allows for more subtlety than the other aspects of life, a court of law allows for less. From our justice system, on which we rely to give us most of our answers about real-life murder, we can only expect the crude discriminations of a yes-or-no, guilty-or-innocent, this-versus-that perspective. Despite its obvious limitations, this either/or structure tends to burst the bounds of the courtroom, extending into all our considerations of murder. There is something adversarial in the very way we think about this crime and its effects: the murderer *versus* the victim; sympathy *versus* condemnation, or (what is not at all the same thing) innocence *versus* guilt; objective reporting *versus* subjective description; television *versus* print, art *versus* news, or news *versus* entertainment; the right to watch killing *versus* the right to die privately; the beneficial effects of witnessing even ugly reality *versus* the destructive effects of becoming inured to violence. Yet these dichotomies belie the actual complexity of murder, and the courtroom insistence on this kind of binary thinking—an insistence that has become so pervasive and ingrained as to be, for most of us, an unwitting habit of mind—makes it very difficult to get at the truth of the matter. Or so I will be suggesting in the exposition of the legal case that follows.

# 2

KQED v.
Daniel B. Vasquez

In the spring of 1991, a California public television station called KQED sued the warden of San Quentin, Daniel Vasquez, for the right, among other things, to bring a television camera into the witness area of a forthcoming execution. KQED was represented on a pro bono basis by the San Francisco civil rights lawyer William Bennett Turner and his associate, Beth Brinkmann; the warden was defended by the state attorney general's office. The three-day trial, held in the federal courtroom of Judge Robert Schnacke during the last week of March, featured a wide selection of plaintiff's witnesses, ranging from television news directors to prison employees, from a former governor's press secretary to a noted journalistic sketch artist, variously supporting the notion that televised executions fell under the First Amendment's protection of free speech. The defendant's witnesses included mainly prison staff—that is, Daniel Vasquez himself, wardens from other states, and several lower-level San Quentin personnel—who all argued that televising an execution would pose a major security problem.

After three days of testimony and two subsequent hearings for the presentation of additional evidence and post-trial arguments, Judge Schnacke delivered his ruling on June 7, 1991. In the course of the two and a half months between the opening of the trial and the judge's decision, the case had

become a major media event, featured on local TV news programs from California to New York, covered at the national
level by Dan Rather, Ted Koppel, and MacNeil/Lehrer, and
discussed in editorial and op-ed columns in the *New York Times*
and numerous regional papers. On the day following the
trial's close, the verdict was given several columns in the
national edition of the *Times*.

One of the things that made *KQED v. Daniel B. Vasquez* an
odd and compelling case is that it was explicitly about one
thing and implicitly about so many others. Explicitly it was
about the First Amendment, and whether and to what extent
the public — in the form of the press, and through reporting by
the press — has the right of access to a public event like an execution. But implicitly it drew in all our feelings about the
death penalty itself, our feelings about the state's right to kill
one of its own citizens. It asked us to examine how we feel
about the presentation of violence — on television, in newspapers, through books and films and photographs — and posed
the question of how we differentiate between real and fictional
violence, real and fictional death. It set our concerns about
individual dignity and privacy, even for an individual who had
been convicted of murder, against the public's right to know.
It posited spectacle versus procedure, excess versus restraint,
bloodthirsty revenge versus bureaucratic enforcement of justice, sleaze versus highmindedness. It mixed up everything
from bad taste to moral depravity, from empathetic concern to
sentimental illusion, from fear and disgust to curiosity and
hilarity; and it did so in a way that had no easy answers.

In the course of this book I will be mentioning specific
details about how the case was played out: who the major witnesses were, what they said in the courtroom, how the judge
eventually ruled, and so on. To begin with, though, I want to
take a look at all the hazy issues raised by the case — legal,
political, ethical, aesthetic, emotional (these aren't necessarily
separable characteristics) — and try to puzzle out how a "rea-

sonable person," that courtroom fiction, might be expected to feel about them, one way or another. But first I will need to lay some historical groundwork.

A story about an execution, as Norman Mailer's "true life novel" demonstrates, is initially a story about a murderer. In the case of *KQED v. Daniel B. Vasquez,* the murderer in question was Robert Alton Harris, convicted of killing two teenaged boys in San Diego in 1978. I will not give any further details about either the murder or the murderer for now, except to say that after a long series of trials and appeals, Harris greeted the beginning of the last decade of the twentieth century from Death Row at San Quentin, where he was awaiting execution in the prison's gas chamber. His execution, if and when it took place, would be the first such death in California since 1967.

In the quarter century since that last California execution, the death penalty had been a vociferously debated point in California politics. The Supreme Court ban on capital punishment throughout America was in effect during the 1974 election of Jerry Brown, the only recent California governor to come out against the death penalty. After the ban was lifted in 1976, thirty-six states independently reinstated capital punishment. In California this was accomplished first through the legislature, over the veto of Governor Brown and under the sponsorship of State Senator (later to be Governor) George Deukmejian, and then through the initiative process, as a popular vote. Though nobody was executed in California during the 1980s—in part because the State Supreme Court, led by the notoriously liberal Rose Bird, did its best to find legal holes in death-penalty sentences—the population's support for capital punishment led to the resounding defeat of Bird as Chief Justice and the election of George Deukmejian and then Pete Wilson, both strong Republican supporters of the death penalty. Wilson's Democratic opponent in the 1990 election, Dianne Feinstein, also supported capital punishment: one of her slogans in the primary was "The only Democrat for the death penalty." Nonetheless, this electoral history conceals a strong undercurrent of anti-capital-punishment sentiment in the state, a feeling probably more concentrated in the liberal environment of the San Francisco Bay Area, where San Quentin is located, than anywhere else.

KQED is the public television station for the San Francisco area. Officially the station has no position on capital punishment. It is supported, however, largely by membership dues and donations from the kind of people one would expect to support noncommercial television in San Francisco, the liberal element of an already liberal community. The station commissions or airs numerous programs on public issues, from homelessness and government arts funding to Central American politics and environmental concerns. KQED's very interest in such matters, in "public" as opposed to "private" welfare, would seem to define the station as left-leaning; but, like other public television stations, it attempts to fulfill its charter by covering multiple sides of controversial topics — by being all things to as many people as possible. Nor is it seen as part of the Bay Area's old-guard left, variously described as "wacky" or "committed" depending on whether you're outside or inside. KQED's implied politics, for instance, are far to the right of the explicit leftism voiced by KPFA radio or the weekly *Express* newspaper, both located in Berkeley. To the right wing KQED may seem to belong to the left, but to the left it stands, at best, for wishy-washy liberalism.

Which makes its role in this controversial case all the more surprising. In early 1990, KQED was in the process of developing a news show about the Robert Alton Harris case. The case was of special interest not because Harris was a particularly grisly murderer (California seems to have more than its fair share of those), but because Harris — originally scheduled for execution on April 3, 1990 — was first in line to die in the San Quentin gas chamber, having been sentenced shortly after the death penalty was reinstated in 1978. In other words, the focus of the show was explicitly on the death penalty, an issue that was important both in news terms (the first California execution in twenty-three years) and in political terms (the result of a popular vote). As part of its coverage, which already included material on Harris's arrest, trial, and sentencing, KQED asked the warden of San Quentin for permission to videotape the April 3 execution. Warden Vasquez refused. KQED responded by bringing a suit in federal district court to compel Vasquez to allow full and impartial coverage of the execution. Because of an entirely different legal issue, a rehearing of one of his appeals, Robert Alton Harris's execution was stayed three days before he was due to die.

The original arguments in KQED's case were based on the First and Fourteenth Amendments, and made essentially two claims: that the selection of which press representatives were allowed to attend executions should not be left solely to the discretion of state officials but should stem from an agreed-upon selection process not subject to political influences; and that the press, in covering executions, should be allowed to use the "tools of its trade"—sketchpads, notebooks, pens or pencils, recording equipment, and cameras. KQED's lawyers, in the trial brief submitted in March 1991, argued that both of these provisions were necessary to ensure the fair and open coverage by the media of a newsworthy event like an execution. ("Newsworthy" is the legal term used to describe occasions when the press's First Amendment rights outweigh considerations of personal privacy, government strategy, public taste, and other competing rights.)

Prior to the suit, in February 1990, Warden Vasquez had issued revised guidelines announcing that press representatives attending the execution were not to be allowed to carry in *any* equipment, including pencils and notepads as well as cameras and recording equipment. He had also left the selection of the fourteen permitted press representatives up to the governor's press secretary, who proceeded to make the selection from hundreds of statewide applicants in a manner that, in KQED's view, invited discrimination against reporters and commentators who had previously expressed doubts about the death penalty. That is, the pro-capital-punishment governor appeared to be using his press office to select media witnesses who would not make the execution an occasion to write anti-death-penalty articles. This seemingly political selection process, as well as the obstacles to accurate reporting embodied in the ban on tools of the trade, gave rise to KQED's initial First Amendment case.

The case was soon to expand, however, when Daniel Vasquez, in explicit response to the lawsuit itself, announced on March 20, 1991, five days before the trial began, that he was now further revising the guidelines for executions and would permit *no* press representatives to attend. The KQED lawyers then added a third prong to their argument: the claim that the press have a right to be present at executions, not only because they have traditionally attended them, but also because, as the public's eyes and ears, they should be allowed to report on this kind of public event.

KQED's case rested heavily on a series of legal decisions made between 1980 and 1986 in which the Supreme Court ruled that press cameras would be permitted in courtrooms where criminal proceedings were taking place, since these criminal proceedings were newsworthy events with a direct bearing on the public. The Court also ruled that televising a criminal trial, even over the objection of the accused, did not necessarily violate the right to a fair trial. These rulings ended the traditional ban on television cameras at criminal justice proceedings and spurred several states, including California, to begin allowing television coverage on a fairly routine basis (always dependent, however, on the permission of the presiding judge). So the very rulings which had already enabled KQED to film proceedings in the Robert Alton Harris case were being used to argue that such coverage should be extended, albeit for the first time in history, to the execution itself.

The state's defense of Vasquez rested on the degree to which press censorship was warranted, in this particular case, by security reasons. The First Amendment is not unlimited in its applications, as the hoary example of a man shouting "Fire!" in a crowded theater makes clear. A recent example of limitations on press coverage attributed to security reasons was the Bush Administration's tight control over the reporting of the Persian Gulf war. In order to win the right to this kind of limitation on the press, the government needs to prove that it is not engaging in censorship per se. In other words, the emphasis has to be purely on *security* (the immediate potential dangers of letting out specific information) rather than on *content*. Whether the information itself is politically desirable or undesirable, tasteful or distasteful, should be no part of the consideration. It therefore became part of KQED's case not only to demonstrate that Warden Vasquez was arbitrarily and illegally restricting press access to an execution, but also to suggest that the state's motive in such restriction had to do with content—had to do, that is, with not wanting people to see what an actual execution looked like. The further implication was that a pro-death-penalty governor and his pro-death-penalty prison warden feared the effect such coverage would have on the population's support of capital punishment.

The legal dispute is perhaps the least complicated of the issues raised by the case. If one excludes political, ethical, aesthetic, and emotional considerations—something which is impossible to do in real life, but which courtroom behavior frequently insists on—one comes down to a legal question about whether the public's right to know about the activities conducted by its government on its behalf outweighs the security considerations of partial or full secrecy. In *KQED v. Daniel B. Vasquez*, the state's argument depended mainly on the notion that televising an execution would inflame the already hot emotions pervading a prison during the time of an execution (since the inmates, who have access to television sets, would also be part of the witnessing public), and might therefore lead to prison riots. There was also the additional claim that individual guards and other witnesses to the execution might be jeopardized by having their identities recorded by TV camera—a fear the KQED side addressed by promising to shoot from unrevealing camera angles and electronically mask any faces, other than that of the condemned man,* which might actually appear on the tape. Finally, the defense suggested that equipment as heavy and unwieldy as a television camera might prove physically dangerous, in that it could knock against and possibly crack the glass walls of the gas chamber, allowing the poisonous gas to leak out into the witness area. (The plaintiff's side pooh-poohed this aspect of the defense, and even the judge made skeptical remarks, during the course of the testimony, about the likelihood of a suicidal cameraman.)

KQED's lawyers, besides attempting to cast doubt on these alleged security concerns, pointed to the long and solid history of press attendance at executions, along with the statutory requirement that at least twelve citizen witnesses be present in the viewing area of the death chamber at each execution. The point of having such witnesses, KQED suggested, was in part to appease the public's need for knowledge of the event. In their March 1991 trial brief, KQED's lawyers quoted the Supreme Court's 1980 decision on the need for open criminal trials with full access by the press. "Civilized societies withdraw both from the victim and the vigilante the enforcement of criminal laws," Chief Justice Burger wrote in *Richmond Newspapers Inc. v. Commonwealth of Virginia*, "but they

---

*Throughout this book, I will use the phrase "condemned man" to refer both to the specific man in this case, Robert Alton Harris, and to the generic person who is threatened with execution. I think the phrase "generic person" goes a long way toward explaining why I have chosen to do this. The gender-free phrases— "the condemned" or "the condemned person" or "the condemned prisoner"—help to deprive the person who is dying of some of the individuality, some of the claim to specific character, that the execution and its accompanying procedures are designed to obliterate. Rather than collaborate with this process of bureaucratic depersonalization, I have chosen to allocate gender to the condemned man. It is not an arbitrary allocation, since the vast majority of people on Death Rows in America's prisons are and have always been men.

cannot erase from people's consciousness the fundamental, natural yearning to see justice done—or even the urge for retribution. The crucial prophylactic aspects of the administration of justice cannot function in the dark; no community catharsis can occur if justice is 'done in a corner [or] in any covert manner.'" An execution, KQED argued, is an extension of the criminal trial process and should be included in this openness, especially now that modern videotape technology makes it possible to bring millions of "witnesses" into the death chamber without noticeably altering the nature of the event.

There is, of course, a huge numerical difference between the relatively small number of witnesses actually in the chamber (who traditionally include not only the statutory witnesses and members of the press, but also up to five people invited by the condemned man himself) and the millions of viewers who would be "present" uninvited through the eye of a TV camera; and this difference raises the issue of privacy. The right to privacy, even for someone judged a criminal and incarcerated in a public institution, was one that was successfully if temporarily upheld against the public's right to know and the press's First Amendment rights in the Massachusetts case regarding Frederick Wiseman's first film, *Titicut Follies*. Initially ruled on in 1969 and continually under litigation until 1991, when the filmmaker finally won the right to show his film, *Commonwealth v. Wiseman* set the only precedent in the history of American film whereby a movie—in this instance, a film about the treatment of inmates at the Bridgewater Correctional Facility for the "criminally insane"—was placed under restraining orders and essentially censored for reasons *not* having to do with either obscenity or national security. I will be referring to this case and this film later, mostly in regard to the aesthetic and moral justifications for such "invasion of privacy."

In legal terms, however, the Wiseman case has no bearing on the KQED situation. The right to privacy in *Commonwealth*

v. *Wiseman* was defined in terms of Massachusetts law (the Supreme Court never agreed to hear the case), and in any event Robert Alton Harris, who by 1990 was already something of a media figure, could be said to have different privacy rights from those of the obscure Bridgewater inmates. More importantly, KQED finessed the privacy problem by declining to push the issue of televising an execution against the condemned man's wishes. If Harris didn't want TV cameras at his execution, KQED promised not to have them there, however the legal decision in the case came out. As KQED's lawyer put it on the opening day of testimony: "KQED has decided that it doesn't want to have to litigate with the condemned person about his privacy interests, and bite that off in addition to . . ." (What else had been bitten off we will never know, because the irrepressibly outspoken Judge Schnacke interrupted at this point to say, "You respect the rights of the condemned man more than you do those of the warden or the state.") In their post-trial brief, the KQED attorneys specifically requested that the judge "not grant more relief than the plaintiff requests"—that he not rule in favor of the press over the privacy interests of the condemned. The brief pointed out that "any competing interests of the condemned person have not been represented in this case," and that such interests would need to be ascertained and explored before the press's First Amendment rights could be weighed against an inmate's right to privacy.

To address the issue of prison security, KQED got a former director of the California, Texas, Virginia, and Utah prisons—an administrator who, unlike Vasquez, actually *had* supervised several executions—to testify in court that there were no valid security reasons for excluding the press and their equipment from an execution. This witness was a feisty, articulate man named Raymond Procunier, who, at the time of the trial, was running Nevada's prison system. The KQED side brought him in to counter the testimony of prison directors from Florida, Texas, and Georgia, all of whom supported

Vasquez's contention that the press should be kept at bay. Procunier, incidentally, was already well known to the legal profession as the defendant in *Pell v. Procunier,* the Supreme Court case that gave prison directors the right to limit media access to prisoners; so his appearance on the pro-media side here had a certain ironic punch.

"Mr. Procunier," William Bennett Turner asked his witness on the second day of court proceedings, "is there any penological reason for excluding the press from witnessing executions?"

"No, absolutely not."

"Are there any security problems with allowing reporters who are allowed to witness executions to use pencils and paper?"

"If handled properly, absolutely not."

Turner then took Procunier through all the other tools of the trade—sketch pads, tape recorders, still cameras, and television cameras—and in each case the prison director responded that they posed no inherent security problem. Finally Procunier was asked, "What about if the condemned prisoners on Death Row—about three hundred of them now in California—were to see an execution on television? Would that cause a security problem?"

"If it did, they're not running San Quentin Death Row properly," he answered.

Ray Procunier obviously supported capital punishment. (Though that "obviously" is not as obvious as it might seem. Clinton Duffy, who supervised over a hundred executions during his term as warden of San Quentin, was adamantly opposed to capital punishment, and spent the period between his retirement and his death testifying against it as an expert witness.) Another supporter of the death penalty, surprisingly enough, turned out to be Michael Schwarz, KQED's director of current affairs. At the time of the trial, Schwarz had already aired one documentary about the death penalty and the Robert Alton Harris case, a KQED-made film called *Appealing*

*Death,* which very effectively presented both sides, perhaps even leaning slightly *against* capital punishment. *KQED v. Vasquez* came about because he now wanted to broadcast another news program that would include videotape of the actual execution.

The first and in many ways primary witness for the plaintiff in this case, Schwarz—a 1975 Yale graduate who had worked in broadcast journalism in Boston, New York, Southeast Asia, and, since 1988, San Francisco—was eloquent if not always persuasive when discussing the power and objectivity of the camera's eye. In his testimony, the legal issue began to blend into the political one. "I think the videotape would enable us to speak to the central question raised by executions," Schwarz said early in the proceedings, "which is whether or not this is an appropriate punishment to carry out for the most horrible crimes that people commit in this society . . . The death penalty tells us who we are as a people. And I think that in order to examine that event most fully, in all its complexity, it's very important for us to be able to look at it." Later, under questioning by his own side's attorney, and over the (overruled) objections of the other side, Schwarz admitted that though KQED as an institution had no position on the death penalty, he himself, while "frankly ambivalent and somewhat conflicted," felt "quite strongly that there are some crimes that warrant" capital punishment. "There are some crimes so terrible that—that people should not be allowed to go on living," Schwarz stammered, adding somewhat apologetically: "I have a personal perspective on this because I myself a few years ago was a victim of a violent crime." The plaintiff's side was anxious to get this into the record in order to demonstrate, defense imputations to the contrary, that KQED's case was not waged by a bunch of pinko peaceniks purely on behalf of an anti-death-penalty agenda.

It became clear early on in *KQED v. Vasquez* that supporters and opponents of the death penalty did not line up neatly on opposite sides of this case. Opponents in the death-penalty battle became allies in support of televised executions, but they did so for opposite reasons, dividing up between themselves Aristotle's classic pair of theatrically induced emotions, pity and terror. That is, some pro-death-penalty types saw televised executions as a deterrent that would inspire terror in potential future murderers, while those against capital punishment hoped that witnessing the condemned man's death would cause viewers (and voters) to pity him.

There is no guarantee that TV executions would do either of these things, just as public executions in the eighteenth and nineteenth centuries did not necessarily have the effects desired by the state that staged them. The novelist Henry Fielding, writing about capital punishment in 1751, noted that terror is not an easy emotion to inspire, for admiration and pity "are very apt to attend whatever is the object of terror in the human mind." Decent people witnessing a public execution, he argued, would be likely to feel sorry for the condemned man, who dies "to make a holiday for, and entertain, the mob." Therefore, if the state truly wished to inspire terror in its audience, it should keep executions hidden; politicians should learn in this respect from poets. "A murder behind the scenes," said Fielding, citing the example of *Macbeth*, ". . . will affect the audience with greater terror than if it was acted before their eyes."

We tend to view public executions as part of the distant and barbaric past, but the last such event in the United States, a Kentucky hanging that took place in front of ten thousand people, occurred as recently as 1936. In California, hangings moved inside the prison walls in 1858, a decade before public executions were permanently abolished in England. According to the historian Thomas Laqueur, this nineteenth-century move away from public executions was not simply the result of humanitarian impulses, for the tasteful humanitarians had been lobbying for privacy for more than a century by then. Laqueur instead attributes the move to a new willingness on the part of the Victorian public to hand its morality-enforcing deeds over to government bureaucracies. This very willingness, and the abdication of personal connection implied by it, provided one of the arguments voiced by those who sought to preserve public executions in England. "It had long been the wise practice of this country for centuries to make people feel that the law was an expression of their own judgment and will," a Member of Parliament said in 1868, going on to argue that executions done in private would seem merely "an act of the executive itself." Something akin to this realization obviously governs the California statute requiring twelve citizen witnesses at an execution: they are there not just to ensure that the deed is actually done, and without excessive harshness, but to represent and embody the wider public in whose name the execution is being carried out.

The argument most often made in favor of televising executions stresses this notion of the public's moral implication. Interviewed for a CBS news segment that aired in May 1991, at the height of the publicity surrounding *KQED v. Vasquez,* Michael Schwarz said: "I think that what people find disturbing about the idea of showing executions on television is that it's our government carrying out the executions, and the only reason our government does it is that we vote for it, so at some level we all carry the responsibility for it." Norman Mailer made a similar point quite differently in his 1964 book *The Presidential Papers of Norman Mailer.* "I would like to see a law passed which would abolish capital punishment," he wrote,

> except for those states which insisted on keeping it. Such states would then be allowed to kill criminals provided that the killing is not impersonal but personal and a public spectacle: to wit that the executioner be more or less the same size and weight as the criminal (the law could here specify the limits) and that they fight to the death using no weapons, or weapons not capable of killing at a distance.... The benefit of this law is that

it might return us to moral responsibility. The killer would carry the other man's death in his psyche. The audience, in turn, would experience a sense of tragedy, since the executioners, highly trained for this, would almost always win.

The gallows humor here, which Mailer was to develop to a pitch of perfection fifteen years later in *The Executioner's Song,* should not be allowed to detract from the seriousness with which Mailer is presenting his notion. Just as he is explicitly suggesting, in this passage, "legislation whose inner tendency would be to weaken the bonds of legislation," Mailer both is and is not in favor of the death penalty—or rather, he favors a version of it so personal, so extreme, that it makes the carnivalesque nineteenth-century hangings look like bureaucratic procedures. The key to Mailer's proposal is in that little word "almost," which leaves open the possibility that sometimes the criminal might win.

Master of doubleness that he is, Mailer raises for us the strongest ethical reason *against* televising executions even as he advocates making such deaths into a spectacle. For the danger of a TV execution is that we would not take it personally. This is not just because the existing procedure is vastly different from the gladiatorial encounter Mailer proposes, though that is certainly the case. Broadcasting a gas chamber execution would show "how cold, how clinical the process of a government taking a human life is," said Joseph Russionello, a former U.S. Attorney who, on the CBS program about *KQED v. Vasquez,* represented the pro-death-penalty viewpoint. Others, particularly opponents of the death penalty, disagree with Russionello's bland assessment, arguing that showing a gas chamber death in all its horror might demonstrate conclusively that this form of execution could be deemed cruel and unusual punishment. When Donald Eugene Harding, the first person to die in the Arizona gas chamber in twenty-nine years, was put to death on April 6, 1992, a newsman who witnessed the death described Harding's six minutes of convulsive spasms and then said: "Obviously, the gentleman was suffering. This was a violent death, make no mistake about it. It was an ugly event. We put animals to death more humanely." But even at its most "humane"—for instance, in death by lethal injection—a contemporary execution is still a long way from the gladiatorial tragedy Mailer wants us to witness; it is instead death as medical procedure.

Beyond that, the very appearance of the execution on television—not present to us in person, as public hangings were—might work to increase the coldness of our reception to it. It's possible that instead of making the killing more real to us, the sight of a condemned person dying on TV might only acclimate us further to such violent images. In its trial brief and, more fully, in its exhibits, KQED's side listed the executions that had already appeared on television in one form or another, ranging from an episode of "L.A. Law" that enacted an execution to the photographs of Ceausescu's killing in Rumania, from a reenactment of the Caryl Chessman execution that took place on Connie Chung's show to the "live" shooting of Lee Harvey Oswald that we all saw—and then saw again, many times over—in November 1963. "This establishes that people under 18, people generally, can see executions on a very frequent basis on television, both real and simulated executions," said KQED's lawyer during the court testimony.

Here, I think, is where the ethical argument most clearly becomes an aesthetic and phenomenological argument. There *is* a difference between planning to watch a real, scheduled murder take place on television, and watching either a simulated execution or a real but unscheduled murder, like that of Lee Harvey Oswald. What differentiates an execution from all other news events, including wars, is that it is the only occasion on which the death of a specific individual will premeditatedly and certainly take place. "This is something well planned, well thought out," said Robert Alton Harris about capital punishment, when he was interviewed for the documentary *Appealing Death*. Those surrounding and witnessing the event, including the media people who are recording it, will not be at any risk (as they are, for instance, in recording war deaths); one person, and only one person, is scheduled to die. To step over this line—the line between simulated or unplanned death and real, scheduled death—is to create a new kind of violence on TV.

It also creates a new kind of voyeurism. We, from the invisibility of our private livingrooms, are given the opportunity to peer into the most intimate event in someone else's life: his death. In this sense, the nonintrusive nature of modern video technology—no bright lights, a relatively small camera—only makes the voyeurism worse. An individual's death is being turned, not into a circus, as it would be if he were made viscerally aware of the spotlight on him and we were made aware of all the other audience members, but into a publicly sanctioned "real death" film. The invasion of privacy is, in this respect, not something that affects the invaded victim so much as the invading viewers.

No one would be *required* to watch the execution of Robert Alton Harris. The question is whether we want to permit large numbers of people to have access to such a sight. That question, with all its implications, was weighed and considered by the attorney for KQED before he even agreed to bring the suit. "I *assume* that it would be degrading in some way for all," William Bennett Turner wrote in a letter to me after the case was over. "For me, the evil is the death penalty. . . . The only thing worse than having executions and watching them is having executions and having our government prohibit us from watching them."

Reasonable and persuasive as this viewpoint is, it fails to take account of our visceral sense of repulsion. "The picture in my mind of California wanting to witness an execution, I just can't comprehend," said Warden Vasquez during his courtroom testimony, voicing some of that instinctive recoil. "I don't want it to turn into any kind of a spectacle," he said later. "I try to put together a procedure that is as respectful as possible, as humane as possible." Though he was pushed by his lawyers to make the argument on the grounds of security, Vasquez couldn't help touching on the moral nature of the event. "We are talking about taking the life of another human being," he pointed out. Speaking about the "tactfulness and precision" required during an execution, Vasquez seemed to be objecting to the possible presence of cameras *not* because they might pose a security risk, but because they were tactless—in short, because they represented an extreme of bad taste.

"Squeamishness about whether it is 'in good taste' to put executions on television, or concern about whether the public might be displeased, obviously is not an appropriate judgment for prison officials (or courts) to make," argued the plaintiff's trial brief. KQED's attorneys went on to quote a 1949 Supreme Court decision which argues, in a manner worthy of Lenny Bruce, that a "function of free speech under our system of government is to invite dispute. It may even best serve its high purpose when it induces a condition of unrest, creates dissatisfaction with conditions as they are, or even stirs people to anger." Yet the federal judge in *KQED v. Vasquez* appeared, during the course of testimony, to be preoccupied with the tastelessness of KQED's proposed broadcast. "Someone once said: no one ever went broke underestimating the taste of the American people," Judge Schnacke commented in court, referring obliquely to the possibilities for commercially exploiting a videotape of an execution. The judge had already remarked to Michael Schwarz, during the latter's testimony, "If you got a scream, that would be a lot more saleable program, wouldn't it?" and in the face of Schwarz's denial had gone on to point out with thinly veiled sarcasm: "Well, you must realize that you're speaking on behalf of every potential television station, I suppose, even including Playboy. ... So they may not all have your extraordinarily high motives."

"Bad taste" appeared to be the key charge of those who favored the death penalty but opposed televising executions. "It is in such extremely bad taste," said the pro-capital-punishment leader of a victims' rights group, when she was interviewed for the May 2 CBS news broadcast about executions on TV. Like a self-defeating character in an Errol Morris documentary, she then went on to list in gory detail the violent images that should instead be projected on the television screen—those that pertained to the crime against the murdered victim. What she was really objecting to, it seems, was not the bad taste of the proposed broadcast, but its potential for eliciting sympathy for the condemned murderer.

Even those of us who oppose capital punishment and who *want* to generate such sympathy can acknowledge, however, that this kind of broadcast would be in extremely bad taste. The question is under what circumstances and to what extent bad taste can be justified. This is both a moral and an aesthetic question, a moral as aesthetic question, since the justification must rest on artistic achievement, which in turn can't be separated from audience response.

Writing about Frederick Wiseman's documentary technique, the technique that governed the making of the state-suppressed *Titicut Follies*, the critic Bill Nichols has said: "Wiseman disavows conventional notions of tact, breaking through what would otherwise be ideological constraints of politeness, respect for privacy, queasiness in the face of the grotesque or taboo, the impulse to accentuate the positive. . . . Wiseman's 'tactlessness' allows him not to be taken in by institutional rhetoric; it helps him disclose the gap between rhetoric and practice. But this lack of tact also pulls Wiseman's cinema toward the realm of voyeurism." Voyeurism, or the risk of it, is the danger into which tactless, bad-taste art—even, or especially, *good* bad-taste art—may lead us. It shows us things we don't want to acknowledge we want to know. In this sense, the threat of voyeurism is not an unfortunate by-product of the tactless work's artistic success, but is central to it. A documentary like Wiseman's that allows us to peer into forbidden places has not only a political value (in terms of telling us truths that pierce through "institutional rhetoric") but also a moral and aesthetic value, in that it impresses on us the high cost of learning such truths.

Art about murder raises the specter of voyeurism in a particularly powerful way when the art is about a real murder, a real death. We have insufficient evidence at this point to say whether a news-generated videotape of a gas chamber execution could be or could contribute to a valuable work of art, but I think it is already possible to say that the fact of its being a documentary would not *preclude* it from being art. Nor would it cease to be art simply by being in very bad taste (and such a videotape would inevitably be in bad taste, however tactfully or responsibly handled; in fact, the tact and responsibility might *exacerbate* the bad taste).

"The words that come to my mind about this kind of thing, televising executions—*morbid, lurid, barbaric, bloodlust,*" said California Attorney General John Van De Kamp, interviewed on an NBC Nightly News program during the course of the *KQED v. Vasquez* trial. He had ample reasons for saying this: not only was his own office defending Daniel Vasquez, but Van De Kamp himself was on record as personally opposing the death penalty—a position that may well have cost him his party's 1990 gubernatorial nomination. Even those who are in favor of televising executions would be forced to agree with Van De Kamp's words, if they are honest. Some might say, as William Bennett Turner does, that the morbidity, the barbarity, inheres in the death penalty itself, so that to televise the event only makes its ugliness more visible. Others might, though with varying degrees of hesitation, admit that bloodlust is a part of the point.

Norman Mailer is, as usual, the least hesitant. "In the flabby American spirit there is a buried sadist who finds the bullfight contemptible—what he really desires are gladiators," he says in *The Presidential Papers* in support of his proposed one-to-one combat between executioner and condemned. "Since nothing is worse for a country than repressed sadism, this method of execution would offer ventilation for the more cancerous emotions of the American public." One can find a similar idea expressed with more restraint by the great British psychoanalyst D. W. Winnicott. "It is impossible to get away from the principle that the first function of the law is to express the unconscious revenge of society . . . ," Winnicott wrote in response to a 1961 official report about punishment in British prisons.

> My own inclination, along with that of a very large number of people at the present time, is to widen as much as possible the range of offence which is treated as an illness. It is because of hope in this direction that I feel like making it quite clear that the law cannot suddenly give up the punishment of all criminals. Possibly if society's revenge feelings were fully conscious society could stand the treatment of the offender as ill, but so much of the revenge is unconscious that allowance must be made all the time for the need for punishment to be kept up to some extent even when it is not useful in the treatment of the offender.

To be sure, Winnicott is not talking about capital punishment here (though that penalty was not abolished in Britain until 1969, eight years after he wrote those lines). But Winnicott's clearsighted acknowledgment of feelings about revenge is a useful antidote to the highmindedness and sentimentality that often appear in discussions about violent crime, and in particular discussions about murder. Elsewhere Winnicott stresses that one of the biggest threats to the advancement of the psychological treatment of criminals "comes from the adoption of a sentimental attitude towards crime. . . . In sentimentality there is repressed or unconscious hate, and this repression is unhealthy. Sooner or later the hate turns up."

I doubt that Winnicott or Mailer would justify the death penalty on the sole grounds that it accurately expresses society's hate. After all, even society must place some restrictions on the exercise of its personal feelings if it expects its constituent members to do the same. But that may well be the *only* grounds for supporting the death penalty. Say we agreed to keep all horrific murderers in jail for life, without the possibility of parole. The cost of imprisoning a man for life, even if he is twenty-five years old when he commits the crime, turns out to be less than the cost of putting him to death, if one includes the lengthy series of trials and appeals that the government must inevitably pay for; so any financial argument in favor of capital punishment collapses. (People do make such fiscal arguments in favor of the death penalty, Gradgrindian as that may seem.) As for the deterrence value of execution, FBI statistics show that the three states which at present have the highest execution rates—Texas, Georgia, and Florida—also have the highest murder rates; these are the same three states, incidentally, whose wardens testified *against* televised executions during the *KQED v. Vasquez* trial. While the statistics do not prove that state violence breeds citizen violence, they fail to prove that execution acts as any kind of deterrent to violent crime.

Remarking on this lack of correlation, the Stanford law professor Robert Weisburg, when interviewed for *Appealing Death,* commented: "If the public gets psychological pleasure and satisfaction out of seeing an execution . . . so be it. The democratic processes, I guess, suggest they're entitled to it. I would simply like to make the more modest point that it is entirely symbolic, and there's no particular *reason* to feel any more in control or any more secure about the public safety because of the death penalty, because it has essentially no connection to it." Weisburg was using the verb "seeing" metaphorically here: he was referring to the existence of executions, not to their actual appearance on a TV screen. But if he is right in feeling that an execution's value is mainly or

wholly symbolic, then one could argue that the symbolic function, the "psychological pleasure and satisfaction" afforded to
society's vengeful elements—which may include unacknowledged elements in the most saintly psyches among us—would
be increased by having the death take place on television.

Or one could argue the opposite: that the sight of the
condemned person actually dying would make us feel compassion, and therefore cause us to turn against the death penalty.
Arguing in this vein on the NBC Nightly News segment
devoted to *KQED v. Vasquez,* Professor John Oakley of the
University of California at Davis, who explicitly opposed capital punishment, said that he would favor televising executions
because of the probable effect on the public. "I think they'll be
educated about the helplessness of a condemned man,"
Oakley said. "We tend to think that the condemned is
someone like Hannibal Lecter in *The Silence of the Lambs,* some
kind of personification of irresistible evil. In fact, it's a helpless
person totally restrained and no threat who is put to death for
no good reason." Though "for no good reason" may be
pushing the point, Oakley's remark accurately stresses the
way in which an execution makes a murderer into a pathetic
victim.

But what Oakley has overlooked—despite his humane
sentiments, or perhaps because of them—is that Hannibal
Lecter is far and away the most compelling and in many
respects appealing character in *The Silence of the Lambs.*
Fielding was right in insisting that admiration as well as pity is
"apt to attend whatever is the object of terror in the human
mind." We feel in regard to our murderers more sympathy,
more identification, than most of us can easily admit; and
therefore we rely on art to admit it for us.

# 3

---

# The Killer Inside Us

One of the central issues in *KQED v. Daniel B. Vasquez* — not necessarily one of the legal problems, but one of the largest surrounding concerns — was the question of how a televised execution would affect our sympathies, our identifications. The state even tried to make this a legal issue when it asserted in Warden Vasquez's defense that seeing an execution on television might cause riot and retribution, both within and outside of the prison walls, among the condemned men themselves and among anti-capital-punishment demonstrators. Mainly, the state attempted to show that broadcasting an execution posed a security threat because the other prison inmates identified so closely with the condemned person.

This position was stated most graphically by Sheila Petrakis, a San Quentin employee who was the state's last witness on the final day of testimony. She was asked by one of the defense lawyers whether she had noticed, on the day before Robert Alton Harris's scheduled 1990 death date, any inmate reaction to the last-minute stay of execution.

"Yes," she answered. "I was walking from my office, which is in the middle of the first tier, so I passed by several inmates' cells. And I was just going to the front of the unit when I heard a loud cheer and yelling, and at that time without knowing particulars, I knew that the stay had been

47

granted." The assumption which Ms. Petrakis was both responding to and affirming was that the people most likely to identify with a convicted murderer were, if not other convicted murderers, then at any rate other criminals.

Later, she described escorting Harris from the vicinity of the gas chamber to another location in the prison. "As we were leaving the North Block Rotunda Area," she said, "the inmates saw who we were escorting. The reception center inmates, many of whom are sitting down on the pavement, as we started walking they stood up and started yelling and cheering how the cops didn't kill him, the pigs didn't kill him, and just cheering and yelling and throwing their arms up." Asked by the warden's attorney to render the prisoners' speech directly rather than in polite paraphrase, she obliged: "Those fucking cops didn't—aren't going to kill you, and well, that was the general consensus that, you know, it was a lot about the pigs, the fucking pigs, and 'You beat them,' which means he won. Things of that nature."

Earlier in the trial, KQED had attempted to counter this sort of testimony by offering Ray Procunier's perspective on the issue of prisoner tension and prisoner identification with the condemned man. "Prison people are historically guilty of creating a lot of myths to make our business a lot more important and a lot more romantic than it really is," said this former director of the California prison system. "And one of those myths is that on Death Row, on Death Day, at a prison, that it's tense; you have to be careful. That is simply not the case."

During the cross-examination, the lawyer from the state attorney general's office asked Procunier, "If there's intense or great community interest, large demonstrations, heavy media coverage, would you take it from that that there would be great interest inside the prison walls?"

"Well, it depends on where these demonstrations are: Berkeley, or—or Beverly Hills," Procunier answered. "In my experience, the kind of interest you're talking about is going to be 'We should have killed him a long time ago.'" Procunier felt this attitude would prevail inside as well as outside the prison. "You're going to have *some* that would identify with the guy, similar to other places. But depending on where you're talking about, you're going to have a different reaction in Berkeley than you're going to have in Sacramento." In other words, the difference between the wacko-lefty sympathy for the murderer and the elected politicians' desire for his blood is going to be no greater than the range of opinions you'd find within the prison walls. What Procunier was doing, in his testimony, was to challenge the presumption of automatic identification between prisoners, between murderers — to suggest that something other than identity of situation makes us identify with people.

Anyone who has ever taught literature at the high school or college level, where adolescent questions of "identity" (to borrow Erik Erikson's term) are so overwhelming as sometimes to obscure all other concerns, will be familiar with this problem of *identify with*. It is a given, but it is not a predictable given. That is, most students enjoy only those books whose characters they can identify with, but that identification may not be based on the obvious grounds. My Santa Cruz students, for instance, only wanted to identify with Richard Wright's black characters; they found it politically and, I gathered, emotionally distasteful to project themselves into white suburban people like themselves. Men students these days find it easy to identify with women characters, while the reverse is not encouraged. At our moment in history, privileged readers like to identify with the underprivileged — the opposite pattern to that portrayed in the Depression-era film *Stella Dallas*, in which Barbara Stanwyck's factory-town character goes to the movies precisely to identify with the upper crust. "I don't want to be like me," she tells her born-to-the-manor escort, "not like the people in this place, but like the people in the movie — you know, doing everything well-bred

and refined." But then, *we* are supposed to be looking at Stanwyck, and identifying with her, from a comparatively upper-
crust position ourselves. At least since *Don Quixote,* one explicit function of art has been to allow people to identify with
something they are not, imaginatively experiencing other
kinds of lives.

Though the phrase "identify with" sounds jarringly
recent, like a remnant of Seventies psychobabble (an idiom
whose chief remnant may well be the word "psychobabble"),
the term is actually hundreds of years old. The *Oxford English
Dictionary* lists usages as far back as the seventeenth century,
with the initial examples pertaining to the transitive sense of
the verb—that is, "to make identical (with) ... to consider,
regard, or treat as the same." But another version quite close
to our present usage appears in the late eighteenth century, in
Burke (1780): "Let us identify, let us incorporate ourselves
with the people." The *OED* defines this version as "to make
one in interest, feeling, principle, action, etc., *with;* to associate
inseparably." It is essential to this version of the phrase that
the items to be associated not already be identical, for in
that case the association would have no meaning; the point is
that "interest" or "feeling" is uniting people who would otherwise remain separate. This seems to me very close to what my
students mean by "identify with," and also to what Ray Procunier means. (The *OED*'s third sense of *identify*—this time
without the *with*—curiously links the verb to the fate of a
criminal. In support of the meaning "to determine or establish
the identity of," the dictionary gives as the earliest known
example a phrase from Blackstone's legal commentaries of
1830: "All indictments must set forth the christian name, sir-
name [etc.] ... of the offender; and all this to identify his
person." This version of the word will become pertinent later
in the chapter, when I look at the notion of mistaken identity.)

What Warden Vasquez and his pro-capital-punishment
allies seemed to fear, and what some people on the KQED side

seemed to hope, was that seeing a murderer executed would cause us to identify with the murderer. This presumes that we do not do so already. But the murder plots we remain most attracted to—from Edgar Allan Poe's tales and Dostoyevsky's *Crime and Punishment* to the latest Oscar-winning movie—are those which assume at least a partial identification with the murderer. Sometimes this identification is deplored or disguised or unwilled or unconscious; sometimes it is brazenly signaled by having the murderer be the work's narrator. But whatever the technique, the presumption of identification is crucial to the story's plot, and to its effect on us.

This tendency is clear in the deservedly popular movie version of *The Silence of the Lambs*. Faithfully conveying Thomas Harris's novel to the screen, the movie contains two serial killers: Hannibal Lecter, who is already locked up in an asylum for the criminally insane, and Jame Gumb, who at the film's beginning, free and unidentified, is out carving up women to make himself a suit of female skin. Clarice Starling, a fledgling FBI agent (played in the film by Jodie Foster), receives as her first assignment the job of interviewing Hannibal the Cannibal and using him to track down the unknown killer. But while Clarice is busy climbing inside Lecter's skin in order to solve the current murders, he gets under hers, and ours. By the end of the movie we find ourselves not only agreeing with her when she tells her friend that the escaped Hannibal wouldn't harm her—"He would consider that rude," she says—but also cheering on Lecter himself when he proposes to make a meal out of his former psychiatrist and jailer, who is by far the most despicable character in the movie. *The Silence of the Lambs* plays on our fears of people like Hannibal Lecter, but it also plays on our even deeper sympathies with them; and the movie so revels in Hannibal's increasingly theatrical antics that poor Jame becomes almost a sideshow, his crimes reduced to providing the necessary but rather perfunctory denouement.

The intense relationship between murderer and detective is a staple of the murder-story genre, but in Thomas Harris's hands it becomes the central motivator of the plot. An earlier book of his, *Red Dragon*, formed the basis for *Manhunter*, a movie that has clear affinities with *The Silence of the Lambs*. Hannibal Lecter figures in both as the "inside" killer who must provide the key to the murderer still at large. In both movies, but much more strongly in *Manhunter*, the detective must mentally become the killer in order to catch him. He (for the earlier detective is a man) must pore over the evidence as if he himself had committed the crimes. He must allow himself to wander to the edge of madness in order to capture the maniac he seeks. If *The Silence of the Lambs*, by giving us a female detective, makes political as well as dramatic hay out of the position of women in a male-dominated outfit like the FBI, *Manhunter* much more terrifyingly suggests the extent to which any man — even, or especially, the most sensitive man — can imagine himself into the mind of a killer of women. And because movies, like other art forms, address their audiences androgynously, I would finally say "anybody" rather than "any man." Watching *Manhunter*, we are all, men and women, asked to identify with the strangely appealing though strikingly repellent killer, just as we are also asked to identify — and this is the source of the thrill, the fear — with the women he kills, or almost kills.

Like *The Silence of the Lambs*, *Manhunter* is impressively faithful to its source novel. But whereas Harris's second Hannibal Lecter novel only lends itself to movie adaptation, *Red Dragon* is integrally tied to the very idea of film, and therefore to the film that came out of it. Visual stimuli, including paintings, photographs, tattoos, and, most important, home movies, are key elements in the plot of *Red Dragon*, key clues to the discovery of the criminal. The detective, Graham, watches home movies made by the slaughtered families in order to learn more about the murder victims; in the process, he finds himself learning more about the murderer as well, and even seeing as if through the murderer's eyes. For the murderer—an odd, isolated, inarticulate, facially deformed but powerfully muscular man named Dolarhyde—has *selected* his victims by viewing these same home movies, to which he had access in the course of his work for a photo lab. Dolarhyde, who identifies himself with a red dragon in a painting by William Blake, and who has had himself emblazoned with a large dragon tattoo to cement the identification, gets his sexual kicks by watching his own version of home movies: the films he makes of members of the murdered families as he kills and violates them. These people, sightless in death, are the only ones he can bear to have as his "audience"; while he is filming, he sets the children up against the wall of their parents' bedroom and props their dead eyes open. Graham, divining this in the early stages of the investigation, manages to retrieve a fingerprint from the cornea of one of the children's eyes.

Despite his gruesome behavior, Dolarhyde comes off as a surprisingly sympathetic figure—if not appealing, then at least pitiable. The novel achieves this feat by placing whole sections of narration within his mind, as if from his viewpoint, though they are expressed in third-person prose, just as Graham's sections are. The movie, appropriately, uses visual means, assigning Dolarhyde's role to a tall, ungainly, albino-pale actor whose physical repulsiveness, as in *The Elephant Man,* comes to seem a Job-like affliction and therefore a stimulus to pity. And in both versions our sympathy for Dolarhyde is created mainly by having him fall in love with a blind woman who works at his lab. Their courtship—he first takes her to pet a sedated tiger, then takes her home to dinner and, at her instigation, to bed—is both the most terrifying and most moving part of the film. We already know he's a serial killer, but she of course doesn't, and her blindness, both figurative and actual, saves him for a while by shielding him from the agony of exposure.

Fictional murderers are traditionally afraid of acute sight, of accurate vision. Oedipus blinds himself after discovering he is a patricidal murderer, Gloucester has his eyes gouged out by his murderous son Edmund, and Edgar Allan Poe has the narrator of "The Tell-Tale Heart" say: "He had the eye of a vulture—a pale blue eye, with a film over it. Whenever it fell upon me, my blood ran cold; and so . . . I made up my mind to take the life of the old man, and thus rid myself of the eye forever." The eye can be the inflicter of violence, as in the movie *Peeping Tom,* where the plot somewhat resembles that of *Red Dragon* (a murderer makes movies of his victims as he kills them, using his camera and a mirror as part of the murder weapon); it can also be the recipient, as in Edmund's "Out, vile jelly!" "Perception's a tool that's pointed on both ends," is how one character in *Red Dragon* accurately puts it. Watching murder, we are pained in a particular way by seeing violence done to the eyes. Dr. Johnson, after exculpating the other forms of violence in *King Lear,* comments: "But I am not able to apologize with equal plausibility for the extrusion of Gloucester's eyes, which seems an act too horrid to be endured in dramatic exhibition, and such as must always compel the mind to relieve its distress by incredulity."

If we were watching an execution on television, we would not be able to relieve our minds in that way. We would not be able to tell ourselves, "After all, he's only acting; this is only a play." And yet we might be obliged to witness something as gruesome as Edmund's attack on Gloucester. An eyewitness to several deaths in the electric chair, a witness whose testimony was cited in the 1985 Supreme Court case *Glass v. Louisiana,* stated: "The force of the electric current is so powerful that the prisoner's eyeballs sometimes pop out on his cheeks." Condemned prisoners know this, and fear it. Randall Adams, the Death Row inmate whose wrongful conviction was the subject of Errol Morris's *The Thin Blue Line,* at one point described to the filmmaker exactly what happens to a man in the electric chair: "His eyeballs pop out, his fingernails pop out, his toenails pop out, he bleeds from every orifice . . ."

Have you been spared the horror of this by being spared the actual sight of it? I think not. Reading also brings things in through the eyes, and words enable us to create sickening mental pictures. *Red Dragon* is in many ways more horrifying, and more horrifyingly visual, than *Manhunter*. Visual artifacts are not just props in a book, as they can be in a movie, where everything is visual; when they are highlighted in words, we are forced to pay attention to them. *King Lear*, in which eyes and sight and blindness pervade the plot and the language, is also the play that, according to Marshall McLuhan, creates "the first, and so far as I know, the only piece of verbal three-dimensional perspective in any literature." In Edgar's description to the blind Gloucester of the imaginary steep cliff, the "arbitrary selection of a single static position creates a pictorial space with vanishing point," says McLuhan. "This space can be filled in bit by bit, and is quite different from non-pictorial space in which each thing simply resonates or modulates its own space in visually two-dimensional form." Even a film or a videotape is finally only two-dimensional. It takes an individual perspective, "a single static position," to give something three-dimensionality, to make it seem fully real—though three-dimensionality is itself an "illusion," a visual convention, as McLuhan, following Gombrich, points out.

Perspective, of the "I" rather than the "eye" variety, is one of the ways murder literature forces us, or lures us, or invites us to identify with the murderer. It is an invitation we readily accept, and not just we of the late twentieth century. Writing to the magazine editor who had printed one of his early first-person horror tales in the 1830s, Edgar Allan Poe remarked:

> The history of all magazines shows plainly that those which have attained celebrity were indebted for it to arti-

cles *similar in nature—to Berenice* ... In the ludicrous heightened into the grotesque: the fearful coloured into the horrible: the witty exaggerated into the burlesque: the singular wrought into the strange and mystical. You may say all this is bad taste. Nobody is more aware than I that simplicity is the cant of the day—but take my word for it no one cares anything about simplicity in their hearts.

Whatever Poe's conscious motives for saying this, marketing zeal alone is unlikely to have given him this degree of insight. The same hypersensitiveness that made him able to write his bared-ganglia tales also enabled him to understand what in us would respond to those tales. Poe's first-person stories of terror—from "Berenice" and "Ligeia" to "The Tell-Tale Heart" and "The Black Cat"—often ask us, grammatically, to identify with a ghoul or a murderer, and thereby invite us to savor the grotesque, the violent, the repellent.

Having devised this form for horror and sensation, Poe then re-used it for detection. He anticipated Thomas Harris by nearly a century and a half, for in Poe's Dupin stories solving the crimes *means* thinking one's way into the criminal's mind. The character C. Auguste Dupin appeared for the first time in Poe's 1841 story "The Murders in the Rue Morgue," and then reappeared in 1844 in "The Purloined Letter." The nameless American narrator who recounts this Frenchman's feats of intellectual wizardry—the Watson, so to speak, to his Holmes—begins the story in which the detective is introduced with a seemingly irrelevant discussion of the game of checkers. In this game, the narrator asserts, "the analyst throws himself into the spirit of his opponent, *identifies himself therewith,* and not unfrequently sees thus, at a glance, the sole methods (sometimes indeed absurdly simple ones) by which he may seduce into error or hurry into miscalculation" (my italics). This is a summary of the technique practiced by the detective we are about to meet, as Dupin subsequently confirms in "The Purloined Letter." "When I wish to find out how wise, or how stupid, or how good, or how wicked is any one, or what are his thoughts at the moment," Dupin tells his interlocutor in that later tale, "I fashion the expression of my face, as accurately as possible, in accordance with the expression of his, and then wait to see what thoughts or sentiments arise in my mind or heart, as if to match or correspond with the expression." Dupin's technique is identification by imitation, an imitation that copies outward appearance to get at inner thought. The key clues are visual, even though the goal is the invisible "mind or heart."

Dupin goes on to explain that in the case of the purloined letter, the police have failed because of their inability to take the correct measure of their opponent's very considerable intellect. What makes his remarks ironic is that Dupin's own ratiocinative success, his first time out in "Rue Morgue," consists of correctly identifying with an orangutan. The murder he solves—a mother and daughter found dead in a locked room, of throat-cutting and strangulation, respectively—is noteworthy for both its brutality and its curious absence of motive. Coupling these with the fact that the murderer requires enormous agility for his escape, Dupin comes up with the proper solution. Before he unveils the answer, however, he has his less astute sidekick guess the identity of the murderer. "A madman . . . ," our narrator responds, "some raving maniac, escaped from a neighboring *Maison de Santé.*"

This is a good guess, not only because, as Dupin confirms, madmen in some ways resemble beasts, but also because the typical murderer in a Poe tale *is* a madman. "True!—nervous—very, very dreadfully nervous I had been and am; but why *will* you say I am mad?" are the opening words of "The Tell-Tale Heart," whose murderous narrator continues to protest too much throughout the story, until his protestations of sanity essentially *become* the story. "The Black Cat" opens with the narrator's assertion that "I neither expect nor solicit belief. Mad indeed would I be to expect it, in a case where my very senses reject their own evidence. Yet, mad I am not"—again, a proposition that the story itself proves questionable. Both the narrator of "The Black Cat," who kills his own favorite pet and then, almost as an unimportant afterthought, his wife, and the narrator of "The Tell-Tale Heart," who murders an old man he purportedly loves, manifest a special kind of madness: the madness of excessive logic, of cold calculation and pure thought devoid of all human feeling. It is a kind of craziness that Dupin himself runs the risk of falling into, for he too is cut off from the run of humanity, and remains so by preference. "Had the routine of our life at this place been known to the world, we should have been regarded as madmen—although, perhaps, as madmen of a harmless nature," comments Dupin's roommate, our narrator, about their nocturnal existence, adding about his friend a page later: "What I have described in the Frenchman, was merely the result of an excited, or perhaps of a diseased intelligence." The connection between madness and murder—madness on the murderer's part, and imitative madness on the part of the detective—is hardly Poe's invention. It is as old as *Hamlet*, as new as *The Silence of the Lambs*. Viewed in light of this tradition, the veiled hints and evasive characterizations offered us by Poe's narrator become something much closer to a direct statement about Dupin's mental condition.

Dupin would deny that he is abstractly, logically mad, deny it not so much by disproving his madness as by showing the manner in which he is not abstract, the ways in which he is solidly and physically connected to reality. He deplores in other detectives—namely, the official Paris police—exactly that disconnection of body from mind which one might see as the identifying flaw in Poe's murderous madmen. Throughout "The Murders in the Rue Morgue" runs a theme of severed heads and headless bodies, evident not only in the actual body of one of the murdered women ("her throat so entirely cut that, upon an attempt to raise her, the head fell off"), but also in the crucial clue that enables Dupin to solve the mystery of the locked room. Pondering the murderer's mode of escape,

Dupin at last discovers how he got out of a seemingly sealed window: "I had traced the secret to its ultimate result, —and that result was *the nail* ... I touched it; and the head, with about a quarter of an inch of the shank, came off in my fingers." This headless nail is Dupin's key to the crime's solution, and it is also the story's most prominent (if not entirely clear) symbol. Even Dupin himself calls on its symbolism when he says at the end, describing the official police technique, that "in truth, our friend the Prefect is somewhat too cunning to be profound. In his wisdom is no *stamen*. It is all head and no body." To discover a murderer who is a beast, or even one who is beastlike, one must use more than one's brain. The detective must *feel* the connection, converting his very facial expression into that of his opponent, as Dupin is able to do even with an ape. If one of the moral flaws in Poe's murderers is their tendency to identify with animals more than with people—a problem most evident in the narrator of "The Black Cat"—then one of Dupin's virtues as a detective turns out to be his ability to do the same thing. Like the murderer, the detective must be able to slide down the chain of being as well as up it, move to a lower level of intellect as well as a higher.

Identification is thus, like perception, a tool that's pointed on both ends. The ability to identify with someone or something we are not is the basis for our most humane behavior, but it can also be the basis for our most inhumane. One must have the capacity to identify with another's feelings if one is to violate those feelings with any degree of personal intensity. As the philosopher Bernard Williams puts it, "cruelty needs to share the sensibility of the sympathetic, while brutality needs not to." This is the difference, say, between the alertly cruel Hannibal Lecter and the solipsistically brutal Jame Gumb. It may also be the difference between those of us who sympathize to the point of identification with a condemned murderer, and those who simply want to see him dead. There is something beyond fearful curiosity in our desire to observe

Robert Alton Harris at the moment of his death. We want him to enact something *for* us; we want to live the terror of death through him, and then be able to leave it safely behind. Carried to an extreme form, we call this kind of identification madness: the inability to tell the difference between ourselves and another, ourselves and the rest of the world. Limited to its usual form, we call it empathy. But even empathy can have its cruel side, as Bernard Williams's remark points out. In Poe, the barrier between empathy and destructive madness seems particularly fragile.

The Poe inheritor who learned this best is the expatriate American writer Paul Bowles. Bowles demonstrates his affinity with his nineteenth-century ancestor not only through his formal language, his macabre plots, and his distant emotional tone, but also in the way his characters are unable to perceive their own boundaries, sometimes even leaving their bodies to adopt the identities of other people, animals, and objects. Failing to distinguish between internal and external reality, Bowles's murderous heroes commit their crimes in a dreamlike state, impersonally wreaking havoc. Like Poe's madmen, they retain a strange sort of innocence by virtue of their failure to understand their own power.

This Poe-like tone is most audible in Bowles's short stories. The crazy but articulate narrator of "If I Should Open My Mouth," informing us with pedantic care about his plans to poison the chewing gum in subway-station dispensing machines, descends directly from the narrators of "The Black Cat" and "The Tell-Tale Heart," though his crime has been updated to suit our impersonal urban existence. The madwoman who is our informant in "You Are Not I" has trouble, as the title suggests, determining where she leaves off and another person begins, just as Poe's William Wilson does. The Arab boy who is the protagonist of "Allal" exchanges identities with a vicious, poisonous snake, terrifyingly making Dupin's technique literal. In all these stories, the central character is both victim and murderer; and all three illustrate that the capacity to identify with another may as easily be violent and harmful as friendly and sympathetic.

Bowles mimics the vacillating motion between identification and detachment in the very rhythms of his prose style. He is a master of the kind of indirect discourse that moves inside a character's mind even while remaining ostensibly outside it. This is particularly true in his novels, where the narration is officially in the third person but the viewpoint flits from one character to another; and of the novels, *Let It Come Down* most strongly suggests the relation between a vacillating narrative viewpoint and an innocently murderous character. It does so largely by converting the personal into the impersonal—by showing us how much emotional power can be released when something human is confused with something inanimate.

This focus on the active inanimate begins as early as the book's title, which, the epigraph informs us, is taken from *Macbeth:*

> BANQUO: It will be Rayne to Night.
> FIRST MURDERER: Let it come downe.
> *(They set upon Banquo.)*

Aside from its delicately emphatic rhythm—its onomatopoetically rainlike, pattering sound, of which Poe would have approved—the title nicely joins together Bowles's nearly contradictory preoccupations: the violence done to humans by other humans, and the subjection of human beings to forces beyond their control. A murderer may feel he has a special kind of freedom and strength, as Bigger Thomas felt after committing his crimes, but actually he is as subject to external forces as anyone else. The First Murderer's imperative statement—about the rain or whatever else may "come down"—will not really ensure the outcome. Isolated in Bowles's quotation, the murderer's remark can be taken as either a grandiose and therefore foolish display of power, or as a resigned and therefore intelligent acknowledgment of fate; it plays both ways.

Bowles is particularly interested in the way a murderer can also be a victim—not just when he is executed, as the more standard account would have it, but even at the moment of committing the murder. Dyar, the hero/villain of *Let It Come Down,* is a man who seems least powerful, least willful, during the very passages when he takes his fate most irreversibly into his own hands. An American in Tangier (like his author), he is—according to his author's introduction—"a nonentity, a 'victim,' as he describes himself, whose personality, defined solely in terms of situation, elicits sympathy only to the extent to which he is victimized." Like all authorial explanations, this one deserves to be handled like a two-edged sword. It's true that Dyar is a wimp, a patsy, but he does not, as his name seems to promise, die. Instead, he kills someone else, and in the course of that murder he gets lifted out of himself, so that while he is indeed the victim of *something*—drug-induced hallucination? guilt-induced paranoia? solitude-induced madness?—he is no longer the schnooky little victim we have come to associate with the person Dyar; like the boy in "Allal," he has become something with fangs. In stressing the extent to which Dyar, at the moment of his crime, becomes something other than his usual self, Bowles implicitly explores the question of who actually commits a murder: is it the person who continues to exist afterward and is generally obliged to take the punishment for the act, or is it some other entity, some other personality or impersonality that comes into being only at the instant of the killing?

Bowles leads up to the murder by suggesting the way Dyar has already moved outside himself. "After a day passed largely in the contemplation of that far-off and unlikely place which was the interior of himself," we are told the day before the murder, "he did not find it difficult now to reject flatly the reality of what he was seeing." This formal, distant style is both the author's bug-collector way of pinning down a character and the character's own way of viewing his "far-off" self. That the two modes are the same becomes even clearer in a later passage, just before the murder: "He gasped a little, and thought of moving. (I must remember to tell myself to move my left hand so I can raise myself onto my elbow . . .)." It is typical of Bowles to withhold from us the total immersion of first-person narration until the moment when the character himself is utterly divorced from his own limbs, his own will.

When Dyar actually does commit the murder—the completely unwarranted killing of his friend and ally, Thami—he is enabled to do so by thinking of his sleeping victim as the same sort of fragmented object he has become himself. "Partly he knew that what he saw before him was Thami, Thami's head, trunk, arms and legs," runs the interior/exterior monologue, shortly before the killing. "Partly he knew it was an unidentifiable object lying there, immeasurably heavy with its own meaninglessness, a vast imponderable weight that nothing could lighten." What Dyar does with this object is rendered with chilling directness:

> A mass of words had begun to ferment inside him, and now they bubbled forth . . . "Melly diddle din," he said, quite loud, putting the point of the nail as far into Thami's ear as he could. He raised his right arm and hit the head of the nail with all his might. The object relaxed imperceptibly, as if someone had said to it: "It's all right." He laid the hammer down, and felt of the nail-head, level with the soft lobe of the ear. It had two little ridges on it; he rubbed his thumbnail across the imperfections in the steel. The nail was as firmly embedded as if it had been driven into a coconut.

Dupin's nail has come into its own, has progressed from a crucial clue, a guiding metaphor, to the weapon itself. While Bowles's rigorously technical description may at first seem to have little in common with Poe's overheated prose, there is a family resemblance between the impersonality of Dyar's action and the efficient manner of the "Black Cat" narrator, who comments after burying his ax in his wife's brain: "This hideous murder accomplished, I set myself forthwith, and with entire deliberation, to the task of concealing the body." The two kinds of hideousness lead in opposite directions: the Black Cat murderer demonstrates logic carried to insanity, while Dyar's is the insanity of the illogical, the babbling nonsense of "Melly diddle din." But Poe's and Bowles's murderers are alike in having divorced themselves from any sense of feeling for the thing they kill.

In this they resemble "the state," which, when it executes a condemned man, needs to view him as no more human than itself. (Less human, from some perspectives: "You respect the rights of the condemned man more than you do those of . . . the state," Judge Schnacke complained to KQED's lawyer.) Ironically, this technique often increases our sympathy for the dying man. A condemned murderer may have a specific, repellent personality of his own that puts us off, but when the state attempts to deprive him of *any* personality, we leap in to provide him with one of our own making. Once we begin to view him as the victim of depersonalization, the condemned murderer instantly becomes more appealing. It is easier to identify with a victimized "it," as Dickens, with his pathetic grotesques, well understood, than with an obnoxious and reprehensible "him."

With Bowles this focus on the "thingness" of the victim is made explicit, and the uncanny precision of his prose style comes through in the use of that tiny word "it." "The object relaxed imperceptibly, as if someone had said to it: 'It's all right.'" The first instance is shocking and chillingly specific; the object, Thami, is no longer a he but an it. The second instance, though, is general, colloquial, and warmly communal, not only in its tone of reassurance ("It's all right"), but in the external reality, the daily omnipresence we attribute to the "it" in such phrases. "It will be Rayne to Night": if there is a God in *Macbeth* or *Let It Come Down,* It is located in that It. Even the sources of comfort in such a world are impersonal, inhuman.*

In reacting against Bowles's vision of impersonal malevolence, some readers have accused him of amorality — as if the author fully shared, to the point of being identified with, the chaotic principles he portrayed. Such readers don't want to give Bowles credit for their own reactions, don't want to acknowledge the extent to which his vision of an amoral universe actively produces a moral response in us. If he deprives his characters of humanity, we lend it to them; if he insists that all is chaos and indifferentiable confusion, we insist on imposing distinctions and attempting to sort things out. Paul Bowles's fictions may affect affectlessness, but they demand a felt response, and in coming up with that response we create our own consolation, to the extent any is possible.

A far bleaker view is offered by one of Bowles's fellow expatriates and near-contemporaries, Patricia Highsmith. The sadness or despair we may feel about the murders in Bowles's novels is utterly absent from our response to Highsmith's work, where the only strong emotion stimulated in us is anxiety. The pleasures of reading Highsmith lie close to the sources of pain, and both have to do with the loss of any feeling but anxious self-preservation.

Most serial authors have a detective for their continuing hero; Patricia Highsmith, in her Ripley series, has a murderer who in each book outwits the police and goes on to kill again, not so much for pleasure as for profit. Highsmith, like Bowles, has created (in her own version of indirectly internal discourse) a murderer who gets away with his crimes. But her

*Paul Bowles himself, in a letter written to me in 1984, said: "It hadn't occurred to me that the act of murder played any serious part in my writing, and I was surprised to see *Let It Come Down* and *Up Above the World* bracketed in that respect. Perhaps the death of Thami in the former never struck me as murder — rather as a kind of inevitable accident."

Tom Ripley is no Dyar. If he is a victim, it is only at the beginning of his career; only in the first novel, *The Talented Mr. Ripley,* do we see him in his chrysalis of orphaned poverty, of American nonentity, from which he emerges to become the sophisticated, well-to-do expatriate who occupies the later books. In the long run, Highsmith is thus even more discomforting than Bowles. If Bowles comes out of Poe, Highsmith comes out of a strange marriage between Poe and Trollope, where the local squire turns out to be a closet killer, but where the Trollopian pleasures of food, travel, and domestic comfort otherwise prevail.

The frightening thing about Highsmith's novels is the way in which we begin almost obliviously to share Ripley's viewpoint and subsequently find ourselves having taken on his guilt as well. This killer is inside us before we know it, and we are inside him. But that's a very odd place to be, because Ripley—especially in the first novel of the series—is most often outside himself. Like a detective who can discover inner truth only through outer appearance, Ripley catches clues to himself in mirrors ("Slowly he took off his jacket and untied his tie, watching every move he made as if it were somebody else's movements he was watching"). He is a constant actor, performing both his own role ("In a large mirror on the wall he could see himself: the upright, self-respecting young man again") and that of others ("He wiped his forehead the way Dickie did, reached for a handkerchief and, not finding any, got one from Dickie's top drawer, then resumed in front of the mirror"). After he kills Dickie Greenleaf, he takes on Dickie's identity and fools everybody, not because they look exactly alike but because he manages to think of himself as Dickie. When things start closing in, he turns back into Tom Ripley—not a return to his "real" identity, but simply another convenient incarnation. For the thing about Ripley is that he has no real identity; he is always improvising. He has turned Dupin's detective technique into a complete mode of existence. "If you wanted to be cheerful, or melancholic, or wistful, or thoughtful, or courteous, you simply had to *act* those things with every gesture," he observes. This is the source of his fascination for us, and it is also the source of his contagious guilt. He is such a permeable vessel that he cannot keep contained within himself his own sense of wrongdoing, but allows it to flood over us as well.

Ripley feels guilty even before he does anything wrong. At the beginning of the novel, when he is just helping out the Greenleafs in their pursuit of their wayward son, he is aware that he "was doing the right thing, behaving the right way. Yet he had a feeling of guilt." It is not that he already knows he's going to kill their son and steal his money; nothing could be further from his mind. He feels guilty only when it's not the appropriate emotion. After Ripley commits his first murder, and the other murders needed to cover up the first one, he ceases to feel guilt and feels instead the anxiety of someone who might be caught. The anxiety too is contagious, and as readers of a Ripley novel we begin to feel anxious that *we* have done something wrong and are going to get caught. Most likely we have; almost everyone has. What Highsmith's insidious style does is to prey on that sense of being far from sinless, to make us begin to feel as if our least crimes are susceptible to the exposure warranted by murder. Ripley's free-floating guilt has left him and entered us.

There is, it must be acknowledged, a certain kind of pleasure to be obtained from feeling the anxiety of guilt, especially when it is someone else's guilt and can be sloughed off at will. The pleasures of reading Highsmith stem from the same antithetical sources as the wish-fulfillment Freud managed to find even in those anxiety dreams we all have about failed exams or missed trains. The wish, the fulfillment, comes when you awaken from the dream and find that you haven't, after all, committed this gross error. Freud insisted that only people who had never failed an exam, never missed a train, would use these plots for their anxiety dreams; otherwise the relief on waking would be incomplete. In the same way, Highsmith's novels must appeal only to those of us who haven't actually committed a murder. It is a luxury to identify with Tom Ripley (or, for that matter, Robert Alton Harris) — a luxury that only the relatively innocent can afford.

Only a small part of the pleasure Highsmith gives us comes from the fact that Ripley gets away with his crimes. That may account for some of the interest, the novelty of her books; but the deepest source of their attraction, the way they gratify us with a guilty anxiety that can be discarded at will, is very close to the attraction exerted by a work of art in which the first-person murderer gets caught — as he does, say, in "The Tell-Tale Heart" or "The Black Cat." These stories allow us to be fully inside the murderer, and fully aware of all the possible risks of exposure. To give us the maximum perception of this risk, the author may choose to put us inside both the murderer and the detective, as Thomas Harris does — or even inside a murderer who is himself the detective.

Jim Thompson gives us exactly this plot in *The Killer Inside Me*, a work which so specifically examines the problem of identifying with a murderer that I have borrowed its name for this chapter. The narrator of Thompson's novel, Lou Ford, is a good-old-boy deputy sheriff in a small Texas town, a man remarkable mainly for his dogged devotion to duty and his overuse of clichés. So he seems, at any rate, to his fellow citizens. Actually he's a child-molester, a girlfriend-beater, and a murderer. Thompson, in this novel, exploits the notion of identification as something relative rather than absolute. We may choose to identify with the murderer, not because he is inherently appealing, but because the people who surround him are so much worse. Lou Ford is not what you would call a likable figure, but just about everybody else in *The Killer Inside Me* is less likable, so we come to depend on him as a twisted sort of Virgil guiding us through Jim Thompson's underworld. There is something congenial in his style, an ease of presentation and self-presentation that makes him an acceptable if not totally trustworthy narrator. He is "inside us" because that voice works its way so insidiously into our heads; and he is also inside us because something about the way he explains his crimes rings true to our sense of the way the world is.

In giving us the murderer from inside, Thompson is careful not to give us everything. He understands the importance of leaving things partially unexplained, of giving us enough insight but not too much. Any explanation for murder that too easily explains away the mystery is likely to strike us as suspect. Thompson even undercuts some of his own offered explanations: the novel's dime-store-psychology analysis of Lou's condition is intentionally unconvincing (there's a good scene in which the clever, medically knowledgeable Lou trounces a visiting forensic psychiatrist), and the childhood trauma Lou recalls—an early sexual experience that consisted of beating the family's masochistic housekeeper—seems inadequate to explain his misdeeds. No, the explanation that rings true to us is the *absence* of an explanation, the sense that all this had to happen and that Lou was merely fate's instrument. "She'd had to be tight," he says of his fiancée, recounting how she reached for her purse at the moment he was kicking her to death, "like any damn fool ought to have known; because there wasn't any other way of being, and that's all any of us ever are: what we have to be." This is offered as self-justification, but also as fact. Elsewhere he takes the idea further—himself not only as instrument of fate, but as the instrument of those who are seeking their own deaths. "It was funny the way these people kept asking for it," he says. "Just latching onto you, no matter how you tried to brush them off, and almost telling you how they wanted it done. Why'd they all have to come to me to get killed? Why couldn't they kill themselves?" This is grotesquely funny, and also patently untrue about at least some of his victims; but there is also a way in which it accurately renders the psychological impact of murder on us, the audience.

Every murder, however unexpected, also seems to have about it a quality of inevitability. Or perhaps our only way of coping with randomness, with complete chance, is to call it fate. Joan Didion harps on this quality of expectedness in her essay "The White Album," where she says of the Charles Manson murders:

> On August 9, 1969, I was sitting in the shallow end of my sister-in-law's swimming pool in Beverly Hills when she received a telephone call from a friend who had just heard about the murders at Sharon Tate Polanski's house on Cielo Drive. The phone rang many times during the next hour. These early reports were garbled and contradictory ... I remember all of the day's misinformation very clearly, and I also remember this, and wish I did not: *I remember that no one was surprised.*

It is not just that Didion's friends, in that era of Kennedy and King assassinations, lived in a world of imminent violence. Surprise was not an appropriate response because even the most seemingly random events were viewed as part of some invisible pattern. About one of the principal participants in the Manson trial, a ditzy New Age type named Linda Kasabian, Didion remarks: "Linda did not believe that chance was without pattern. Linda operated on what I later recognized as dice theory, and so, during the years I am talking about, did I."

Perhaps in reaction to the kind of rational and insufficient explanation satirized in the person of Jim Thompson's forensic psychiatrist, Didion has thrown away all efforts to explain murder. The murderer Didion identifies with, or sees herself as continuous with in affect and attitude, is not Charles Manson himself, who barely makes an appearance in this essay. It is the Los Angeles that gave rise to him — Los Angeles as a state of mind and a moment in history as much as a physical location. In this essay Didion has taken into herself, as her "killer inside," the senselessness that permeated the city in which the Manson murders took place. In such a context, cause and motive become pointless. Internal connections, seeming coincidences, random events forced into a pattern, are all that matter. "I was no longer interested in whether the woman on the ledge outside the window on the sixteenth floor jumped or did not jump, or in why," Didion says, in the most nakedly unembarrassed admission of her generally narcissistic approach to events. "I was interested only in the picture of her in my mind." Didion goes on to argue:

> In this light all narrative was sentimental. In this light all connections were equally meaningful, and equally senseless. Try these: on the morning of John Kennedy's death in 1963 I was buying, at Ransohoff's in San Francisco, a short silk dress in which to be married. A few years later this dress of mine was ruined when, at a dinner party in Bel-Air, Roman Polanski accidentally spilled a glass of red wine on it. Sharon Tate was also a guest at this party, although she and Roman Polanski were not yet married. On July 27, 1970, I went to the Magnin-Hi Shop on the third floor of I. Magnin in Beverly Hills and picked out, at Linda Kasabian's request, the dress in which she began her testimony about the murders at Sharon Tate Polanski's house on Cielo Drive ... I believe this to be an authentically senseless chain of correspondences, but in the jingle-jangle morning of that summer it made as much sense as anything else did.

Why do I find Lou Ford's untrammeled narcissism amusing and persuasive, whereas Joan Didion's strikes me as deeply offensive and filled with bad faith? Only partly, I think, because Lou Ford and his victims are fictional characters, while both Joan Didion and the people she describes are real. This is, however, an important difference. When one is dealing with murder, there is something liberating about the fictional mode, and something conversely restrictive about choosing to deal with reality. Reality imposes certain obligations, and also certain obligatory feelings. We are obliged, for instance, to value the least human life over the greatest artwork: if we could save a potential murder victim, *any* murder victim, by destroying Michelangelo's *Pietà*, we would be obliged to dispense with the statue. Yet even to pose the situation in this adversarial manner shows how impossible it is to weigh such things. What is the "least" human life, and what kinds of human life would count as greater? To acknowledge the validity of this sort of measurement is to violate the very obligations the example hopes to demonstrate; even to be asked to make such a choice is morally sickening.

This jarring incommensurability becomes evident whenever fictional violence and real violence are discussed in the same breath. I love David Cronenberg's movies, but there is something that makes me want to renounce them all, some fatal flaw of tone, in the story he tells about making *Scanners:*

> Inevitably the first day was the most disastrous shooting day I've ever had. We went out, and there was nothing to shoot ... We were shooting along the expressway, and the traffic was jamming up. A guy in a truck was watching us shooting by the side of the road and didn't notice that everyone in front of him had stopped. I turned round in time to see his truck climb on top of this little Toyota. Our grips had to jump the fence and drag these two women out of their car and lay them on the verge. Dead. It was hideous ...

Somehow "the most disastrous shooting day I've ever had" does not seem adequate to cover this, and the introductory "Inevitably" only makes things worse. The story causes one to think in a different way about the violence in Cronenberg's films, as if (though this is patently untrue) that transcendent fictional experience of violence had been bought at the cost of real human lives. This is not to say that Cronenberg should stop making films as some kind of penance for the car accident; simply that he should refrain from telling this story.

But this tonal problem—this moral confusion wrought by the claims of reality when they are brought to bear against the claims of the artist's own inner life—is only part of what I object to in Didion's essay. Her crime against the Manson murders, her refusal to grant them the integrity of a separate existence outside herself, is just one element in what's wrong with her prose. What truly offends me is that Didion thinks she can get away with the self-indulgence of a fictional character, an actor in someone else's plot. Lou Ford is, after all, only a narrator, and behind even the most intense moments of our communion with him we sense another viewpoint, the ordering viewpoint of his author. However high on the pinnacles of egotism Lou ascends, he cannot injure us in his fall, because Jim Thompson is holding a safety net beneath us.

Joan Didion acts as if she has this freedom, as if she is just the narrator, as if we can't hold her responsible for authorship. She orders events for us, she composes the narrative, she makes the connections, and then she insists that all narrative is "sentimental," all connections "equally meaningful, and equally senseless." Yet hers is the determining sensibility by which we are asked to abide. She apparently acquires this right to senselessness, to lawlessness, by incorporating into her own mind the atmosphere that led to the Manson/Tate killings; but she acquires this right without having gone to the limit herself, without having committed the actual crime and risked punishment, as Lou Ford does. So her attempt to be our Virgil in the underworld of murder is doomed to failure. At her best—and in this essay she is not at her best—she can only be a Persephone, paying seasonal visits to death's realm and then fleeing back to the comforts of everyday life, the shallow ends of Beverly Hills swimming pools.

Since she sees herself as afflicted by self-consciousness to an almost paralyzing degree, it seems perverse to accuse Joan Didion of a lack of self-awareness. But it is finally this flaw

that most severely damages her essay; Lou Ford, by comparison, comes off as a persuasive and unsentimental narrator.
One can see the difference most clearly in their respective use
of banalities. Banalities are a constant in the telling of murder
tales, which all, sooner or later, come to rest on clichés (like
"sooner or later"). Both Lou Ford and Joan Didion have a
fondness for cliché, but Lou Ford is its master, Didion its servant.

I'm not just talking about Ransohoff's and I. Magnin, the
stereotypical shopping haunts of women of Didion's background. I'm not even talking about the spilled red wine,
though if anyone but herself had tried that one, Didion would
have leapt on him for being a sentimental symbol-mongerer.
I'm talking about the use of the phrase "jingle-jangle morning"
in the final, supposedly emphatic line of the passage I quoted
earlier. This phrase, which worked perfectly well in the refrain
of Bob Dylan's "Tambourine Man," becomes an instant cliché
in Didion's hands: she takes a piece of living cultural effluvia
and kills it dead on the page.

Part of the problem is Didion's lack of concern about
whether we recognize the source of the words. This problem
is tied to what I have been calling Didion's narcissism, her
failure throughout the essay to keep track of who *we* are, out
there in her audience. At times she tells us major historical
facts as if we've just arrived from Mars; at other times she
expects us to recognize unquoted allusions to popular song
lyrics. If in this case we *don't* recognize the words—if we don't
know they come from a song that also contains the lines, "I'm
not sleepy and there is no place I'm going to"—they mean a
different thing, in this essay about nighttime murders, from
what they do otherwise. And if we *do* know the song, the
words seem twisted out of context here, for "Tambourine
Man," despite its drug-related story line, is possibly the most
tuneful, the least "jangly" of Dylan's compositions, and the
rhythmic and lulling tone of the music utterly conflicts with
the ragged, jagged string of events Didion is here patching

together. By using the phrase as if it were purely menacing rather than allowing it to retain its teasing ambiguity, Didion converts it into a mere jingle-jangle of sound, an empty phrase, an unwitting cliché.

Lou Ford, in contrast, uses his clichés like a hidden stiletto, goading his victims without ever letting them know they're being intentionally gotten at. In the first few pages of *The Killer Inside Me*, we see him unleash this weapon on a relatively benign fellow citizen. "I liked the guy—as much as I like most people, anyway—but he was too good to let go," Lou tells us. "Polite, intelligent: guys like that are my meat." He then lets loose with a string of clichés that runs from "A man doesn't get any more out of life than what he puts into it" through "The boy is father to the man" to a final fusillade that includes "Every cloud has a silver lining," "Haste makes waste," and "I like to look before I leap." About this last cluster, Lou remarks in an aside to us: "That was dragging 'em in by the feet, but I couldn't hold 'em back. Striking at people that way is almost as good as the other, the real way"—by which he means (though we don't know this yet) murder.

Words as actions, banality-mongering as murder: this is Lou Ford, but it is also Jim Thompson, offering us a hint about the kind of pleasure it gives him to hook us on a story like this and make us squirm. ("I could hear his shoes creak as he squirmed," Lou says about this first victim of his battery of clichés.) We who are attracted to murder stories are asking to be victims ("It was funny the way these people kept asking for it"), begging to be tortured with yet another banal story, told in banal language, about this banal crime. Part of our enjoyment lies in the banality: that too is one of the suspect pleasures, like feeling vicarious guilt, which the murder story offers us. The banality of evil is also the fascination of evil, and clichés can sometimes be true. In Lou Ford's case they often are, tellingly so, as the string I've already listed suggests. In this story of a teenaged child-molester and woman-beater who grew up to be a murderer, the child *is* father to the man; and he does indeed look before he leaps, as his well-plotted murders reveal.

If murder is a cliché, then that is partly because the hack pens of journalists have so long been applied to it. Thompson makes this point too, later in the novel, when Lou is reading over the newspaper reports on the murders of his first victims. "As usual, the papers had given me all the breaks ... they had me down as a kind of combination J. Edgar Hoover-Lombroso, 'the shrewd sheriff's sleuth whose unselfish intervention in the affair came to naught, due only to the unpredictable quirks of all-too-human behavior.'" Lou laughs at this, as we do, and then considers calling up the papers

> and complimenting them on their "accuracy" ... I could say something—I laughed—I could say something about truth being stranger than fiction. And maybe add something like—well—murder will out. Or ... the best laid plans of mice and men.
> I stopped laughing.
> I was supposed to be over that stuff.

It is the cliché-mongering, as much as the brutal murdering, that Lou can't escape, the "sickness" he can't get out from under. The clichés rushing unbidden to his mind are, as usual, all about his own situation. One of them, the one about truth being stranger than fiction, is even about him in a way he can't possibly comprehend, for despite his vast reserves of intelligence, Lou doesn't know he's only a fictional character.

Yet in a way he does know this—knows, at least, that he's the main character in the tale he's telling us. Unlike Didion, he understands the responsibilities of narrative and unshirkingly takes them upon himself. He understands that part of what draws us to a murder story is an admiration of craft, and he undertakes to deliver that expected or hoped-for level of detailed workmanship. "In lots of books I read," Lou tells us toward the end of his own book, the writer seems to go haywire every time he reaches a high point. He'll start leaving out punctuation and running his words together and babble about stars flashing and sinking into a deep dreamless sea. And you can't figure out whether the hero's laying his girl or a cornerstone. I guess that kind of crap is supposed to be pretty deep stuff—a lot of the book reviewers eat it up, I notice. But the way I see it is, the writer is just too goddamn lazy to do his job. And I'm not lazy, whatever else I am. I'll tell you everything.

The murderer who is an author, who becomes an author to tell us the story of his murder, is the governing model in all these narratives about murder. The model even structures stories that are told by another author about a real-life murderer, for in that case, whether the author is Norman Mailer or Joe McGinniss or Ann Rule, the writer takes on the life of the murderer as a way of taking on material, enters the mind of the killer so as to have a good story to tell us. Lou Ford's "I'll tell you everything" could be the motto of *The Executioner's Song* or *Fatal Vision* or *The Stranger Beside Me*, as Rule acknowledges by echoing Jim Thompson's title in her own. These authors identify themselves, though sometimes resistantly, with their murderers; they feel that the connection is somehow fated or inevitable.

Throughout her book on Ted Bundy, Ann Rule repeatedly ponders the curious and coincidental intimacy between herself and her subject. "Not even a television script could make it believable that a crime writer could sign a contract to write a book about a killer, and then have the suspect turn out to be her close friend," she comments about the coincidence that shapes her book. (What makes it seem even more ludicrously overplotted is that they met as fellow workers at a suicide hot line.) Bundy, though still in some ways just a casual acquaintance, was more than Rule's friend. "I doubt that Ted will understand the depth of my feeling for him," she writes toward the end of the book. "The knowledge that he is undoubtedly guilty of the grotesque crimes attributed to him is as painful to me as if he were my son, the brother I lost, a man as close to me in many ways as anyone I have ever known."

In *The Executioner's Song*, Mailer brings Gary Gilmore to life by making him a Maileresque figure, a character who is by implication his own narrator—for elsewhere Mailer writes about himself in the third person, as here he does about Gilmore. Like the Mailer we have come to know from such autobiographical works as *Advertisements for Myself* and *Armies of the Night*, this Gilmore is both an individual citizen and a historically significant personage who embodies within himself the cultural conflicts of America. He is an expressive, eloquent writer and a lover of feminine beauty. He is, moreover, a master of gallows humor, not to mention a firm believer in reincarnation, of the sort that Mailer subsequently espoused in *Ancient Evenings*. If we are fascinated by the Gary Gilmore of Mailer's "true life novel," it is in part because he offers us so many of the same rewards we get from Mailer's more explicitly autobiographical works. The miracle is that in *The Executioner's Song* Mailer accomplishes this act of identification without once setting foot on the stage himself. We are so used to his dominating presence that his very absence seems a commentary, a vacuum that demands to be filled with the larger-than-life figure he gives us instead.

Conversely, a true-crime author may borrow qualities or incidents from his murderer and apply them to himself, even though his identification with the murderer may be unwilled, unconscious, or concealed. Joe McGinniss does this, for instance, at the end of *Fatal Vision*, in the 1985 Afterword to the book, when he describes wiping his nose with his hands one night in the winter of 1980:

> As I switched on the bathroom light and looked in the mirror, I saw that it had not been a runny nose but a

bloody nose, and that I was now standing at the sink of my hall bathroom with my hands covered in blood. And then it came to me what day it was, and I ran back to the bedroom to check the time; it was 3:30 A.M. on the morning of February 17, 1980—ten years to the minute from the time that Jeffrey MacDonald had stood at *his* hall bathroom sink at Fort Bragg with the blood of his wife and children on his hands.

McGinniss is remarkably obtuse about his own motivations, and here he makes too little of this story, using it only to show "how deep my involvement in this business really was." It is up to us to conclude that, in bringing Jeffrey MacDonald to permanent life on the page, McGinniss unconsciously felt himself to have become an accomplice, a perpetrator who had "the blood of [MacDonald's] wife and children on his hands."

Like the Didion example, the McGinniss version of entering the mind of the murderer is filled with bad faith: he wants credit for plumbing the abysses, and yet he hasn't had the nerve, if that's the right word, actually to go to hell himself. For the author-as-murderer story to work, we need to get the feeling that the narrator really *has* killed somebody, which means that the most satisfying versions of this plot are likely to be the fictional ones. Mailer realized this, which is why he made his book a true-life *novel*. We want to hear about the murder directly from the person who committed it, but we also want to hear that story shaped as literature.

The clearest and most powerful version of the murder story fictionally told from the inside—portraying the viewpoint of a realistic murderer, but with all the shaped beauty of art—is also one of the oldest examples of the genre: Dostoyevsky's *Crime and Punishment*. If, as Dostoyevsky said, all Russian literature of his era comes out of Gogol's overcoat, then we in turn may say that all modern killer-inside-me tales come out of Raskolnikov's shabby old student coat. From the opening lines of *Crime and Punishment*, we are offered a prose of vacillation and anxious inconsistency, a prose that is simultaneously outside and deeply within the sensibility of the murderous hero. (I will quote, unless otherwise noted, from David Magarshack's persuasively intense translation, but the same tendency is also evident in the Constance Garnett version, as well as in the recent translation by Richard Pevear and Larissa Volokhonsky.) "On a very hot evening at the beginning of July a young man left his little room at the top of a house in Carpenter Lane, went out into the street, and, as though unable to make up his mind, walked slowly in the direction of Kokushkin Bridge." The book's first sentence, in that phrase "as though unable to make up his mind," captures Raskolnikov's eternally recurrent condition, and yet does so in a way that seems only to be hazarding a guess from appearances. Farther down the page we learn that "He was up to the neck in debt to his landlady and was afraid of meeting her," and the mention of this fear now begins to hint at omniscient, soul-seeing authorship. Yet the language itself, the overwrought "up to the neck in debt" (Garnett has "hopelessly in debt"), sounds more like a formulation of the young man himself; and a few lines farther on we are told, "As a matter of fact, he was not the least afraid of his landlady, whatever plots she might be hatching against him. But rather than be forced to stop on the stairs and listen to all the dreary nonsense which did not concern him at all, to all those insistent demands for payment . . ."

We are now well inside Raskolnikov's own inconsistencies: his paranoid (though, it turns out, justified) fears of "plots"; his cockeyed sense that "those insistent demands for payment" have nothing to do with his debt, do "not concern him at all"; and most of all his sense, vacillating wildly in the course of a single paragraph, that he is both afraid of his landlady and "not in the least" afraid of her. But we have come into this deeply internal terrain by way of a narrator outside Raskolnikov, one who is as capable of floating into the consciousness of a conceited prig like Luzhin or a satanic genius like Svidrigaylov or a goodhearted, passionate man like Razumikhin as he is into the tortured soul of this murderer. Like Raskolnikov, the narrator of *Crime and Punishment* seems to have no firm idea of where his dreamlife leaves off and others' reality takes over; like Raskolnikov, he embraces vacillation and inconsistency "as though unable to make up his mind." It is this curious authorial voice which makes the open-and-shut case of Raskolnikov's crime so unfixed, so contingent, so mysterious. To vacillate is, after all, to prove that one is still alive, capable of changing one's mind at any moment. Only the finality of death brings fixity. So if vacillation induces elements of anxiety in us — anxiety at not knowing exactly where we are going to settle — it can also be pleasurable, reminding us of the fluidity of life, the freedom to be different things at different times and *not* know how it will all turn out.

Behind and against the voice of this narrator, who believes in change and fluidity, lies something terrifyingly fixed: the threat of murder, or execution. In Dostoyevsky's hands, the two categories begin to merge together. "Crime" and "punishment" are not sequential events, the latter an external act of the justice system, brought about in response to the former. They are simultaneous and internal: both belong to the murderer himself. Raskolnikov's crime *is* his punishment, looming over his head, dooming him. This is not, strictly speaking, a question of remorse. Remorse in this novel is a sentimental indulgence, as practiced most noticeably by the drunken Marmeladov, who deplores his own careless destruction of his family ("But, my dear sir, do you really think that my vile and unprofitable life doesn't make my heart bleed? A month ago, when Mr. Lebezyatnikov laid his hands on my dear wife while I lay blind drunk in the same room, do you imagine for a moment, sir, that I did not suffer?"). Raskolnikov's suffering is of a purer, less self-displaying sort, but even Raskolnikov's more persuasive suffering is called into question by the existence of a figure like Marmeladov.

In Raskolnikov's case, the decision to commit the murder, the act of committing the murder — though "decision" and

"act" both overstate the function of his will—are themselves
the source of his victimization. He has, so to speak, put his
own neck into the noose. "He entered his room like a man sentenced to death," we are told the day before the murder, when
circumstances for the first time seem to favor his plan to kill
the old pawnbroker. The image of execution invades Raskolnikov's sensibility at the very hour of the killing ("'It is like
that, I suppose, that the thoughts of those who are led to execution cling to everything they see on the way,' it flashed
through his mind" as he approached the pawnbroker's house),
and colors his fear of discovery and retribution afterward:

> "Where was it," thought Raskolnikov—"where was it I
> read about a man sentenced to death who, one hour
> before his execution, says or thinks that if he had to live
> on some high rock, on a cliff, on a ledge so narrow that
> there was only room enough for him to stand there, and if
> there were bottomless chasms all round, the ocean,
> eternal darkness, eternal solitude, and eternal gales, and
> if he had to spend all his life on that square yard of
> space—a thousand years, an eternity—he'd rather live
> like that than die at once! Oh, only to live, live, live! Live
> under any circumstances—only to live! How true it is!
> Good Lord, how true it is! Man's a scoundrel! But
> anyone who calls man a scoundrel is an even bigger
> scoundrel himself!" he added a moment later.

Like the self-accusation in the last lines, this passage doubles
back on itself, reflecting a sense of life's value for the women
Raskolnikov has murdered as well as his own desire to keep
living, to remain untrapped, unaccused.

There is nothing facile about the way Dostoyevsky has
converted his murderer into a victim, though people have
used his discovery to mouth platitudes. Primo Levi, the great
Italian-Jewish writer who survived Auschwitz, quoted one
such mouthing in *The Drowned and the Saved:* "The film director
Liliana Cavani, who was asked to express briefly the meaning
of a beautiful and false film of hers, declared: 'We are all victims or murderers, and we accept these roles voluntarily. Only

Sade and Dostoevsky have really understood this.'" Levi's answer to this is eloquent and profound. "I do not know, and it does not much interest me to know, whether in my depths there lurks a murderer," he says, "but I do know that I was a guiltless victim and I was not a murderer. I know that the murderers existed, not only in Germany, and still exist, retired or on active duty, and that to confuse them with their victims is a moral disease or an aesthetic affectation or a sinister sign of complicity; above all, it is a precious service rendered (intentionally or not) to the negators of truth." I said earlier that perhaps only the relatively innocent can enjoy an identification with murderers. Here I want to stress the "relatively," and point out that the purely innocent—in particular those who have actually been victims, like Primo Levi—probably have no access to such enjoyment.

It is dangerous, as Levi says, to confuse murderers with their victims. But is it not possible for murderers to be a different kind of victim on their own, without usurping the role of the people they themselves have victimized? This, I think, is what the case of Robert Alton Harris made clear. Harris did not cease to be a murderer, and the boys he killed did not cease to be pitiable victims, when he was sentenced to the gas chamber at San Quentin. But he nevertheless became a victim himself—at the very least, of the slow-grinding judicial system that was inexorably, though with numerous digressions and brief cessations, dragging him toward his death. The threat of execution converts a murderer into a victim without allowing him to cease being a murderer.

Dostoyevsky himself well understood the threat of execution, for in 1849 he had been led before a firing squad in the Semyonovsky parade ground in St. Petersburg—perhaps as a kind of cruel joke on the part of the Czar, who apparently never intended to carry through on the killing. Dostoyevsky was sentenced to death, at the age of twenty-seven (Raskolnikov's approximate age in the novel), for publishing anti-government propaganda. He was saved only at the very last

minute by a commutation of his sentence, delivered on horse-
back and read aloud at great length by a stuttering soldier—a
truly Dostoyevskian touch—which reduced his punishment
to four years in Siberia. (Raskolnikov, in the end, got eight.)
So when Dostoyevsky repeatedly refers to his hero as a man
who feels about to be executed, he is emphasizing the bonds of
identification between this particular author and the murderer
he has created.

As well as those between reader and murderer. For if we
find it hard to acknowledge a potential murderer inside us,
either because we deny it entirely or because we consider it an
"aesthetic affectation" (to use Primo Levi's term), we certainly
have no trouble locating in our hearts the potential victim of
the criminal justice system, that terrified creature who can't
escape the workings of the blind, inexorable judicial machine.
"As though he had been caught in the cog of a wheel by the
hem of his coat and was being drawn into it"—that's Dostoyevsky talking about Raskolnikov, but it could apply just as
well to K. in Kafka's *The Trial,* to Highsmith's Tom Ripley, to
George Stroud in Kenneth Fearing's *The Big Clock,* to the
Henry Fonda character in Hitchcock's *The Wrong Man,* to the
Susan Hayward character (based on the real-life Barbara
Graham) in *I Want To Live,* and to Randall Adams in Errol
Morris's *The Thin Blue Line.* The odd thing about this sense of
entrapment, and our identification with it, is that it has very
little to do with whether the accused actually committed the
crime.

Janet Malcolm, in her book *The Journalist and the Murderer* (which chronicles Jeffrey MacDonald's lawsuit against
"his" author, Joe McGinniss), has a psychoanalytic explanation for why we so easily identify with murderers:

> This reason can be stated as a corollary to society's need to
> punish the transgressor, which is the need to forgive the
> transgressor. The crime of murder is one we have all
> committed in our (conscious and unconscious) imagina-

tions. We have all dreamed about the violent deaths of our families; we have all said about people we love "I could kill him" (or her). In our old literature, we have Medea, Clytemnestra, and Oedipus acting out these fundamental fantasies; more recently, and thus more veiledly, we have Raskolnikov killing his mother and sister through the murder of two strangers. And as we need to be punished and then absolved of our guilt, so do we punish and then absolve those who actually do what we only dream of doing.

However truthful it may be at its core, the Freudian viewpoint on murder inevitably manifests the fatal flaw of reductiveness—especially when set beside the overwhelming complexities and subtleties of a novel like *Crime and Punishment,* or even of daily life. In many if not most murder stories, from *The Killer Inside Me* to *Psycho* to *The Silence of the Lambs,* from *The Thin Blue Line* (which features a sequence about "Doctor Death," the capital-punishment-inducing courtroom psychiatrist) to Janet Malcolm's own book (which skewers Dr. Stone, McGinniss's expert psychiatric witness), the psychiatrist is the easy butt of the joke, the know-it-all booby who hasn't a clue. The fact that the vastly intelligent Hannibal Lecter is himself a former psychiatrist is the exception that proves the rule, for does one really want the honor of the profession to rest in the hands of a cannibalistic murderer? Even *Crime and Punishment* contains one of these satiric figures, in the form of the well-meaning, well-fed, officiously opinionated Zossimov, the medical student who suspects that Raskolnikov may be mad. That Raskolnikov may indeed be mad—or, like Hamlet, playing so hard at madness as makes no difference—does not subtract from the sum total of Zossimov's boobiness, which consists partly of being right for the wrong reasons.

What Errol Morris shows so skillfully in *The Thin Blue Line* is implied in all these works: the justice system and the psychiatric system have a natural affinity with each other because both prefer diagrammatic, black-and-white, instantly comprehensible renderings of reality to the messy, difficult tangles of truth. I think we identify with the murderer partially because we see him as the victim of both these misrepresenting systems. The justice system needs to misrepresent, for its own purposes, exactly *what* he did, with each side in the adversarial arrangement correspondingly heightening or depreciating his actions and motives; and the psychiatric system inevitably misrepresents *why* he did it. The reductive machinery, the inexorable cog in the wheel, makes the accused murderer a figure we can identify with on our own terms; for we too have felt trapped, in one context or another, by the machinery of our social setting. We don't have to imagine ourselves as murderers to identify with him. We need only imagine ourselves as victims.

This holds, strangely enough, whether the accused murderer is in fact guilty or innocent of the crime, though it holds in a different way in each case. If we believe him to be guilty — as I believe Robert Alton Harris to have been guilty of pulling the triggers in the murders he was accused of — we can nonetheless identify with the condemned man's victimization at the hands of the justice system. In that case we may feel that the punishment is inherently too cruel to be practiced on anyone, however heinous the crime; or that the murderer was in some way the victim of external circumstances, and therefore not fully responsible for the crime; or that the process of conviction was rigged or unfair, with insufficiently thorough defense for the murderer; or that the selection of this particular punishment for this particular crime was arbitrary, given the punishments assigned to other convicted criminals; or that there remains some mystery at the heart of the crime, something we still don't know about how it happened, so that even if we are sure that *this* man pulled the trigger, we don't know what else was involved. All of these arguments were raised, in one way or another, in the case of Robert Alton Harris. All of these arguments have to do with the gap between the vacillating uncertainties of reality and the dead certainty of capital punishment.

But the greatest gap arises when the wrong man has been convicted of the crime. Appeals lawyers sometimes argue, with varying degrees of sophistry and sophistication, that their client on Death Row is no longer the same person he was when he committed the crime; that remorse, or rehabilitation, or the simple process of aging in prison, has made him cease to be "identical" with the murderer of a decade earlier. This is one version of executing the wrong man. But another, less legalistic version is that the wrong person was arrested in the first place, either through honestly mistaken identity or lying witnesses or incompetent police or corrupt prosecutors, or any combination of the above. According to Roger Keith Coleman (admittedly a biased source, since he was speaking from Death Row only fifteen days before his execution date), there are at least twenty-three cases in this century of people who were proved innocent *after* they were executed. Jim McCloskey, who works full time to free wrongly convicted prisoners, estimates that up to one-tenth of the people in American prisons are innocent of the crimes they've been jailed for. Whatever the exact figures, these cases come to light with sufficient frequency (two such wrongful murder convictions were overturned in California in March 1992, after the condemned men, Clarence Chance and Benny Powell, had spent thirteen years in prison) to make us wonder about all the other cases. They make us wonder how we can ever be certain, when we threaten to execute a murderer, that we are not about to make a terrible mistake.

The appeal of such stories, when they are conveyed to us in book or, more commonly, movie form, is very different from those about a guilty murderer. They are more painful—not only because the injustice is extreme, but because the victim is closer to ourselves in nature. He is relatively innocent and so are we; ergo, this could happen to us. Again, let me stress the "relatively": the victim in these cases is usually guilty of *something*, if only of being inarticulate, or apathetic, or careless, or transient, or friendless, or unemployed, or just plain odd. Our identification with him — or, in the case of Barbara Graham, her — is therefore of a different nature from our feeling in regard to a guilty person. We are willing to let ourselves enter into the victim just so far; at some point, we insist on detaching ourselves, saving ourselves. This tension between identification and detachment is what makes such movies pleasurable, but it is also what can make them anxiety-producing to the point of tedium. We have trouble staying the course with an innocent victim, especially if the mistake becomes irrevocable — that is, if the wrongful conviction leads all the way to death. And even if the mistake is finally rectified — as it is, say, when the Henry Fonda character is at last released in *The Wrong Man* — the filmmaker is likely to make us feel that what has been lost by the mistake can never be fully restored.

*The Thin Blue Line* is about one such mistake. The documentary filmmaker Errol Morris, snooping around the Texas prison system in pursuit of another story, came upon a man who, he realized, had been wrongly imprisoned for a murder he had not committed. In the course of several years' investigation and filming, Morris made a movie whose effect was ultimately to free Randall Adams (though this effect is not contained within the movie; the film ends, that is, with Adams still in jail). Using his own quirky documentary format, Morris created an artwork that drew on all the usual sources of interest in a fictional murder tale. We are asked, as the audience to this fragmented, complicated, rigorously un-self-explanatory film, to be the detectives piecing together the true Randall Adams story; and we are asked to identify, at different times, with both the wrongly accused man and the actual murderer. Morris is following directly in Dostoyevsky's footsteps when he asks us, in particular, to understand how even an innocent person might act and appear guilty, as the housepainter Nikolay does in *Crime and Punishment*. "'What were you frightened of?' 'That I'd be found guilty of the murder.' 'But why should you be frightened of that if you knew you were innocent?' Believe it or not, Zossimov, but they actually put that question to him, and literally in those words," says the kindly and intelligent Razumikhin, acknowledging how easy it is for blind justice to make such mistakes.

Like all protagonists of murder stories, from Oedipus onward, Randall Adams seems the victim of a preordained, foreshadowed plot. "It's as if I was meant to be here," he says the first time we see him onscreen, before we know he's in a Texas prison, before we even know who he is. The actual murderer, David Harris, says of Randall Adams toward the end of the movie: "Heard of the proverbial scapegoat?" Adams is presented not just as the scapegoat for David Harris's youthful crime spree, but for all of us who may ever have taken up briefly with an unsavory character, been in the wrong place at the wrong time. And "fate," very self-consciously, is presented as the way we sometimes try to justify or rectify or explain away to ourselves the bad mistakes that are due to human error.

Morris's vacillating, eccentric, colloquial film style, filled with gallows humor and other forms of grotesque comedy, is the visual and auditory equivalent of Dostoyevsky's anxious prose style: it's funny, but it's also terrifying. "I'm trying to speak for you. I'm trying to speak for all of you. I *am* the student body," says a silly blonde actress in a tacky, semi-pornographic cheerleader movie that Morris has Randall Adams and David Harris watching together at a drive-in on the night of the murder. (This is in one of the many "reenactments," a plot device that Morris used with self-conscious irony before television took it up as a straightforward means of reportage.) The remark is ridiculously laughable, and it is also chilling in the way it seems to apply to Randall Adams's own position as representative victim. Yet we need to be careful—the movie teaches us to be careful—about accepting the offer the remark suggests: that Adams can be our stand-in sufferer, our collective scapegoat.

The heroic knight-errant figure in this movie, as in *The Silence of the Lambs,* is a woman: Edith James, Randall Adams's "lady lawyer," as all the other characters persist in calling her. The fact that she is a woman, a denigrated outsider in the good-old-boys world of Texas law, might seem to be an unfair play for sympathy, or *would* seem so in the hands of a filmmaker less complex than Morris. But unlike Jodie Foster's glamorous Clarice Starling, this heroine first appears onscreen as yet another butt of our audience ridicule. Heavy-set, wearing glasses, and speaking with a twangy, high-pitched voice, Edith James initially comes off as corny and possibly incompetent. "I hate to be considered some kind of dummy who believes in the innocence of her clients, whatever . . . I *am* kind of gullible," she says. But she is the first person in the film to call Randall Adams by name—to locate this story and identify its main character for us—as well as the first person in Texas to recognize Adams's innocence. It was she who took his case through the lower courts, losing through no fault of her own ("Any prosecutor can convict a guilty man. It takes a great prosecutor to convict an innocent man," is one of the Texas jokes the movie tells us); and it is she who explains to us, in a few sentences, the legal processes whereby Adams had his death sentence commuted but remained locked up in prison without the possibility of a new trial.

This movie also has its Hannibal Lecter, its Svidrigaylov: not the central, pathetic, somehow more innocent murderer but the *other* one, the particularly guilty one, who by virtue of his unrepentant and deep-seated evil earns our intense fascination. In this case that role is played by David Harris, whose friendliness and articulateness mark every scene with him, and whose willingness to render the right affect makes him so much more congenial, on a superficial level, than the rather deadpan Randall Adams. As a boy of sixteen, David met up briefly with Randall Adams, killed a Dallas policeman shortly after dropping Adams off at a motel, confessed the murder to a few of his friends, and then helped the state frame Randall Adams for the cop-killing. "Little David," as Edith James repeatedly calls him, seems rotten to the core. Yet even he is given his moment of sympathy in the movie, when Errol Morris, against a quick montage of old family snapshots of two towheaded boys, allows David to describe the accidental childhood drowning of his brother and his own subsequent sense of survivor's guilt. This is offered neither as psychiatric explanation nor as mitigating circumstance; it is simply offered as a fact about David, one that enlarges our view of him and momentarily makes us feel something for him.

At the end of the movie, Morris gives David Harris the crucial piece of dialogue. "What do you think about whether or not he's innocent?" an offscreen Morris asks David Harris about Randall Adams. (The interview takes place in yet another prison, to which David has been sentenced for yet another murder; he was never accused of the Dallas cop-killing.)

"I'm sure he is," answers David.

"How can you be sure?"

"'Cause I'm the one that knows."

This is a scene from real life, but it is also straight out of *Crime and Punishment,* where Raskolnikov comes to tell Sonia who killed the pawnbroker and her half-sister:

> "How do you know?" she asked quickly, as though recollecting herself suddenly.
> Sonia was panting. Her face was getting paler and paler.
> "I know."

If David, the guilty murderer, can be Raskolnikov for a moment and thereby achieve some level of grace and forgiveness, then Randall Adams, the innocent, wrongly accused man, can sometimes sound like the depraved killer Lou Ford.

Describing in detail the gruesome manner in which someone dies in the electric chair, Adams discusses his own fear at the prospect of such a death: "You get numb. It's like a bad dream. You want to wake up, but you can't do it." Lou Ford, talking in *The Killer Inside Me* about his plan to kill his fiancée, says: "It was like being asleep when you were awake and awake when you were asleep." Even Adams's numbness has a curiously guilty quality to it, like the emotional numbness we have come to associate with Poe's Black Cat murderer, Bowles's Dyar, Highsmith's Ripley. This is not at all to say that Randall Adams was actually guilty of the crime of murder. But Errol Morris is too good an artist to let Adams, or us, fully off the hook. *The Thin Blue Line* gives us a very special kind of killer-inside-us: the kind who didn't actually commit a murder but could have been executed nonetheless, an unintentional scapegoat for all our relatively innocent human sins. Yet can there be such a thing as an *unintentional* scapegoat? If we don't purposely use him as a vehicle for our self-shriving, the innocent man's death will fail to have its cleansing effect. It will instead compound our sins, turning everyday faults like carelessness and hypocrisy into something far more mortal.

# 4

## The Sleaze Factor

One of the everyday frailties shared by most of us is curiosity about the lurid details of murder. True-life murder stories like *The Thin Blue Line* ask, much more pointedly than fictional ones, the question of whether there is something inherently depraved in our curiosity. This is a question that threatens to expose the character of both the author or filmmaker and the reader or viewer, both the purveyor of the sleaze and its consumer.

A version of this question — one might call it, in this context, the question of motive — colored the whole course of the *KQED v. Vasquez* case, both within and outside the courtroom. What kind of television station would want to broadcast an execution? What kind of person would want to watch it? What kind of society would permit it? (Perhaps I am over-sensitive to this concern because I also felt another, unspoken question lying in the background: What kind of person would be interested in writing about it?) The judge himself appeared to be influenced by this perspective, this sense that KQED's case was somehow unseemly. "He acts kind of mad at us," is how one KQED employee characterized Judge Schnacke's manner in the courtroom, "as if we shouldn't even be bringing the suit in the first place."

I had asked about the general feeling around KQED in regard to the case. "Oh, we're all pretty much in favor of it," said this employee. But elsewhere I had heard rumors that the organization's board and management were seriously divided over the seemliness of the lawsuit. I knew that KQED had lost a number of memberships and donations because of the case: the angry letters accompanying these cancellations followed a predictable how-can-you-be-involved-in-such-sleaze pattern. Every time the case hit the newspapers or the airwaves, which happened many times between the March 25 opening of the trial and the June 7 verdict, KQED's public relations office braced itself for a new onslaught. One morning, as a group of us waited in the hallway outside Judge Schnacke's courtroom for the hearing to begin, I heard Joanne Sutro, KQED's public relations director, compliment William Bennett Turner, the station's *pro bono* lawyer, on his TV appearance the night before.

"I worry that every time I open my mouth you lose another hundred members," Turner joked.

"Yes," Sutro responded, "but every time anyone *else* opens his mouth, we lose even more."

At this point someone mentioned that the "Geraldo" show was planning to cover *KQED v. Vasquez* that very day. "Geraldo!" groaned one of the KQED people. "I wonder if he has any idea how often his name has come up during this case."

Geraldo Rivera has been performing the role of representative media sleaze at least since Mailer wrote *The Executioner's Song,* over a decade prior to the *KQED* trial; as recently as May 1992 he was the cameo murder victim in a made-for-TV Perry Mason movie that capitalized on his distasteful reputation as a tell-all talk show host. But Geraldo only represents a particularly visible example of what exists everywhere in the broadcasting profession: a tendency to convert journalism into entertainment. Speaking on an ABC News "Nightline" episode about what would happen to a videotape of an execution, the *San Francisco Examiner* journalist Stephanie Salter said:

"By the time it's been dissected and analyzed and shown again and again on news programs, and by the time it makes its way to MTV and some sort of musical video that's supposed to make us think deeply about ourselves as a society, so what, it won't—it will lose its power to scare us and stop us and make us think about, hey, we're killing a guy today." Anthony Lewis, in the op-ed column he published in the *New York Times* during the *KQED v. Vasquez* trial, argued the same point: "Television will not make the business of official killing real to the viewer. It will trivialize executions—reduce them to the level of entertainment, to be clicked on and off." Newspapers, on the other hand . . .

A condemnation of the whole media profession became part of the record in *KQED v. Vasquez* when Florida prison superintendent Thomas Barton responded to cross-examination by Beth Brinkmann, Turner's associate.

"In your opinion," she asked him, "the press don't give a damn about the truth?"

"The majority of them are interested in selling the point," he said, "whether it—their story—whether it be electronic or written print." He sarcastically characterized the widely distributed coroner's photo of the electrocuted Ted Bundy (submitted in this case as Plaintiff's Exhibit #29) as "another one of the expos of the media," and admitted that as prison superintendent he "certainly" tried to stay as far from the news media as he could.

Journalism's interest in murder and death as a grotesque form of entertainment is not a twentieth-century invention. The *National Police Gazette,* founded in New York in 1845, was printing 150,000 copies a week by the late 1870s; its distinctive pink pages, containing an ever-rising quota of blood and sex, were a staple of the reading matter available in barber shops, hotels, saloons, and other pleasurable gathering places. The equivalent publication in England was such a hit with the mass readership that Dickens, in *Our Mutual Friend,* could have the illiterate Betty Higden say of her orphan charge, "You mightn't think it, but Sloppy is a beautiful reader of a newspaper. He do the Police in different voices," and expect his 1865 audience to understand the reference to the *Police Gazette*. Similar papers existed in other European countries, and one such newspaper worked its way into Poe's "Murders in the Rue Morgue" as the source of all Dupin's information. The story's narrator tells us that he and Dupin "were looking over an evening edition of the 'Gazette des Tribunaux,' when the following paragraphs arrested our attention." The paragraphs in question—quoted in full, so that they take up eight pages of a forty-page story—are luridly headlined: "EXTRA-ORDINARY MURDERS." That such information affords entertainment to Dupin is made explicit in a subsequent remark: "As for these murders," the amateur detective is quoted as saying, "let us enter into some examinations for ourselves, before we make up an opinion respecting them. An inquiry will afford us amusement." The narrator immediately adds: "[I thought this an odd term, so applied, but said nothing]."

Poe's congenitally naive narrator may be shocked at the idea of someone finding amusement in a murder story, but Dostoyevsky's characters are far more sanguine. Raskolnikov, it is true, fears that his excessive interest in newspaper reports of the pawnbroker's death will be seen as not only morbid but highly suspicious. Still, Raskolnikov is an evident paranoid. "You're interested to know what I was reading about, what I was looking for in the papers, aren't you? See how many papers I've asked the waiter to bring me! Suspicious, eh?" he says to the policeman Zamyotov when he runs into him in a café. "I declare to you, or rather *I confess*, or better still, *I am making a statement* and *you are taking it down* ... that I was reading—I was interested—I was looking for—searching ... searching for news—and that was what I came in here for, of the murder of the old widow of the civil servant."

Zamyotov's reply suggests that there is nothing inherently suspicious about such behavior. "'Well, what if you have been reading about it?' he cried suddenly, perplexed and impatient. 'What do I care? What of it?'" This answer is a bit disingenuous, as we learn later; by this point in the plot Zamyotov and the other inspectors have already begun to suspect Raskolnikov. But it is not Raskolnikov's reading habits in themselves that are suspicious. It's his display of guilt and paranoia about them. As for reading about the murders, everyone else in St. Petersburg is doing it too, so that each time Raskolnikov wakes up from his fever-induced sleep, he hears his caretakers—Zossimov, Razumikhin, and the others—obsessively discussing the latest details of the crime and its investigation. This is not guilt, but human nature.

Or perhaps the two are not so easy to tell apart. Errol Morris gives us a good lesson about this in *The Thin Blue Line.* It's also a lesson about the dangers, and allures, of confusing fictional murder-mystery stories with real ones.

At a crucial moment in the film, we learn that Randall Adams's fate, his wrongful conviction for murder, hinged largely on the testimony of a "surprise witness" who appeared on the last day of the trial. An alleged eyewitness, this woman (one Mrs. Miller) insisted it was Randall Adams she saw shooting the cop—or sitting in the driver's seat of the car, shortly about to shoot the cop—as she drove by on the other side of the street. By this point in the film we already feel that Randall Adams is innocent, so we doubt her testimony; and, for reasons that come out later in the film, this turns out to be a correct assessment. But our initial reason for doubting Mrs. Miller is that she herself, speaking to Errol Morris a decade after the trial, seems to be such a suspicious character. "When I was a kid," we hear her saying, "I used to want to be a detective all the time, because I used to watch those detective shows on TV." Then we see her for the first time, a creepy-looking woman with glassy eyes, virtually colorless bleached hair, a weird little smile, and badly applied makeup. Morris intercuts shots of her with snippets of old black-and-white Keystone Cops movies, as we listen to her speak about her amateur detection. "I listen to people," Mrs. Miller says, "and I'm always trying to figure out who's lying or telling the truth."

This is Morris at his most risk-taking. He seems to be setting this woman up, cruelly mocking her and inviting us to join in the laughter. And to a certain extent he *is* doing that: this is not an Edith James situation, where our initial skepticism about the "lady lawyer" proves totally inappropriate and the character is utterly vindicated. But it turns out, in the case of Mrs. Miller, to be we who are really being set up, we who deserve to be mocked. For in our feelings of superiority and self-righteousness—"*This* is the witness who convicted Randall Adams, this strange, affectless idiot who can't tell the difference between movies and real life?"—we momentarily forget that we are guilty of some of the same sins she is. (Not all of them, however: we are not bearing false witness, for one thing. Our "sins," if that's what they are, remain those of private pleasure rather than public harm to another person.) Like Mrs. Miller, we enjoy trying to figure out, just by listening and watching, who's lying and who's telling the truth; we have already decided, for instance, that she's lying. Like her, we evidently enjoy watching detective movies and murder stories—such as this one, *The Thin Blue Line*, the one we're watching as she speaks.

Morris is asking us to do something subtle and complicated here. He is asking us to appreciate the form he has cast his story in—the detective-story format—and also to resist that form. He even implies that we have an *obligation* to resist the forms of art, or of argument, that we automatically find alluring. If we accuse Mrs. Miller of falling too easily into the role of murder-movie viewer, confusing fiction with reality, then we who are absorbing as art the true though artfully shaped story of Randall Adams's conviction must be included in the accusation. It is an accusation, moreover, in which Errol Morris, with his self-consciously sleazy use of various film devices, implicitly includes himself. We are all guilty of being fascinated by Randall Adams's fate, entertained if also horrified by his tragedy.

Why "guilty"? There's nothing wrong, most of us would agree, in being interested in detective stories. There's not even anything unusual, as Dostoyevsky points out, in taking an intense interest in the details of a recent murder, as supplied by the daily newspapers. So when does this fascination edge over into something more reprehensible, something that might be subject to the accusation of voyeurism? To be an offensive voyeur, as opposed to a participant in mutually agreed upon sex games, one must derive pleasure from witnessing other people's activities without their permission. The essence of voyeurism is its secrecy, its hiddenness: the voyeur peeps at his object, his victim, from a place of relative invisibility. This is why fictional murder stories and other imagined artworks can't really engender voyeurism (though they can attempt, as some do, to simulate the atmosphere of voyeurism). Fictional characters can neither withhold nor grant permission for us to view them. To fictional characters, we are neither invisible nor visible; we simply don't exist at all for them. In the case of real people transmitted to us on the page or the screen, though, we are learning something about them while remaining completely unrevealed ourselves. We *do* exist for them—at least in the abstract, as other people inhabiting the same universe—but they can't see us or know anything about us. We, on the other hand, know incredibly intimate things about them.

This is not exactly voyeurism in its sexual sense, but in *The Journalist and the Murderer* Janet Malcolm makes a connection between that more traditional version of secretive gratification and the pleasures of finding out about someone else's murder. "Although none of us ever completely outgrows the voyeurism of childhood," she says, "in some of us it lives on more strongly than in others—thus the avid interest of some of us in being 'insiders' or getting the 'inside' view of things." Reading Gary Gilmore's letters to Nicole Barrett, hearing David Harris exculpate Randall Adams, watching as a condemned person dies in the gas chamber—these are all versions of getting an abnormal "inside" view, seeing things from which we would normally be excluded if the people in question were just acquaintances of ours. As social acquaintances, they would be protected by the rules of ordinary politeness from our probing and peering; but as strangers caught up in the cogs of law and journalism, they are completely exposed to us.

*The Journalist and the Murderer* is in large part about the discomfort we feel with the "sleaze factor" in murder stories—even, or especially, those of us who are avid consumers of such stories. The background to Malcolm's book is that Joe McGinniss and Jeffrey MacDonald, the title's journalist and murderer, had entered into a contract whereby McGinniss would be offered an exclusive inside view of MacDonald's trial, in return for which MacDonald would get a cut of any money McGinniss made from his book about the case. When the book, *Fatal Vision*, eventually came out, McGinniss—having all along kept his opinions to himself, and having continued to pump the now-convicted MacDonald for information, under the guise of an enduring friendship—announced his firm belief that MacDonald was in fact guilty. MacDonald, in the initial contract between them, had signed away the right to sue for libel, but he proceeded to sue McGinniss for fraud. The case was settled out of court, after a hung jury failed to resolve it. This lawsuit was Janet Malcolm's essential subject, but she used it as the springboard for a wide-ranging discussion of law and ethics, fiction and nonfiction, unforgivable lying and normal deception, and other subjects pertinent to the pursuit of journalism. (I was going to say law *versus* ethics, and so on, for the pairs I've cited are presented in Malcolm's book as oppositional notions. But it is important, especially when discussing a trial, to avoid the simple adversarial structures that trials offer us, to see things as related in more complicated ways—as Malcolm herself acknowledges in calling her book *The Journalist and the Murderer.*)

What Joe McGinniss was really on trial for, as he seems not to understand in the impassioned epilogue he has now added to *Fatal Vision,* was being a sleaze. This is not a convictable crime. It is not the same, legally speaking, as fraud, though it has something to do with what we mean when we say about someone's character: "He's a total fraud." As the First Amendment lawyer Floyd Abrams said on a TV talk show in regard to a hypothetical version of the MacDonald-McGinniss case, it "raises a nice issue of the difference between the sort of situations which the law ought to deal with and the sort of situations which allow us to pass a moral judgment on somebody but which the law, as such, is not designed to deal with." The judge and jury, to the extent they did not simply dismiss MacDonald's claim outright, seemed to be in sympathy with his sense that McGinniss had done something ethically despicable. Even a convicted murderer, as the KQED lawyers mentioned in their brief, may have a right to a certain degree of privacy, of integrity; and even a murderer may deserve not to be lied to.

Malcolm appears to find McGinniss personally despicable, but she also sees in his behavior the root of all relations between journalists and their subjects. A lie of omission—that is, the failure to say "I may betray you"—is at the heart of all such encounters, she feels, and there is something rotten in every contract, written or unwritten, between journalist and subject. She received a lot of criticism from the journalistic community for expressing this view, and her position in this regard is indefensibly extreme. But *The Journalist and the Murderer* is nonetheless a skillful and intelligent exploration of the inherent anxiety we feel about the sleaziness of the writer or filmmaker or newsperson who gets involved in chronicling a murder story.

One level of that anxiety derives from a naive belief (naive because we see it disproven all the time, yet manage to hold onto it nonetheless) that we cannot learn The Truth, or even some truths, from a liar. If an author lies to her subject, how can we be sure she is not lying to us as well? And even if she doesn't *mean* to lie to us, will such a person be capable of collecting and transmitting the truth? Margaret Mead expresses this ethical concern very movingly in her anthropological book *New Lives for Old*, where she explains that she does not have any baseline data about childbirth from her previous trips to New Guinea with which to compare her postwar data: "For, in 1928, no woman who had not herself borne a child was permitted to witness a birth, and I believed then, as I do now, that in field work it is essential not to deceive those from whom one wishes to learn the truth. I had never had a child and so I saw no childbirth."

I have always loved those sentences (part of what I love is the stirring ring of the phrase "I believed then, as I do now"), but I have come to feel that they cannot adequately deal with all situations. Or perhaps it's just that rules which were meant to apply "in field work" cannot be transferred to the courtroom, the true-crime story, or the evening news. Particularly in cases involving murder, where the best potential witness, the victim, is no longer around to tell us his side of the story, we are constantly required to learn the truth from people who are either lying or being lied to by us. Even if our only lie is silence—and we who are viewing these events from the audience seats of the courtroom or the movie theater have no option but to be silent—we are still implicated in the exchange of untruths. Part of the fun of detective stories, as that creepy Mrs. Miller said in *The Thin Blue Line*, is "trying to figure out who's lying or telling the truth." Sometimes we even learn more from the liars—as Errol Morris does from David

Harris, as jury members do from the witness who makes a crucial slip, and as readers of true-crime books do from accomplished fictionalizers like Truman Capote and Norman Mailer.

However, lying is not the only ethical crime McGinniss committed, though it was the one he was officially on trial for. His other crime, equally non-convictable, was taking money for his voyeuristic work, exploiting a real-life tragedy for purposes of his own financial gain. This may be even more common than lying: it could accurately be said of any writer who focuses on murder stories, from Norman Mailer and Ann Rule to Janet Malcolm and me. To the charges of sleazy amusement-seeking and voyeurism incurred by her readers, the writer or creator of a true-life murder story thus inevitably adds the charge of exploitation. She's making money off someone else's story, swooping in for the kill like some ugly old buzzard. That this has become so common as to be parodic does not make it any the less distasteful. A recent episode of the TV show "48 Hours," which covered the current life of a "reformed" and therefore highly endangered gangster, asked about the man who shadowed his footsteps: "Is he a bodyguard? A federal agent? No, he's an author." Nor does the symbiotic nature of the parasitic relationship make it any more palatable. In fact, the discovery that the criminal is benefiting too ("You mean you're splitting your advance with a convicted *murderer?*") is likely to make the audience even more suspicious of the exploiting author.

The problem of exploitation, whether for money or for some other kind of gain, continually resurfaced in the case of *KQED v. Vasquez*. It lay behind Judge Schnacke's remark (echoing Mencken) that "no one ever went broke underestimating the taste of the American people." It also appeared in his reference to the Playboy channel and his suggestion that the execution videotape would be "a lot more saleable" if the dying man screamed. It colored the judge's attitude toward

television journalism in general, as evidenced by his inter-
change with George Osterkamp, the San Francisco–based
producer of CBS News who was one of the plaintiff's witnesses. Osterkamp had said in his testimony that it was
unlikely that CBS News would want to broadcast an execution live—that is, while it was actually happening.

"But, obviously," Judge Schnacke egged him on, "it
would be a feather in your cap to have the first live broadcast
of an execution in California, wouldn't it?"

"We always like to get on the air," Osterkamp admitted.

"Sure," said the judge, presumably satisfied that he had
succeeded in eliciting the truly crass motives of the media.

Nor did the judge limit his imputations of sleaze to the
commercial media. He seemed to feel that KQED, though a
public television station, was equally capable of going after
the lowest common denominator in its audience. During the
state's cross-examination of Michael Schwarz, for instance,
Judge Schnacke interrupted at one point to say to Schwarz,
"You could do a lot of editing with the camera."

"The potential for abuse always exists," KQED's current
affairs director agreed, "and I would be the last person to deny
that. I myself have seen it happen on television."

"Probably done it yourself on occasion," the judge noted.

To counter this image of television as exploiter, KQED
repeatedly emphasized its position of highminded poverty. As
a public television station, KQED saw itself as being in an
especially strong moral position to bring this lawsuit, since,
unlike commercial stations, it did not rely on selling advertising during its programs. An execution broadcast on KQED
would be less lurid and grotesque than on commercial news
stations; it would not, at any rate, be punctuated or bracketed
by ads for denture fixatives and analgesics. "Television need
not trivialize or sensationalize such an obviously important
news story," stated the media packet that KQED handed out
to journalists at the May 3rd hearing of the case. "KQED
believes television is capable of serious and responsible cov-

erage of controversial issues. KQED has demonstrated that responsibility in the past." Elsewhere in the same packet, the station acknowledged that commercial television might not be as responsible: "Under the traditional rules of pool coverage, the footage will be made available to other stations. And while we cannot guarantee that they will use it with the same discretion as KQED, we will strongly urge other stations to follow the same restrictive guidelines which we have placed on ourselves."

In court and outside it, the plaintiff's side stressed the extent to which money was *not* the dominant motive in public TV. In poverty, these statements suggested, lay virtue. On the first day of testimony, the KQED team brought in a sample of the kind of videotape camera that would be used in the coverage, but proposed to leave only photographs of the camera in evidence. "So we want you to see the camera," William Turner explained to the judge, "but we'll leave the pictures."

"You know, we've had more expensive things than that," Judge Schnacke joked, provoking a round of laughter from the courtroom.

"Not brought by a public television station," Turner answered.

A similar joke arose in the press conference that followed the final hearing in the case. After the judge had delivered his verdict, one reporter asked Schwarz and Turner if the KQED management had exerted any pressure to end the lawsuit, perhaps feeling that it was costing the station too much.

"No, the board of directors and KQED management are behind this one hundred percent," Schwarz asserted.

"It's not costing too much," Turner added drily, obliquely reminding everyone that he was handling the case *pro bono.*

William Bennett Turner's willingness to carry the legal costs of waging this First Amendment lawsuit constituted part of his ammunition against the "sleaze factor" in this case; his own legal background was another part. Bill Turner had a history of taking on civil rights causes. In the late 1970s and early

1980s he had brought a groundbreaking and successful lawsuit against the Texas prison system on behalf of the prisoners, charging that the conditions of their incarceration (including poor medical care, overcrowding, guard brutality, and so on) violated the Eighth Amendment's rule against "cruel and unusual punishment." More recently, he had handled a number of First Amendment cases, including an appeal by Dannie Martin, the federal prisoner who was prevented by the prison administration from writing articles about prison life under his own byline in the *San Francisco Chronicle*. Unlike Michael Schwarz of KQED, Turner personally opposed capital punishment, and had been active in death penalty cases on behalf of the condemned; in fact, one of his current clients, at the time of the *KQED* case, was only a few steps behind Robert Alton Harris in the queue to the California gas chamber. Turner also had a longstanding interest in journalism: in recent years he had taught courses on law and journalism at UC Berkeley, and before that he had hosted a series of television programs (not coincidentally, on KQED) about publicly important legal issues. So Bill Turner was in many ways the ideal attorney for the plaintiff in this case. As he made clear in his post-trial brief, he did not see *KQED v. Vasquez* as a case that pitted prisoners' welfare or dignity against First Amendment rights; rather, it set the press's and public's right to know against the right of the government to control or limit news coverage.

If Turner's highmindedness made him the perfect lawyer for KQED in this lawsuit, it also made him seem occasionally oblivious to the wider implications of the case. "This case is *not* about whether executions should be broadcast on TV; it is *not* about whether the American public should be forced to watch them," he emphatically stated on a local news program the evening of the May 3 hearing. "It is about the First Amendment, and whether the press should be allowed to practice with the tools of its trade." One fully understands

Turner's desire to combat the scare tactics about KQED "bringing executions into your living room," as Dan Rather had put it on the CBS news the night before. But it seems obvious that in practical terms the case *was* about whether executions would be broadcast on TV. By May 24, when he appeared as Ted Koppel's guest on "Nightline," Turner had refined his assertion somewhat, pointing out that

> the question is not whether executions should be tele-
> vised but who should make the decisions about whether
> and how the news is covered. And in a country that cele-
> brates the 200th anniversary of the First Amendment this
> year, we ought to be reminded that the whole purpose of
> the thing is to have those kinds of decisions made by jour-
> nalists, about whether and how the news is covered, and
> not by government officials who are themselves involved
> in the process. I think that's the point that's been over-
> looked here.

This may sound either complacent or naive about the recti-
tude we can expect of journalists, but legally it is accurate, and strategically it was the intelligent thing for KQED's lawyer to say. I would simply add that it's not the whole story. But the law, being adversarial, doesn't ever intend either side to tell the whole story, and most often prevents them both from doing so.

I hope I do not seem to question the sincerity of KQED and its attorney if I also point out that this kind of highmind-edness *always* accompanies involvement in the sleaze of murder stories. I, for instance, drag in Dostoyevsky and all sorts of other high-class literary models, attempting to make an intellectual subject out of what some might see as just a gruesome preoccupation. Ann Rule, in her book about Ted Bundy (a book that, as a physical object, is almost too embar-rassing to read in public places, with its bright-red cover fea-turing a grim shot of Ted Bundy's eyes and the words "HIS SHOCKING TRUE STORY—INCLUDING INTIMATE DETAILS OF

THE SERIAL-KILLER'S FINAL MOMENTS ...”), starts off with a quotation from Book Nine of *Paradise Lost*. Joe McGinniss also quotes from Milton, but he prefers the *Areopagitica* — "he who destroys a good book, kills reason itself, kills the image of God, as it were, in the eye" — which is invoked in *Fatal Vision*'s 1989 epilogue as a means of raising McGinniss above both Jeffrey MacDonald's lawsuit and Janet Malcolm's insinuations.

It is in McGinniss that we begin to see how such high-mindedness can really backfire. Toward the end of *Fatal Vision* itself, McGinniss tells us that at first, sifting through these people's personal lives and intimate tragedies, he'd felt "that this was a violation of privacy so gross in dimension that no end, however meritorious, could justify it. Eventually, however, this squeamishness gave way to an acceptance of the fact that if this was where the path had led me, then, for the moment, this was where I would be." In the epilogue, after summarily trashing both Malcolm and MacDonald and making himself appear sleazier than ever, McGinniss reveals to us this higher path, this end that justifies the means. "If you are going to be a non-fiction writer," he sniffs, "you must be willing to go where the story leads you, even if it isn't where you want to be. And, as the occasion demands, you must be willing to publish unpleasant truths — rather than pleasant untruths — about your subject." The use of the pronoun "you" isn't enough to disguise the aura of self-congratulation. As in his court case, the mistake McGinniss makes here is to think that what's on trial is his veracity, whereas what we actually condemn him for is his tone. In his case, the banality of evil has become the evil of banality.

It is hard to attack someone's excessive piousness, as I have attacked McGinniss's, without coming across as excessively pious oneself. The highmindedness is as contagious and as unattractive as the sleaze. One way for an author to evade the dangers of both the inevitable sleaze and its accompanying highmindedness is to relocate them onto other characters in the murder story. Janet Malcolm cleverly accomplishes this in *The Journalist and the Murderer,* where McGinniss becomes the vehicle for the sleaze and Dr. Jeffrey Elliot, a witness who testified on MacDonald's behalf in his suit against McGinniss, represents highmindedness. Not surprisingly, the two serve as foils for each other, dividing up between them the objectionable qualities of a journalist in pursuit of a good story.

Dr. Elliot's high standard of journalistic truth and seriousness turns out to irritate Malcolm almost as much as McGinniss's duplicity does. "It is rare to be in the presence of someone as grudging of himself as Elliot is," she comments when she finally meets him. What she has earlier objected to in McGinniss is his failure to hold himself in, his insistence that in his interview with her "we play the old game of Confession, by which journalists earn their bread and subjects indulge their masochism." For a while this balancing act works, and together McGinniss and Elliot divert our attention from Malcolm, who is playing both games at once, reveling in the sleaze and calling the revelations "unpleasant truths." But eventually we notice that she is doing this, and at this point, depending on how manipulated we feel, we may begin to resent her tactics. We may also feel that Malcolm is unwittingly playing out with McGinniss a plot that really started elsewhere, just as she accuses McGinniss of doing when she says: "McGinniss's confession to me was not a new one. Someone had been there before me, and something was being repeated with me." It is Malcolm herself who, with her ever-vigilant Freudianism, has given us the equipment necessary to see through her technique.

One of the things that enraged people about *The Journalist and the Murderer,* when it first appeared in serial form in *The New Yorker,* was that Janet Malcolm seemed to be holding back a crucial bit of information about her own interest in the MacDonald/McGinniss lawsuit. For Malcolm herself had recently been sued (the case, as of this writing, is still in the courts) by one of her own subjects, Jeffrey Masson. Joe

McGinniss, Jeffrey MacDonald, Janet Malcolm, Jeffrey Masson: as if to acknowledge and indeed cement the J. M. pattern, Malcolm featured the words *J*ournalist and *M*urderer in her book title. We would expect a relentless Freudian to call the connection between the two cases overdetermined. Malcolm, uncharacteristically, defends herself in the afterword to her book by calling it irrelevant. What she doesn't seem to realize is that sleaze rubs off, even on the slightest contact. Having lowered herself into the pit of *MacDonald v. McGinniss* to give us a journalistic report about journalism's evils, she can't simply rise up unsullied herself. She offers us McGinniss and Elliot as scapegoats, but they aren't enough. We want to see her sacrificed on truth's altar as well. As penance for her (and our) voyeurism, we want her to come out of hiding, expose something of herself. We want to hear her guilty confession.

Malcolm, however, claims to have an alibi: it wasn't she who was at the scene of the crime, but her double, her fictional look-alike. She tries to persuade us, in the afterword, that "the 'I' character in journalism is almost pure invention. Unlike the 'I' of autobiography, who is meant to be seen as a representation of the writer, the 'I' of journalism is connected to the writer only in a tenuous way—the way, say, that Superman is connected to Clark Kent." This is clever and amusing, but unconvincing.

A far more persuasive witness is Norman Mailer, who in his 1968 book *Armies of the Night* testifies on the other side, showing us how all the authorial selves (the fictional, the journalistic, the autobiographical, the historical) contribute to and enrich the truth-telling power of each one:

> So the Novelist working in secret collaboration with the Historian has perhaps tried to build with his novel a tower fully equipped with telescopes to study—at the greatest advantage—our own horizon. Of course, the tower is crooked, and the telescopes warped, but the

instruments of all sciences—history so much as physics— are always constructed in small or large error; what supports the use of them now is that our intimacy with the master builder of the tower, and the lens grinder of the telescopes (yes, even the machinist of the barrels) has given us some advantage for correcting the error of the instruments and the imbalance of his tower.

Sentences like these are what make Mailer great: as a stylist, and also as a chronicler of reality (a realm that, at least in his case, encompasses fiction as well as nonfiction, autobiography along with history). He elevates himself with capital letters and diminishes himself with reference to his errors. He is both the master builder and the lowly machinist. He is our only source of truth, and an admitted liar, or at least exaggerator. Joining us in "our" intimacy with the novelist/historian, he yet alludes to himself in the third person, from outside; his relationship to language itself is so intimate that his very grammar helps him grind the lenses of our perspective. He gives us a portrait that is also a self-portrait, a telescope that is also a mirror.

It is this gift that has enabled Norman Mailer to be the only author of a true-life murder story who fully gets away with it. In *The Executioner's Song*, he doesn't just acknowledge the sleaze factor; he makes it the subject of the book. Using Malcolm's displacement technique, he relocates the lurid, exploitive, questionable side of authorship onto all the other "carrion birds" who swarmed in to devour Gary Gilmore's body. Yet he does so in a way that fully admits his own implication in the crime.

"Eastern Voices," the second half of *The Executioner's Song*, is—like the second half of *Don Quixote*—both a continuation of the first half's story and a commentary on how that story was received by the public. "Western Voices" is the direct rendering of the murder story, "Eastern Voices" the mediated version, with the emphasis very heavily on the media. Once

Gary Gilmore announces he wants to be executed, thereby becoming the first person likely to be put to death after the ten-year Supreme Court–imposed hiatus on capital punishment, he becomes national and international news; but "news" is hardly the word for the grotesquely sleazy form this interest takes. The depths of the media depravity are probably best represented in Mailer's humorous little story about the *National Enquirer:*

> After dinner, Ian Calder of the *National Enquirer* called from Miami, to say that he had an idea that might be worth *six figures.* "Get Gary," said Calder, "to agree to submit two small personal objects that are at present in his possession, and have him write twenty-five words, whatever they are. We'll send a bonded messenger to pick up the sealed envelope and put it in a vault. Before Gary dies, we will tell our worldwide network of seers and clairvoyants to key in on the exact moment of his execution. Then we'll see how close they come to guessing what those two objects are, or what the words in Gary's message might be."

Like Lou Ford's jokes, this story is amusing partly because it is horrible and grotesque. Which element is *more* grotesque — the six-figure purchase price, or the proposed "clairvoyant" intrusion on Gary's most intimate moment — is hard to say, but both recall Poe's remarks about magazines "which have obtained celebrity" by featuring "the ludicrous heightened into the grotesque: the fearful coloured into the horrible: the witty exaggerated into the burlesque," and all the other elements that routinely draw us to such murder tales.

The *Enquirer* is not the only potential purchaser that wants a piece of Gary. Everybody else descends on Provo, Utah, for essentially the same purpose. Sometimes this piece is literally of his body: a young blind man asks to be willed his eyes; Gary's niece is to get his pituitary gland. This gives a new twist to Hannibal Lecter's cannibalism, for here it is the murderer who is being cannibalized by the public rather than vice versa. The media too is in a feeding frenzy, a frenzy that runs the gamut, from the highmindedness of David Susskind (who only wants to do the Gilmore story until everybody else starts bidding it up, at which point it becomes, "in Susskind's view, a very sensational, malodorous, exploitative mess") to the legally doubtful maneuvers of Dennis Boaz, a New Age crank who initially becomes Gary's attorney in order to write about the execution. Yet even Boaz is not beyond the range of Mailer's self-mocking sympathy. After Dennis is taken off the case, he begins "thinking that he might have to call his character Harry Kilmore, not Gary Gilmore ... Might make a good novel." This is Boaz at his most banal, but it is also a satiric version of what Mailer himself is doing in this "true life novel."

The central character in "Eastern Voices" is Larry Schiller, known in his profession as "the journalist who dealt in death" because of his previous work on such stories as Jack Ruby and the Manson trial. If Schiller hadn't existed, Mailer would have had to invent him (as perhaps he partially did), for Larry Schiller is both the perfect deflector and the perfect stand-in: he does all the advance dirty work, sewing up all the "exclusive rights," and then he hands the story over to Mailer to write. It is Schiller who gets called a "carrion bird" in a *New West* article by Barry Farrell, a journalist who later comes to work for Schiller on the *Playboy* interview of Gary Gilmore — a clear case of the pot calling the etcetera.

When we first meet Larry Schiller, we see him ("It was as if you'd taken the head of Fidel Castro and plugged it into a wide body") through the kookily self-righteous view of Dennis Boaz, who has heard Schiller is a "super-hard salesman ... Gets in when people are dying." But Schiller, for the purposes of this book, *is* Mailer, and Mailer suggests as much in a striking passage of internal monologue:

> Other reporters would be on the phone, checking back to
> hear what was going down, but Schiller sat and relaxed

and let the heat of the room pour over him and the
fatigues of twenty-five years perspired slowly, a drop and
another drop from the bottomless reservoirs of fatigue,
and he sat there quietly thinking, and let his sins and
errors wash over him, and reviewed them. He considered
it obscene not to learn from experience.

In all this thousand-page book, with its flat sentences and
fragmentary paragraphs and cacophony of various voices, this
is one of the very few places where Mailer speaks to us in the
characteristic rhythms of his sinuous, self-extending prose. It
is also the only point where anyone, in this novel of extreme
violations, thinks over his own "sins and errors"; and when it
happens here, we feel that the mood of acknowledgment and
atonement applies to Mailer as well as Schiller. We are also
likely to be moved by the conjunction of "sin" and "error," for
part of our anxiety in reading this tale comes from wondering
at exactly what point an error (mistaking real people for
fictional characters, as we are prone to do, or allowing oneself
to sink too deeply into solipsistic despair, as Gary does)
becomes a sin (depriving people of their integrity, or their
life). It is not that our errors lead directly to Gary's: we don't
kill anyone by enjoying this story as a novel. But we would be
missing an important part of how this novel works on us if we
did not recognize that Mailer is purposely comparing different
kinds of sinfulness, different kinds of error.

Larry Schiller may be a buzzard, but he practices a buzzard's special code of honor, and Gilmore, who has his own
brand of sinner's honor, responds to that in him. Gary deals
with Schiller, sells his story to Schiller, answers Schiller's
interview questions, because on some level he trusts Schiller's
integrity (if "integrity" is not too strange a word to apply to a
murderer's assessment of an exploiter). Like Hannibal Lecter
and Clarice Starling, Gilmore and Schiller share a version of
honor—not just honor among thieves, but honor among the
emotionally wounded. It comes to seem no coincidence that

this murderer and his journalist have both become famous for their dealings with death.

One way to respond to murder, especially official, state-imposed murder, is to be pious and aggrieved about it, as David Susskind and his writer Stanley Greenberg are. Their proposed movie "could offer a wonderful statement about capital punishment and how godawful it is, eye for an eye. I even think that reaching a large audience can probably save the guy's life," Mailer has Greenberg say to Susskind. But another way is to respond with humor, with irony—as Gary Gilmore does, as Larry Schiller occasionally does, and as Norman Mailer, constructing them both as fictional characters, does throughout the second half of the book. The tone of "Eastern Voices" is, literally, gallows humor.

This tone is by no means unique to Mailer. Joe McGinniss, for instance, uses it when he writes to the convicted Jeffrey MacDonald in prison. "I am glad to see that you are able to write—to describe and analyze both what happened to you and your own feelings about it," says McGinniss, as quoted in *The Journalist and the Murderer.* "Also, I'm glad you didn't kill yourself, because that sure would have been a bummer for the book." This is funny partly because it hints at the sleazy nature of their connection, so it functions as an inside joke, a friendly dig in the ribs—though McGinniss, by the time he came to publish *Fatal Vision,* had become too pious to acknowledge such complicity. A more sophisticated and ironic version of the same joke appears in *Crime and Punishment,* where the inspector Porfiry Petrovich, after urging Raskolnikov to turn himself in and confess all the details, ends his plea with a little request:

> "It's rather a ticklish thing to ask, but it's important. What I mean is that if you should decide (mind you, I don't believe for a moment that you will, and, as a matter of fact, I don't believe you're capable of such a thing), but if you should decide during the next forty or so hours to

end it all in a different way—I mean, put an end to yourself (quite an absurd idea, and I apologize for even suggesting such a thing), I'd be glad if you'd leave a little
note with all the particulars."

This joke is *from* us as well as *to* us. We, the readers of a
murder story, are hanging on the suspense and would be
furious if the criminal died before he had a chance to finish the
story for us. So this form of gallows humor is actually more at
our expense ("we" in this case being the author and the reader
together, as represented by the detective) than at the murderer's. There is nothing wrong with wanting to know the end
of the story, but there may well be something wrong with
valuing that knowledge more than a human life, even, as in
this case, a suicidal murderer's life. Without suggesting that
we are in any way killers, the joke manages to draw a connection between our own sleazy curiosity and Raskolnikov's willingness to commit murder—both being tendencies built on a
compulsion to pursue predetermined plotlines and an inability
to abide uncertainty.

There is another form of murder-story humor, however,
that takes just the opposite tack, mocking the killer for his
own highmindedness, his own sense of ethical superiority. In
*Crime and Punishment,* this kind of joke embellishes one of the
exchanges between Svidrigaylov and Raskolnikov. Svidrigaylov, intentionally eavesdropping from the next room, has
overheard Raskolnikov's confession to Sonia and now confronts him with this knowledge. "You don't mind listening at
keyholes, do you?" Raskolnikov says with the icy superiority
of a gentleman, to which Svidrigaylov replies, laughing:

> "And now you're telling me not to listen at keyholes. If
> that is so, then why don't you go and tell the police what
> an extraordinary thing happened to you: you made a little
> slip in your theory! But if you're really convinced that
> you mustn't listen at keyholes, but you may crack open
> the skulls of old women with the first blunt instrument

you happen to get hold of, then you'd better go off to America at once."

America, to Svidrigaylov, stands for the absence of moral rules, or perhaps rules of any kind. Mailer, who has based his murder story partly on Dostoyevsky's—Nicole, at any rate, is definitely a version of Sonia—would seem to agree, and in *The Executioner's Song* he has a very Svidrigaylovian joke. After Gilmore has answered a long series of questions about the two vicious murders he committed, the interviewer asks, "Well, what led you to the City Center Motel, where Bushnell worked? We're just trying to understand the quality of this rage you speak of. It wasn't a rage that might have been vented in sex?" Gary's reply is worthy of Raskolnikov at his most self-righteous: "I don't want to mess with questions that pertain to sex. I think they're cheap."

Jokes about the relative seriousness of murder and other offenses are usually at the murderer's expense, but not always. In *The Stranger Beside Me*, Ann Rule quotes a note from Ted Bundy that plays self-mockingly with this kind of comparison. Writing in December 1976 from a Utah prison (this was, coincidentally, the heart of Gilmore territory, one month before Gilmore's execution), Bundy wrote, "Now I am attempting the impossible: suggesting all us hardened cons sing carols on Christmas Eve. Thus far, I have been designated a sicko degenerate for such a perverse idea." Bundy explicitly meant the joke to be about his fellow prisoners, since he wasn't admitting any guilt himself; only from our retrospective position, therefore, does the remark gain its full ironic punch. Yet even an innocent man can make jokes of this sort. In *The Thin Blue Line*, Randall Adams describes sitting in a Texas prison being interviewed by Doctor Death, prior to being sent to Death Row. "It was April 15, tax time," he recalls, deadpan. "I think I was filling out my taxes at the time. Afraid I might be late." Afraid of what? That the government might send him to jail for tax evasion? It is this same sort of beyond-the-law humor that informs Mailer's description of the judge's reaction to Gary Gilmore's disrespectful court-room behavior: "Bullock ignored the remark. How could you sentence a man to Contempt when he was already bound over to execution?"

Humor is a form of freedom in the face of powerlessness. It offers a chance to break the unbearable tension, to thumb one's nose even at the prospect of death. If Gary Gilmore's embrace of his execution was one way of pre-empting official control of his life—of saying, "I'm dying because I want to, not because you want me to"—then his frequently displayed humor about the execution itself was another. He even issued a joke "invitation to the beheading" in a postcard to his former cellmate Gibbs:

> BANG!                                    BANG!
> *A Real Live Shoot' em up!*
> Mrs. Bessie Gilmore of Milwaukie, Ore
> cordially invites you to the execution of her son:
> Gary Mark Gilmore, 36.
> Place: Utah State Prison. Draper, Utah
> Time: Sunrise
> EARPLUGS AND BULLETS WILL BE FURNISHED

In its imitation of a wedding invitation, this note slyly suggested that the principal actor of the occasion, rather than the nominal host or hostess, was really the one who had made the decision to go ahead with the event. Gary was meeting death like a bridegroom—perhaps with a trace of cold feet, but by his own choice.

Gilmore also used his gallows humor to mock the media circus his death had become, especially in one tape he sent to Schiller and Farrell:

Oh, hey, man, I got something that'll make a mint. Get aholda John Cameron Swazey right now, and get a Timex wristwatch here. And have John Cameron Swazey out there after I fall over, he can be wearing a stethoscope, he can put it on my heart and say, "Well, that's stopped," and then he can put the stethoscope on the Timex and say, "She's still running, folks."

This tape, when Farrell and Schiller played it, "got them laughing so hard they almost slid off their chairs. It had to be the tension." They felt guilty at laughing about such a serious occasion; the joke in itself couldn't possibly warrant such hilarity. Yet how can a joke exist in itself? Humor is in part a response to tension, feeding on it and making sense only in relation to that tension. Laughter is one way of coping with the sleaze factor, of acknowledging one's embarrassed fascination with gruesome subjects. But it also ups the ante. It makes us wonder what kind of person not only would be interested in such material but would find it funny. Even if the answer is "Just about anyone," the question itself causes us to squirm a bit.

One could feel this confused, embarrassed hilarity pervading the *KQED v. Vasquez* trial, where an underlying level of hysteria seemed ready to burst out any time the judge made a slightly humorous remark. The most pointed of these occasions was, not surprisingly, during one of the most emotionally charged moments of testimony: a description of the last execution which had taken place in California, that of Aaron Mitchell in 1967. It was a moment when all the issues bound up in the case—from sleaze to propriety, from inflamed sympathy to cold justice, and from hesitantly recalled testimony to viscerally rendered presence—seemed to break their bounds at once.

Philip Guthrie, the former press officer for San Quentin, was describing the event under cross-examination by the state's attorney, Karl Mayer. "Once the process started, was there much movement in—if you can recall—in the room?"

Mayer asked, referring to the witness area surrounding the gas chamber itself.

"No," Guthrie answered. "There was one person who was overcome with emotion, and that created a slight stir in the background, but there really was not much."

"Do you recall who that was?"

"It was a female, a woman reporter who was not there as a reporter but rather as a—a person who had gotten to know the—Mitchell during the time he was in prison, as I recall. I don't remember her name."

At this point Judge Schnacke interrupted. "Were most of the women there female women?"

"Yes, sir. Yes," Guthrie answered, relaxing into the joke as the courtroom exploded in laughter. "I can't think of one that was not, in fact."

"All right. I find it a little hard to imagine myself," said the judge, playing to the audience's guffaws. ("More laughter," the transcript demurely mentions.)

# 5

# The Trial

If I have portrayed Robert Schnacke as something of a "character," that has not required any exaggeration on my part. The judge in *KQED v. Vasquez* was, in many of his mannerisms, reminiscent of an Eli Wallach role on "L.A. Law": tyrannical in his own little courtroom fiefdom, wayward in his inconsistent insistence on decorum, and eccentric to the point of occasional nuttiness. One morning, for instance, as we waited for the cases before *KQED* to be heard, the assembled legal and media community was witness to a surprise wedding between a prisoner and his girlfriend. Apparently the prisoner, due to appear before Judge Schnacke that day, had been unable to find anyone else to perform the ceremony, so Schnacke had offered to do so. He married the bride and groom, then heard the groom's case and sent him back to jail.

It was odd to see a real-life judge mimicking the eccentricities of a television character. But then, for someone like me who has never even served on a jury, the judicial process itself seemed like an imitation of TV or the movies. "All rise," said the clerk as Judge Schnacke came in. "Move to strike on grounds of hearsay," said one of the attorneys. These lines were extremely familiar to me: from "L.A. Law," from "Matlock," from "Law and Order," from "Perry Mason," from all the courtroom dramas I've ever watched on a big or little screen. As a result, they felt like fictional constructs rather than real life.

To a certain extent, this fictional quality inheres in the rituals of the courtroom itself. The legal version of reality is much more limited than our usual, daily-life version. As in a sports event, strict rules govern how each side may play the game. Moreover, each side, through the legal process known as "discovery," knows in advance what moves the other side is going to make. So the reality that is presented in this context has a stripped-down, starkly meaningful, suited-to-the-ritual quality. It is not as messy and meandering as our normal reality. The courtroom version of reality is unusually teleological, in that those who are shaping the reality (the lawyers on both sides) have a very specific aim, and that aim is to win. Winning and losing are the only two possibilities here; the vast middle ground, which most of us occupy most of the time, is absent.

In *The Executioner's Song,* Mailer comments on this feature of the judicial process through the consciousness of Earl Dorius, one of the lawyers from the Utah State Attorney General's office: "By Friday morning, with the execution not seventy-two hours away, Earl Dorius knew a number of legal actions were going to be filed. Law was always, to some degree, a game, and that was one good reason, Earl had long ago decided, to keep its processes slow and orderly. It helped to tone down the sporting and competitive aspects." Yet what keeps us reading, in this long and detailed account of the legal maneuvers surrounding Gary Gilmore's execution, is our interest in the "sporting and competitive aspects," even though we know the final outcome in advance.

With a murder story whose endpoint is an execution, the sporting quality of the legal proceedings will reflect and anticipate something about the gruesome conclusion itself—that is, the execution also becomes a part of the game, an aspect of the competition. Mailer points this out when he quotes from an edition of the *Salt Lake Tribune* that came out the day before Gilmore's death: "The execution of Gary Mark Gilmore has turned into a 'super bowl of violence,' an Episcopal priest charged Saturday." Yet, as Mailer had already suggested in his *Presidential Papers*, a contemporary American execution is a very strange version of a sporting event, because one side is always doomed to lose; the ground rules are literally unsporting. What makes the Gilmore execution resemble a football game is not the uncertainty of the outcome but the fact that millions of fans are anxiously awaiting that outcome. It is the spectators, not the participants, who convert an execution into a sporting event, and their interest is not so much in the competition as in the final results. Theirs is the spectatorship not of football but of foxhunting or bullfighting or (to recall Mailer's presidential recommendation) gladiatorial games.

In presiding over *KQED v. Vasquez*, Judge Schnacke eerily echoed both of these *Executioner's Song* quotations about competitive sports. He picked up the lawsuit-as-sporting-event metaphor in his opening remarks. "Well," he said at the beginning of the first day of testimony, "we pride ourselves on providing a level playing field for litigants here, but apparently we can't provide a stationary one. I'm not sure what game we're playing or what field we're playing on this morning. Every time we address the problems here, the circumstances appear to change." Schnacke was referring to the fact that five days before the opening of the trial, Warden Vasquez had entirely altered the terms of the lawsuit by banning all media witnesses from the execution. The briefs and witnesses prepared beforehand thus became nearly obsolete, and the trial focused on a different set of arguments from what the litigants had planned.

The second echo, in which Judge Schnacke unwittingly quoted from the *Salt Lake Tribune* story on the Gilmore execution, took place later on the first day of the trial. Michael

Schwarz of KQED was being cross-examined by Paul Gifford, one of the lawyers from the attorney general's office, who was attempting to show that KQED didn't really *need* to have a camera at the execution. As an analogy, Gifford referred to the trial itself, where the assembled reporters — even those from TV stations — were taking old-fashioned pen-on-paper notes. "Is it fair to say that KQED could report the proceedings occurring in this courtroom without the benefit of a videotape?" he asked. "Would a report by KQED about the proceedings in this courtroom not supported by a videotape not be accurate?"

"Not as accurate as a report that included a videotape would be," Schwarz carefully replied.

Gifford went on to ask the same kinds of questions in various ways about the execution itself. In the midst of one of Schwarz's painstaking attempts to answer the questions in all their complexity, giving full due to the "very serious" act of interpreting an event like an execution, the judge interrupted impatiently to say to Gifford: "Counsel, I think your questions are answered if you'll ask yourself whether you would rather listen to a radio broadcast of the Super Bowl or watch a television broadcast."

In general, Judge Schnacke had little patience for complex explanations, or at least other people's complex explanations. Earlier in Schwarz's testimony, the plaintiff's attorney had asked what he personally felt about the death penalty and, over Gifford's objection, the judge had permitted him to answer. However, about halfway through Schwarz's complicated response, which included the information that his feelings were "frankly ambivalent and somewhat conflicted," Schnacke got tired of listening.

"Okay," he interrupted.

"But I haven't finished answering the question," Michael Schwarz pointed out.

"I think you have," said the judge.

This was truly the judge as umpire, if not the Judge as Empire. As Gifford's questions noted, there were no cameras in the courtroom during *KQED v. Vasquez.* Nonetheless there was a way in which Judge Schnacke seemed to be playing to an audience: at the very least, the large audience of media people who had been attracted to the case by its more lurid aspects. Or perhaps he was simply behaving as he habitually does in court, as the lead actor in his own courtroom drama.

Part of the trial's fiction-like quality can be attributed to the theatrical nature of the legal process itself. Courtroom procedure has been useful material for the theater since Aeschylus put Orestes on trial in the "Eumenides" section of *The Oresteia.* Trials form the climactic scenes of Shakespeare's *Merchant of Venice,* where Portia gets to do her star turn as a young advocate defending Antonio from Shylock, and Shaw's *Saint Joan,* where Joan of Arc appears before the Inquisition. Bertolt Brecht and Arthur Miller used historically famous trials to make contemporary social comments in, respectively, *Galileo* and *The Crucible.* And Hollywood movies from *Mr. Deeds Goes to Town* to *Anatomy of a Murder,* from *To Kill a Mockingbird* to *The File on Thelma Jordan,* have hinged on the outcome of a dramatic courtroom scene.

But to this backlog of courtroom theater has recently been added a plethora of real-life television trials that further blur the distinction between judicial proceedings and popular entertainment. The Supreme Court decisions that were used as the legal basis of *KQED v. Vasquez*—the decisions ending the ban on cameras in the courtroom and allowing some proceedings to be filmed with the presiding judge's permission—have resulted in a whole new form of television program. On July 1, 1991, an entire channel, the Courtroom Television Network, began presenting twenty-four-hour judicial programming, consisting of unedited, often live trials from around the country. As the *New York Times* TV critic commented on July 3, "Court TV seems to be onto something, combining the

inherent appeal of courtroom drama with an effort to open up
the workings of the law." Much of the material appealed to
interests other than the legal and the educational: "Last night
brought the trial of Marlon Brando's son, Christian, for the
killing of his sister's lover," the same *Times* piece noted. Is it
only my imagination, or is there something bizarrely circular
about having the real-life murder trial of a movie star's son, a
boy presumably named after his father's role in *Mutiny on the
Bounty,* appear as the evening drama on the nation's television
sets?

It is against this background that a proposal to broadcast
executions on television must be considered. Decorum was
frequently invoked as an issue in *KQED v. Vasquez,* both legal
decorum, particularly as it applied to the death penalty, and
television decorum, or the lack thereof. The value of decorum
should not be underestimated, in daily life or in works of art.
It is sometimes what *makes* daily life seem worth commemo-
rating in works of art, as Thom Gunn notes in a brief essay
called "Writing a Poem." "When I saw the naked family I
didn't know why they satisfied me so much, why I had that
strange sense of what I have called decorum . . . ," Gunn says.
"But I did know that I had certain clear and strong feelings
about them that I wanted to preserve, if possible by preserving the experience that elicited them." It makes sense that
law and TV—both, in their different ways, preservatives of
experience—should be interested in the notion of decorum.

But the boundaries of decorum, in both legal and television terms, are being stretched all the time. The same *New York
Times* entertainment section that carried a review of the
Courtroom Television Network also included an article on
"The Grudge Match," a new show wherein "people who might
otherwise be in small claims or divorce court are entering a
boxing ring and going three rounds against each other,
cheered on by a studio audience that picks the winner." This is
Mailer's gladiator dream come true, though on a much lower

level of criminal seriousness. The show's tastelessness, which at first seems shocking, turns out to be a sign of the times:

> Mr. Melcombe said he came up with the idea for "The Grudge Match" in 1987, when he was working for Turner Broadcasting and the network's owner, Ted Turner, asked him to develop some sort of program that could run in tandem with the network's wrestling shows. But when Mr. Melcombe presented the idea to Ted Turner, "Ted laughed and said, 'Rich, come on,'" Mr. Melcombe recalled.
>
> Since then, however, both television economics and audience tastes have changed. "The Grudge Match" costs relatively little to make, thanks to a fixed set and low overhead, and is expected to appeal to the same viewers who have made solid successes out of the so-called reality-based cop and rescue shows on the Fox network.

The Courtroom Television Network, too, is applauded by its producers for its low production costs. One can foresee a time when public tastes will have altered even further, and video-taped executions (which now provoke, at best, a "Rich, come on" response) will be seen as good, cheap, educational enter-tainment. While this is not something to be welcomed, neither is it something that can easily be averted by judicial or legisla-tive action—unless, indeed, that action results in the abolition of executions themselves.

"The Grudge Match" still seems a far cry from the normal decorum of a courtroom trial; but, as the sporting metaphors suggest, the two may not be so distant after all. Perhaps it makes sense to view a trial, especially a criminal trial, as a ritualized, "sporting" way for society to work out its collective grudges. So, at least, suggests Gary Bostwick, the lawyer who handled Jeffrey MacDonald's side in his suit against Joe McGinnis. Speaking to Janet Malcolm, Bostwick observes about the judicial process: "People feel that it's a search for truth. But I don't think that is its function in this society. I'm convinced that its function is cathartic. It's a means for allowing people to air their differences, to let them feel as if they had a forum. You release tension in the social body in some way, whether or not you come to the truth."

Certainly, if one's aim were to elicit the whole truth and nothing but the truth, one could (one imagines, in flights of self-congratulatory fancy) design a more effective means than the Anglo-American legal trial. For all the reasons I've already suggested—its ritualized format, its competitive insistence on win-or-lose finality, its inability to encompass complex viewpoints or gray middle areas—the trial does not seem the ideal mechanism for yielding up truth, especially complicated truth. And truth is almost always more complicated than the legal system wants it to be, as the exchange between Michael ("I haven't finished answering the question yet") Schwarz and Judge Robert ("I think you have") Schnacke suggests.

A version of the murder story that stakes out as its central subject matter this incompatibility between law and truth is Elizabeth Hardwick's 1955 novel *The Simple Truth*. Hardwick herself, in the afterword to a recent edition, insists that her novel is "in no sense a murder story or a mystery." But in its portrait of two people who, for reasons of their own, avidly attend the daily sessions of a murder trial in a small Iowa town, *The Simple Truth* holds up a mirror to those of us who find ourselves obsessed with murder, whether real or fictional. The novel does not offer explanations or give solid answers; on the contrary, it's about the way truth resides in the avoidance of such explanations, such answers. "The two fictional characters whose emotions have become engaged by the trial," Hardwick remarks in the afterword,

> are not so much persons of ideas as ones in whom a certain cluster of feelings leads to wishes about the outcome. A murder that might not have taken place the day before or the day after or if the telephone had rung or some other commonplace intervention had occurred does often

arouse sympathy in a way that has little to do with the command that justice proceed from the available evidence. Otherwise responsible people sometimes do not welcome justice or they see the exercise of it as too narrow, revengeful, lacking in all those allowances a busy imagination offers to motive. I cannot think this altogether a bad thing for a mere observer, even if it cannot be recommended as valid for a juror.

In this respect, we who consume murder stories are all "mere observers," seeking out more than just an innocent or guilty verdict. Like Anita Mitchell and Joseph Parks, the two people who follow Rudy Peck's trial in *The Simple Truth*, we want to sympathize with murderers or apparent murderers, to guess at the irresistible forces that may have made them commit their crimes, and possibly even to imagine ourselves in their situation, or them in ours. As observers, we want to note the subtle gradations that make up the broad spectrum linking innocence to guilt—a spectrum on which we may imagine the accused to lie somewhere in the middle, as do we.

Both Anita, an overeducated, underemployed housewife, and Joseph, a dilettantish graduate student from a wealthy background, find themselves drawn to the pathos of Rudy Peck's situation. A poor boy from an Iowa farm family, he was dating Betty Jane Henderson—an attractive sorority girl, daughter of a prosperous Des Moines banker—when some set of circumstances (their exact nature is under debate in the trial) led to her death by strangulation. Anita, who has a strong Freudian bent, is drawn to the love-hate quality of the relationship; Joseph, a well-meaning but essentially armchair Marxist, focuses more on the class difference. Both Anita and Joseph believe Rudy to be more innocent than the evidence suggests. This is not to say that they think someone else murdered Betty Jane (there are no other suspects); rather, they feel the circumstances are so extenuating as to make Rudy less than a cold-blooded murderer. Fearful of what they see as the probable harshness of the parochial, class-biased, small-minded Iowa jurors, these two outsiders cling to the slightest suggestions that Rudy might be innocent. Praising the coroner's testimony about the autopsy as "extremely fair-minded," Joseph Parks reports to Anita:

> "He finally said . . . and it seems to be literally true . . . that she died because the flow of air was cut off. That's the end of it you might say . . . From the medical point of view at least."
> "Yes, but how did the air get cut off? It wouldn't take much sense to figure out that such a thing wouldn't happen of its own accord!" Anita smiled warmly as she said this.
> "Of course you're right," Parks said. "But still these things are slippery. The doctor didn't rush right in and say he was sure she was choked to death by Rudy Peck! It seems hopeful somehow . . ."

It is typical of this novel, in which all truths are rendered more complicated than they may initially seem, to assign the phrase "literally true" only to such a carefully meaningless piece of testimony.

But Anita and Joseph's hope and trepidation turn into something more like perplexity or even dismay when the jury delivers the unexpected verdict of "Not Guilty." In part, as Anita's friend March points out to her, this reaction stems from her shock at the fact that the jury turned out to be as "sophisticated" as she. "It is really unnerving to live in a world where *everyone*, just *anybody*, takes as complicated a view as the most clever people!" March teases her. "When everyone sees things in all their paralyzing ambiguity—that's not so pleasant and comfortable after all! There's no one to uphold common sense!" Yet Anita's reaction, as she thinks about it afterward to herself, involves more than just a sense of wounded *amour-propre*. It has to do with the inadequacy of the legal choices in the face of a complex situation. "Society had declared him innocent. Facing this idealistic decision, Anita acknowledged at last that she had not *quite* thought Rudy innocent—nothing so bald and clear as that. She had thought him innocently guilty." The phrase "innocently guilty," at once so comprehensible in moral terms and so meaningless in legal terms, captures well the law's inability to encompass or address reality's complex range of truths.

As you can see from the bits I've quoted, *The Simple Truth* is a rather cold book, "a sad kind of comedy," in Hardwick's phrase, that pokes dour fun at the ways in which Anita and Joseph—and, by extension, we the readers—feel sympathy for murderers. When I taught the book in my "Murder" course at Santa Cruz, most of the students reacted badly to it. They had no interest in the feelings of these white, upper-middle-class observers of a murder trial. They much preferred *Native Son* and its poor, black protagonist, Bigger Thomas. Coming from students who resembled Joseph Parks to a T, such remarks were amusing in themselves; but they also pointed to something important in the murder-story genre. This brand of literature (or movie, or TV show) is supposed to take you out of yourself and into an alien world you have no normal access to, the world of murder—that is, the bare act, the thing itself. In this sense Hardwick is right to say that hers is "in no sense a murder story," for it withholds from us this core of unobtainable experience, turning us back instead on ourselves, the curious observers.

Still, all murder stories have this element of distance, of circularity, of being about us, the observers, instead of them, the killers. It's even there in *Native Son,* in the external views of Bigger Thomas that the novel generates: the Communist Party view, the cops' view, the newspapers' view, and so on. To portray murder—even as if from inside, as Edgar Allan Poe and Jim Thompson do—is to acknowledge the distance between the act of murder and its rendering. The murder story is always in part about this distance. This is also true of murder trials; as Hardwick's novel suggests, the trial is just a rough sketch of what happened, an incomplete and inadequate portrayal, not the thing itself. If this is true of an ordinary trial, how much more so of *KQED v. Vasquez*, which was itself a trial about the portrayal of a murder (that is, the scheduled execution of Robert Alton Harris). This dizzying circularity came to me as I sat in the courtroom feverishly taking notes on testimony about the inadequacy of note-taking as a technique for recording events. It came back to me again on the last day of the trial, as Howard Brodie—the well-known sketch artist who had earlier testified about witnessing and drawing Aaron Mitchell's 1967 execution—sat in the press box and sketched Judge Schnacke as he delivered his verdict. Witness had become reporter, the judge had replaced the condemned man as the subject of reportage, and the entire judicial process had swallowed its own tail. The trial was about the idea of looking at murder as directly as possible, being taken into the very heart of the event, *seeing the thing itself*; and yet the legal process inevitably led us outward and away, to the act of portraying, of reporting, of testifying about things that had happened or would happen elsewhere.

Something of this sense of circularity and evasion is piercingly rendered in Kafka's "Before the Law" parable, which comes toward the very end of his novel *The Trial*. The parable, which is told to K. by a priest in the chapter called "In the Cathedral," begins:

> Before the Law stands a doorkeeper. To this doorkeeper there comes a man from the country who begs for admittance to the Law. But the doorkeeper says that he cannot admit the man at the moment. The man, on reflection, asks if he will be allowed, then, to enter later. "It is possible," answers the doorkeeper, "but not at this moment."

The man, after ascertaining from the doorkeeper a few more facts about the extensive security arrangements, sits down on a stool to await admittance. He waits for years, repeatedly pestering the doorkeeper and repeatedly being refused; and finally, as he is about to die, he beckons to the doorkeeper, who bends down to speak with him:

> "What do you want to know now?" asks the doorkeeper, "you are insatiable." "Everyone strives to attain the Law," answers the man, "how does it come about, then, that in all these years no one has come seeking admittance but me?" The doorkeeper perceives that the man is nearing his end and his hearing is failing, so he bellows in his ear: "No one but you could gain admittance through this door, since this door was intended for you. I am now going to shut it."

In true Talmudic (not to say legalistic) fashion, K. and the priest tease out the possible meanings of the parable by focusing on various technical questions: Was the doorkeeper the man's servant or his master? Did the doorkeeper deceive the man, either through ignorance or malice, or was he telling the truth at all times? Are there contradictions in the doorkeeper's statements? and so on. Like the characters in the story, the explanations circle around the central point without ever going inside it. The center of the tale lies in the emotion it both renders and creates: a sense of frustrated longing, of being both chosen and refused, of failing to attain the single object that one was personally destined to attain. Like John Marcher in Henry James's "The Beast in the Jungle," the man in Kafka's parable has been frustrated in his single-minded pursuit of his own fate; but unlike Marcher, he has more than himself to blame. The paradoxical quality of the parable lies in the fact that the man's fate is at once so singular and so universal.

The presence in this chapter of the priest and the cathedral would seem to indicate that this "Law" is at least in part a religious notion, a semblance of God, but the book's title and our own normal usage allow us, I think, also to give a more secular meaning to the term. In any case, the two settings, a law court and a cathedral, may not be as far apart as we normally think. Commenting on Kafka's work in a book called *The Built, the Unbuilt, and the Unbuildable,* the architectural historian Robert Harbison has pointed out that

> some of the most interesting actual structures are fictional . . . , pretending to infinite extent or perhaps just occupying more space than one can find any rational warrant for them to do. It is so common for certain types of enclosed space to be bigger than any conceivable crowd or set of activities which will ever occur there, that it is hardly thought of as a fiction. A law court or a cathedral *without* a void at the centre would seem peculiar.

To this short list of fictional structures we might add an execution chamber and its witness area.

Like Randall Adams, K. is someone who is both the singular victim of his own fate and a randomly selected wrong man on trial: the doom is both for him alone and not intended for him at all. This is true of doom, of death, in general. That too is what is being referred to in the "Before the Law" parable. Our death, which is intended for us alone, is the one experience in our life we can't directly experience (if that verb connotes the chance to contemplate afterward what the experience meant, as the noun—in its opposition to innocence—implies.) We can have access to the event only indirectly, by extrapolating from the experience of others. This is what Walter Benjamin means when, talking about a death in a novel, he describes how "this stranger's fate by virtue of the flame which consumes it yields us the warmth which we never draw from our own fate." With a fictional character, this dying-through-another seems a reasonable solution. With a real person, it seems nothing short of ghoulish, as if in sharing among ourselves the dying man's singular fate we make it less singular, less his own. This is why our collective presence at a condemned man's execution would be such a violation; it is also why we so much long to be there.

# 6

# Being There

Of course, we would not really be there, not bodily, not in person. We would be present at the execution only by virtue of the television screen. "You Are There": that was the title of a show aired during the early years of TV, when the medium represented a miraculous degree of presence, compared to radio or newspapers or even movies. The title seems to have been intended unironically, but no irony was necessary, because at that point—with black-and-white television images, limited broadcasting hours, and hand-cranked special effects—nobody feared that you could mistake TV for reality. "You Are There" was a self-acknowledged form of exaggeration, an acceptable level of false advertising.

By 1971, when Jerzy Kosinski published his novel *Being There*, the irony of the notion that to watch television *was* to "be there" had become more overt, more intentional, and certainly more comprehensible. Kosinski's parable for our times is about a human automaton whose only contact with social reality has been through watching TV. This conceit, after more than two decades of regular broadcasting, had become understandable enough to be both frightening and funny. Kosinski's simpleminded but handsome young protagonist is initially called Chance the gardener, as if to underline the randomness of his fate (a poor authorial pun, but un-authored life makes even poorer ones, such as naming a California man who spent thirteen years in jail due to a mishap "Clarence Chance"). When he joins the rest of the world, however, Chance the gardener's new upper-crust companions, mistaking him for one of themselves, call him Chauncey Gardiner: "Chance noticed that she had changed his name. He assumed that, as on TV, he must use his new name from now on." Of the character's inner life, Kosinski remarks: "By changing the channel he could change himself . . . By turning the dial, Chance could bring others inside his eyelids. Thus he came to believe that it was he, Chance, and no one else, who made himself be." This pathetic hero, who becomes a nationally celebrated political and economic guru as a result of his gnomic utterances about world events, has no direct knowledge of or desire for anything, not even sex. "I like to watch you" is all he can say, repeatedly, when the beautiful young wife of his aging sponsor attempts to seduce him. Reality, for him, is what he can watch, either on TV or as if on TV.

An updated Chance character appears, briefly and interestingly, in the otherwise tedious film *Slacker,* a 1991 low-budget portrait of late-blooming Texas hippies. One of the fictional "slackers" who inhabit this movie is a young man whom we meet in a darkened room—a room completely filled with television screens, VCRs, and other video equipment. The nameless character even wears an operating TV screen strapped to his back as he zooms about the room in a wheelchair. Speaking about a real-world event, a public disagreement that he witnessed a few days before, he complains, "But I didn't feel I was really *seeing* it—I mean, I couldn't rewind it or freeze-frame it or anything like that—it was all over before I knew what was happening." Television, he feels, is the only truly reliable form of access to reality.

Some of the witnesses in *KQED v. Vasquez* occasionally sounded as if they felt the same way. Testifying in favor of a television camera's presence in the execution chamber, Michael Schwarz said, "I think a camera alone can provide a true and clear and complete and accurate picture that is unmediated by an individual's personal interpretation of that event." Given the black-and-white, yes-or-no requirements of a court case, this stark presentation of Television as Truth may not have represented Schwarz's full and final views. Nonetheless, it was a viewpoint that was echoed by other witnesses on the KQED side. George Osterkamp, the CBS news director who testified on behalf of the plaintiff, contrasted print journalism with TV coverage by saying that in the absence of a television camera, "we'd be able to cover [the execution] only through second-hand or third-hand testimony. It would be filtered through people who had knowledge, or who had knowledge of people who had knowledge. We'd be denied the best evidence of the event, which is actually seeing it and covering it with videotape." In this last sentence, Osterkamp grammatically equated "actually seeing it" and "covering it with videotape," granting them the same degree of reliability or credibility; he implied that videotape was "first-hand testimony," the equivalent of seeing something with one's own eyes and hearing it with one's own ears.

Later in his own testimony, Osterkamp stressed the importance of videotape to "the historical record," saying that without videotape there could be "no solid record of what happened."

"You don't find it too hard to believe that Lincoln was shot at the Ford Theater, do you?" asked the ever-mischievous Judge Schnacke.

"No," replied Osterkamp, "but there are a lot of questions I have about that . . ."

"The television camera would have answered all of those?" said the judge.

"Well, I think it would have answered many of them." Then Osterkamp refined his position without in any way backing down: "The television camera is simply a tool, but a wonderful tool."

What Osterkamp was trying to do, in this final remark, was to say: Look, I'm not a fool; I know the camera can't help us know the unknowable, but it *can* give us more evidence than we've ever had before, and thereby help us know about things that previously seemed insoluble mysteries. It brings us closer to actually being there than any other form of journalism—print, radio, still pictures—that we've ever had access to. Television may not be reality, but it can help us see reality, because it transmits things to *our* eyes and lets *us* be the judge of what happened.

That's a reasonable position to hold, I think. But the problem is that television doesn't lend itself to the reasonable. It insists on its own specialness, its own near approach to the truth—even, or especially, when it is dealing with something as arguable as the historical record. I say "it insists," following the prevailing tendency to cede supernatural or at any rate human powers to the medium. But television is not its own advocate; the people who work with it and in it are, and they do it a disservice when they exaggerate its claims. "Television news has the power to transmit the experience itself rather than information about the experience," announce Robert Donovan and Ray Scherer, the authors of *Unsilent Revolution,* a 1992 book about television news and its effect on public life since 1948. In *KQED v. Vasquez,* the plaintiff's side took this deeply embedded attitude and gave it another turn of the screw. Ostensibly arguing that television, as one of the several important tools of journalism's trade, should be allowed equal access to a publicly important story like an execution, KQED drifted instead into the position that television was *uniquely* qualified to capture the news. Aside from being a difficult proposition to prove, this stance made the plaintiff vulnerable to exactly the attacks it was in the process of legally deploring. For if television is different in kind from all other forms of journalism, mightn't that give Warden Vasquez the right to exclude this branch of the media on reasonable and considered and *not* arbitrarily discriminatory grounds?

KQED's special case for television focused heavily on the idea of the camera's objectivity. In doing so, the plaintiff's side appeared to confuse two different senses of the word: on the one hand, our sense that an objective report is disinterested, honest, reliable, impartial; and, on the other hand, the sense that only something which is not subjective—which does not partake of the individual human viewpoint—can be fully objective, neutrally conveying things and events that are out in the world without the distorting coloration of human consciousness. A good newspaper reporter can be objective in the first sense (reliable, honest, and so on), but only a machine like a television camera could possibly be objective in that second sense. And even that possibility seems remote. It's not clear how we could use Schwarz's "true and clear and complete and accurate picture that is unmediated by an individual's personal interpretation of that event," for in order to become a functional picture of reality, even television's images need to be absorbed by our particular minds. The picture itself can have no meaning until viewers make something of it, as the jury verdict in the Rodney King case and the outraged response to that verdict demonstrated. We depend on people to give objective—in the sense of disinterested and impartial—interpretations to videotape, and are justifiably outraged at the people, not the videotape, when they fail to do so. Objectivity, in the first of the two senses, is a quality that only the human mind can have.

George Osterkamp, in his *KQED v. Vasquez* testimony, limited his praise of television to his assertion that it is simply an excellent recording tool, providing a fuller and more detailed record than any single set of handwritten notes or any single picture could. In Osterkamp's view, the objectivity of television is a function of its capacity to substitute for the individual eyewitness. Yet nothing, as those investigating Lincoln's assassination could no doubt have told us, is as unreliable as an eyewitness. These two facets of the television camera — its role as a neutral recording tool, and its substitution for or collaboration with the ever-interpreting human eye — are in direct conflict. Yet this paradox is repeatedly glossed over in the accounts of news professionals, who stress the extent to which "being there" through the camera will mean seeing things more accurately.

At the opening of *Nightline*'s coverage of *KQED v. Vasquez*, for instance, the ABC newswoman Jackie Judd summarized the issues in a voice-over: "Through the eye of a television camera, we would go into the San Quentin gas chamber and actually watch a condemned man die. It wouldn't be happening in some far-off country and it wouldn't be happening in the middle of a violent conflict. It would be the most close-up look ever of how our society chooses to punish some of its most violent criminals." Her primary metaphor was that of the camera's eye (a metaphor to which we are so habituated that we no longer view it as metaphorical), but there was also an overtone of historical record-keeping — in the reference to faraway world-shaking events, in the scrutinizing term "close-up look," and even in the oddly chosen preposition "of" (implying that this is the look *of* an execution, not merely a look at it). The camera, she suggested, is our own eye made more powerful, more scientific, more *objective*. That underlying impression was then confirmed in a brief commentary by Michael Schwarz, who asserted that the camera in the death chamber could be used "almost in the way you might use a surveillance camera, to provide a complete and accurate record of the event."

But having set up Schwarz's position, Judd proceeded to knock it down. (So much for the impartial objectivity of television reporting, at least as practiced on *Nightline*.) She pointed out that "no one else in the debate, on either side, believes that a powerful tool like television could ever be a neutral witness." The other participants in the interview then aired various arguments against showing us a televised execution: that it would blunt our moral sensibilities, that it would horrify us, that it would be pornographic or disgusting, that it would be viewed as casual entertainment. (Some of these, like the arguments in favor of television's accuracy, logically conflict with each other: if the images continue to horrify us, our sensibilities will not have been blunted; and if we find something pornographic or disgusting, we are likely to view it as more, or less, than "casual" entertainment.) The most profound objection came from David Bruck, a defense attorney who had actually witnessed two executions and who staunchly opposed capital punishment. He challenged the *truth* of what the camera would show. "The thirty seconds or sixty seconds or two minutes that the public would see is almost no part of the death penalty," Bruck said. "The death penalty is the process of waiting for death for years and then measured by the calendar and then finally by the clock. The death penalty is going to the families—to the motel room where the man's parents or his wife and children are waiting afterwards. None of that would be on TV."

Not only would the experience as portrayed on television be contextless and therefore false, as Bruck suggested; it would also be pure spectacle, unmediated by the understanding and knowledge that convert spectacle into experience. Far from "being there" with the condemned man, we would be completely outside of him, viewing him as an easily liquidatable object: "if you don't believe that people can be converted into junk in as long as it takes to shut a drawer or cut off an electric light, just watch this," Bruck had asserted earlier in the interview. What we really want to know, when we ask to be taken into the gas chamber, is not just what it looks like when we kill a person; we also want to know what it feels like. The camera alone can't give us that. It can only give us something approaching the sensations of Bowles's character Dyar—the sense of how effortless, how easy it is to kill a person who has become an "it."

And even that level of interior experience—that portrayal of an automaton's viewpoint, inflected by an author's judgments and choices—is finally beyond the news camera's capacity. The camera's objectivity, in the sense of its inability to be subjective, is its downfall in this regard. Being there, inside someone else's experience, is a function of projective imagination. But the journalistic TV camera has no projective imagination. Far from neutral it may be, but the television news camera is relentlessly external. This is not so much a function of the machine itself as of the people who wield it. Videotape *can* be a personal expression of individual viewpoint, in the hands of a master documentarian like Frederick Wiseman or Errol Morris; but it is not used this way on television news, where all sorts of factors (time availability being one) conspire against the expression of the personal. If you pointed this out to broadcasting executives, they would not see it as a problem. On the contrary, their characterization of the news would echo Schwarz's—that it should aspire to the unmediated. Yet the television news camera, purporting to give us unmediated reality, all the while leaves out something crucial. This is what David Bruck meant when he said in his closing remarks on *Nightline,* "The truth of the matter is that the public's imagination of what this must be like—and I say this having seen two of these executions take place—the public's imagination is much truer than what they would see on TV."

In his passionate commentary on the KQED case, Bruck may have hit on the central characteristic of the murder story. It is about what must be imagined, what can't actually be seen—what can't, in any verifiable way, be known. Even when the murder story involves the solution of a mystery, that solution can't resolve all our questions: if it does, we get the flat, disappointed feeling so many murder mysteries give us, where the solution seems a dead end that greets us at the conclusion to a wild, hurtling journey. On the other hand, a mystery can't arbitrarily refuse to offer complete solutions either — that route is simply infuriating, the way the trail of unexplained red herrings in "Twin Peaks" was. The murder story must do its best to answer all the answerable questions, and still leave something open or unresolved in the end.

*The Executioner's Song* is exemplary in this respect. It gives us more than we could ever have expected to know about how Gary Gilmore killed his two victims, who he was at the time of the murders as well as before and after them, how he dealt with his own crime and punishment, what his friends and relations thought, and so on. But the book doesn't pin down, in any final way, *why* these murders took place, or even exactly how Gary felt about them; and it lightly mocks the people, such as the jailhouse interviewers, who tried to get answers to those questions. It helps a great deal that Mailer had the freedom of fiction in which to maneuver, allowing the Novelist to assist the Historian with any necessary adjustments to the telescope. And — a corollary feature — it helps that Mailer never met Gilmore, that he had to imagine him instead.

The author of a murder story resembles a homicide detective: he has to imagine what must have taken place, based on the physical evidence. This is different from a scientist's work, or a lawyer's, which involves proof. The author and the detective are allowed to take leaps into the unknowable. They are allowed to — they *must* — ask questions that have no hope of certain answers. Poe commented on this feature of authorship and detection in the epigraph to "The Murders in the Rue Morgue," which was itself the first example of authorship about detection. (About detection per se: I exclude from this category earlier works, such as Sophocles' *Oedipus*

*Rex* and William Godwin's *Caleb Williams*, in which the detection of a murder is merely a by-product of some more central passion on the part of the searcher.) The "Rue Morgue" epigraph is taken from Sir Thomas Browne: "What song the Syrens sang, or what name Achilles assumed when he hid himself among women, although puzzling questions, are not beyond *all* conjecture."

A recent murder story that transformed this conjecturing principle into an obsession was the Dutch movie *The Vanishing*, released in America at around the same time as *The Silence of the Lambs*. As the film critic Craig Seligman has noted, "The peculiar theme of *The Vanishing* is the terrible need to know." A young couple are on vacation; the woman inexplicably disappears; years pass, and everyone assumes her to be dead. Meanwhile, her boyfriend—who, after briefly leaving her alone in a pitch-dark tunnel, swore, in an earlier scene in the movie, never to abandon her, and in particular never again to leave her in dark, enclosed places, which terrify her—continues to search for her, to the exclusion of all else in his life. Also meanwhile, we are introduced to the odd, repulsive, but strangely engaging figure whom we take to be the abductor and (increasingly, as the movie progresses) the murderer. He is a murderer with the soul of an accountant: in a series of flashbacks, we see him measure each step of his procedures in meters and seconds, planning his crime to perfection. *His* terrible need is to know whether and how such a crime might be executed, and we get the definite feeling that the successful execution of a Plan accounts for a large portion of his satisfaction.

Acting, in a way, on behalf of the desperately curious audience, the boyfriend also has a "terrible need to know": so terrible that he is willing to trade his life for the knowledge. He puts himself in the hands of the suspected murderer, knowing that he will discover his girlfriend's fate only by submitting to it himself; and in the last scene of the movie he finds himself buried alive in a coffin. As Seligman puts it: "Anything, he tells himself, is better than not knowing—and at the end, horribly, he knows." But the horror, it seems to me, is not in *his* fate. Unless we are neurotically susceptible to fears of being buried alive—and some of us are: horror is always partly personal—his fate alone will be insufficiently terrifying to live up to all our horrific expectations. The horror lies instead in our imagining of his imagining of what his girlfriend felt when she found herself in that buried box, she who was so frightened of dark tunnels, of being left alone. Having willingly, even willfully put himself in the hands of the murderer, he seems less deserving of our sympathy. It is only she who is the completely innocent victim, the completely pitiable one.

For me, the end of *The Vanishing* failed to work emotionally: I was irritated at the hero for letting himself get checkmated, and thereby, by proxy, letting *me* get checkmated; and I was also annoyed at the faux-Poe quality of the final "horror." But my reaction appears to be a minority one, and I suspect that's because I failed to see the strapping young woman who played the girlfriend as an endangered, potentially weak creature. (A child, now: if it had been a child I probably would have walked out of the movie before it was over, unable to bear either the offered knowledge or its suspenseful withholding. But that would be a different sort of artistic failure, or success.) Another way of putting this is that I found the female lead an insufficient container for my projective imagination. I did not want to be there, inside her.

This is not, I think, because I am a woman. As I said in talking about *Manhunter* and *The Silence of the Lambs,* my own feeling is that we are all, men and women, asked to identify with both the (predominantly male) killers and the (usually female) victims in murder movies. Imagining ourselves inside the murderer enables us to feel a kind of power. Imagining ourselves inside the victim enables us to yield ourselves to a certain defenselessness. The murderer's desire for power, in the most interesting of these stories, is one which also includes a desire for that defenselessness. He too seeks to be inside his victim. (This is the point of the ladyskin suit in *The Silence of the Lambs*, and also of the murderer's assumption of his victim's identity at the end of Paul Theroux's *Chicago Loop*.) That this is an intrusive sexual feeling as well as a sense of intruded-upon, masochistic identification is made explicit in *The Killer Inside Me*, where Jim Thompson echoes his title in an argument between Lou Ford and his fiancée Amy. "You screwed her. You've been doing it all along," Amy yells at Lou about the local prostitute. "You've been putting her dirty insides inside of me, smearing me with her." We know — "we" being Lou and the reader — that this "her" is the woman he's just killed. Amy doesn't know this, but our knowledge of it is part of what makes her graphically disgusting (and true) remark even more disgusting.

Only part, however. Another large part has to do with the repellent physical image of sex as a diabolical medical procedure, the same idea that underlay David Cronenberg's brilliantly terrifying *Dead Ringers*. Lou is, after all, a doctor's son, and I hear echoes of "pap smear" in that "smearing me with her." "Putting her dirty insides inside of me" is more than promiscuous; it is taxidermical (*Psycho* enters in here) and dehumanizingly intrusive. People's inner selves are getting mixed up together; personal integrity is being violated, and secret recesses are being exposed. It's akin to what happens when we consume the lurid details of a murder, putting ourselves in the place of both participants.

Where sex and violence overlap, as they do in so many of these murder stories, our projective imagination is bound to entail a disturbing level of prurience. "The concept of prurience," said Christopher Ricks, apropos Racine's *Phèdre* and its English translations,

> implies an attitude toward one's own impure, lewd or las-
> civious imaginings, an impurity not of the imaginings but
> of the attitude toward them, an attitude of cherishing,
> fondling, slyly watching, or preferring (preferring imag-

ining to acting). Art is obliged to be especially interested in prurience, since prurience is a disease of the imagination; prurience is not unimaginativeness, a failure of imagination, but a corrupt success of it.

Prurience is, specifically, the disease that afflicts those of us who enjoy murder stories—those of us who, identifying with both victim and murderer, messily put our insides inside of them. The itch to do this (the word "prurience" stems from a verb meaning "to itch") is linked to the voyeurism Janet Malcolm detected in murder stories, "the avid interest of some of us in being 'insiders' or getting the 'inside' view of things." We want to be inside but also removed, fully involved but also safely hidden, getting the experience from behind a protective wall of glass—or a television screen. We want to be *there*, not here.

Frank Bidart's poem "Herbert White," a dramatic monologue spoken from the point of view of a serial killer, contains a stanza on exactly this subject (if "stanza" is the right word for Bidart's idiosyncratic segmentations). The poem itself is about prurience and uses prurience—both the secretly hoarded, privately fondled, necrophiliac passions of the killer himself, and our own itch to know about those passions. There is something embarrassingly private about our experience of this poem. Bidart is an especially powerful reader of his own dramatic monologues, but I can't imagine this poem read aloud: it would be like watching Herbert White commit his secret, nighttime, hidden crimes in public.°

°Having written this sentence, I decided to ask Frank Bidart whether he ever read "Herbert White" aloud. The answer was, essentially, "Never again." He said he read it aloud once, on request, to a group of college students, and he was already so nervous about it that he prefaced the poem with a long introduction about how it was a *character* speaking, the whole poem was in *quotes,* he himself was not Herbert White, and so on. After he began reading the poem, a latecomer arrived and, without benefit of the excessive explanation, sat down to listen. In two minutes she got up again, shocked and offended, and left. Bidart was mortified.

The particular stanza I'm singling out is bracketed by two of the more horrific passages in the poem: one where Herbert describes how he

> saw a little girl—
> who I picked up, hit on the head, and
> screwed, and screwed, and screwed, and screwed, then
>
> buried,
>          in the garden of the motel . . .

and another where he quotes his mother: "Mom once said, 'Man's spunk is the salt of the earth. . . .'" But the stanza itself is comparatively innocent:

> —You see, ever since I was a kid I wanted
> to *feel* things make sense: I remember
>
> looking out the window of my room back home,—
> and being almost suffocated by the asphalt;
> and grass; and trees; and glass;
> just *there*, just *there*, doing nothing!
> not saying anything! filling me up—
> but also being a wall; dead, and stopping me;
> —how I wanted to see beneath it, cut
>
> beneath it, and make it
> somehow, come alive . . .

The passage harps on the juxtaposition of nearness and distance: "just *there*, just *there*." Like the viewers of a television execution, Herbert White is separated from reality by a pane of glass, a transparent but deadening wall. Reality, in this version, has no sensations of its own; it is "doing nothing!" It is up to White to "*feel* things make sense," to "make it / somehow, come alive." (Remember Kosinski's version of being just there: "Thus he came to believe that it was he, Chance, and no one else, who made himself be.") Paradoxically, the form that this life-giving impulse takes in White is to kill—to murder little girls and "screw, and screw, and screw, and screw" their dead bodies. Because of that dead glass wall separating him from the world of feeling, Herbert White's access to real life is death.

If White is, in this respect, like the viewers of a televised execution, he is also like the readers of his own tale. We are separated from his fate and feelings by a transparent pane of words, the very medium through which we also have access to those feelings, that fate. We enter Herbert White through our projective imagination, making him "somehow, come alive." So, even more, does Frank Bidart, taking on the killer's own voice to bring about the poem. Bidart too has given life to death, immortalizing a murderer and his crimes. The speaker he gives us in this poem sounds painfully near to us—our access to White is as direct as imagination can make it (which is more direct than life can make it)—and yet that nearness has been achieved through the distance of carefully wrought art. Bidart has had to withdraw into himself, looking away from the bare realities for a moment, in order to plunge us into Herbert White's existence.

A video camera can record while it "watches," but a human being must look away first. One of the smaller ironies of the Rodney King case was that the man who recorded King's beating didn't even know what he had "seen" until he played the tape on his VCR. This may make the machine seem more powerful, but in that failure to look away also lies its weakness, its limitation, its stupidity. The machine alone cannot lend to recorded experience the imaginative imprint that transforms "there" to "here," for that imprint can take place only in the space between looking and looking away.

Howard Brodie, the journalistic sketch artist who testified on the side of the television station, explicitly made this point during *KQED v. Vasquez.* A famous and respected chronicler of public events, including wars, trials, and executions, Brodie had watched and recorded the last gas chamber execution to take place in California—that is, Aaron

Mitchell's death in 1967. He was willing to testify on KQED's behalf because, as he told Ted Koppel on *Nightline,* the Mitchell execution had been "my most dehumanizing memory in civilian life," and he felt people should understand and take responsibility for what the state was doing in their name; "it's not the governor, it's not the warden, it's not the law—it's you and I who execute," Brodie pointed out. Television, he felt, would show people exactly how dehumanizing an execution was. What Brodie ended up demonstrating, though, was the difference between an artist's sketch and a camera's rendering, a difference that lies, among other things, in the human lag between watching and recording, in the necessity for the artist to look away.

In his testimony, Brodie stressed that although he was permitted to bring a sketchpad into the witness area to make visual "notes," his drawings of Aaron Mitchell's execution were actually made from memory. "I found it extremely valuable to sketch from memory," he said, "because instead of just my eye and my hand working, I began to observe what was happening. . . . I felt that I'd better intensely focus on this execution, which I thought would take, frankly, a moment or two—a minute or two . . . I felt that I'd better not waste a moment by taking my eyes away from the subject." Drawing from memory is not, he suggested, a technique practiced only by him; all journalistic artists do it to some extent. Brodie gestured to the artists sitting in the press box as he testified, the artists who were at that moment engaged in sketching *him* ("I presume they're sketching me and not you," he said in a friendly aside to the judge. "I don't know why I presume that") and pointed out that even they were "drawing from memory," since they had to take their eyes away from him every time they focused on their sketches. I registered the truth of this observation myself as I sat in the courtroom, looking away from the events when I looked down at my page of notes.

In the Mitchell case, Brodie used a longer-term kind of visual memory. "How long after the execution itself did you make your sketches?" Bill Turner asked him on the stand.

"Until the emotions had subsided within me," he answered. "I didn't want to have my emotions affecting my drawing ... It may have been a week; it may have been ten days, two weeks. I don't know ... If things are burned into my mind, I can draw." Brodie emphasized that what he produced were rough sketches without much detail because "I didn't want anything in here unless they were things that were precisely in my memory."

Howard Brodie's commitment to objectivity is admirable, and his faith in his accuracy no doubt warranted. But because he is a human being rather than a mere recording machine, he cannot have something "burned into" his mind that does not in turn involve his "emotions." It may be a very cooled down, precise, transmogrified kind of emotion, such as Frank Bidart must have used to create his artful portrait of Herbert White, but it is emotion nonetheless, and comes across to us all the more powerfully because of its rigorous submersion in art.

George Osterkamp suggested as much in his own testimony. He pointed out that an eloquent newspaper reporter with a good memory could convey a great deal about an event, "and a courtroom artist, like Howard Brodie, can convey something that's indelible, and that may be closer to the truth than anything else that comes out."

"Including a television camera?" interjected the judge.

"Including a television camera," the CBS newsman confirmed. "A television camera is only a tool."

Later the judge remarked to him, "You appreciate that Howard Brodie did an awful lot of editorializing in his drawings."

"Well, I do think you see emotion in them, which is an important part of the event ..."

"Mr. Brodie's emotion," said the judge.

Howard Brodie's sketches of the execution of Aaron Mitchell. "These two were the key drawings: the condemned man was first upright, then, immediately, went down, then slowly sat up again for several long minutes, then went down for a final time." (Howard Brodie, letter to Wendy Lesser, January 27, 1993)

"Well," said Osterkamp, "it's hard to separate Mr. Brodie's emotion from the emotion of the event, I think. They blend."

Osterkamp's intelligence, which took the form of his willingness to grant the ambiguities of a situation, made him a less-than-ideal witness for the plaintiff. In this instance, the truth and subtlety of his observations laid him open to the defense lawyers' most telling thrust. Judge Schnacke (who repeatedly told Howard Brodie how honored he was to have him in his courtroom) had just finished saying, "So you have to be a genius to do it the way Brodie did," to which Osterkamp replied: "There are some video geniuses too, Your Honor, I think, who are ready to do this with the help of videotape, who can come very close to the truth."

At this the cross-examining attorney, Paul Gifford, saw his opening and leapt in. "Does that mean that these video geniuses would be supplying some interpretive element to the videotape, as Howard Brodie does to his drawings?"

"Well, I would hope they would amplify it," Osterkamp answered, cautiously using a less loaded term. But somewhat later, when speaking about the emotion in Brodie's sketches, he added: "And I think you would see emotion in videotape, which is important."

In one blow, Osterkamp undid the testimony of his fellow expert Michael Schwarz, who had previously asserted that the television camera "can act as a neutral witness." Schwarz had distinguished between a reporter, who "needs to put the story into his or her own words, and that in itself constitutes an act of interpretation," and a camera, which "does not require that kind of filter. A camera can give us a direct and unmediated recording of what, in fact, happened at the event." Schwarz's statement was the useful, professional thing for a plaintiff's witness to say; Osterkamp's was the complicated and possibly damaging truth. Yet it need not have been damaging. Because of Schwarz's initial testimony, KQED's case against Warden Vasquez had been set up in terms of the special qualifications of television to report impartially and accurately, and the unnecessarily biased reporting that would therefore ensue if television were excluded from the death chamber. But what if television had been presented, not as different from the other forms of reporting, but as continuous with them, in all their human frailties? Such a perspective, while it might tarnish videotape's uniqueness as a form of journalism, would certainly enhance its possibilities as art.

# 7

# Rendering Reality

The whole underlying thrust of the plaintiff's case in *KQED v. Vasquez* was that news is different from art, that news is objective, neutral, capable of rendering experience directly, whereas art is subjective, biased, a personal interpretation of experience. Yet it might have made the plaintiff's case easier to prove, and would certainly have made it more truthful, if KQED and its attorneys had considered the extent to which the rendering of an execution, on television or on film, would be acceptable—ethically, aesthetically, emotionally acceptable—only if that newsworthy portrayal fell into the category of art. I am not surprised that the KQED people didn't consider this; the adversarial thinking of a lawsuit is not conducive to boundary-blurring ideas. But if they had observed Judge Schnacke carefully, the plaintiff's representatives and lawyers might have noticed that the judge himself granted to art a special sort of dispensation.

This was especially apparent in Judge Schnacke's treatment of Howard Brodie. Quick to suspect the motives of even the nonprofit sector of the press, the judge never once asked himself, or anyone else, whether there was something unseemly or distasteful or exploitive about Howard Brodie's desire to see and sketch an execution. This was partly because Brodie defused such reactions by explaining on the witness stand his economic relations to the Aaron Mitchell drawings.

156

"I have never copyrighted them," Brodie said of his widely reproduced pictures. "I—to me, they belong to whoever wants to use them." Whatever small fee he received for doing this work, Brodie refused to keep: "I said to the state at the time that, if I did receive money, any money for any of these things, they would go to Aaron Mitchell's mother. And really, I must have gotten in my life maybe—I don't know, a hundred, two hundred, or whatever it is. And whenever I got a check, she— I sent it to her." Howard Brodie also revealed the way in which he valued other people's feelings over the importance of his own work. "I did have one proviso," he testified. "I said that I did not wish anyone to publish these unless the mother of Aaron Mitchell sees them first and okays them. And then I met her minister and met the mother and she said, 'I want them published.'"

All of this made Brodie a much more sympathetic figure than any of the TV news people, convinced as they were of the unimpeachable public value of their revelatory acts. But Brodie's testimony is not sufficient in itself to explain the judge's reverent attitude toward the artist. Before he had said anything at all about the Aaron Mitchell pictures, and only shortly after he had been put on the witness stand, Howard Brodie became the object of Judge Schnacke's lively and somewhat irrelevant interest. In answer to the attorney's opening questions aimed at establishing the witness's credentials, Brodie had said that he was an "artist/journalist" who had been reporting on news events for quite a long time—"offhand, I'd say at least fifty years."

"Who do you work for now?" the judge interrupted. When the artist responded that he was now independent and only semi-active, the judge continued, "I just thought I'd mention. I must confess I haven't seen any of your work for a long, long time and I miss it."

"Well, I'm honored, Your Honor," Brodie said.

"TV can do a good job on things like the Big Game,"

Schnacke added, once again reverting to his sports obsession, "but never quite as good a job as you did on it."

Judge Schnacke's affection for Howard Brodie's work may have contained a strong personal element—including memories of his own younger days, when he had last seen those pictures—but it also partook of a more widely held attitude toward art, an attitude that came out in the judge's exchange with George Osterkamp. Brodie, they both agreed, was a "genius" at conveying the "emotion" of an event—both his own and that of the event itself. Howard Brodie's "editorializing" was, in this sense, the essence of his art. In his testimony Brodie noted that although TV news stations, before they could get cameras into courtrooms, had simply viewed the sketch artist as "a substitute for a camera," other places— in particular, certain magazines—had valued his work for itself: "They felt that an artist added a human element to the coverage." As the exchange between Schnacke and Osterkamp and then between Gifford and Osterkamp made clear, this "human dimension" does not just involve a distortion or lessening of the truth. It can actually increase the truthfulness of an event's representation, making it more faithful to the emotions of the participants and the in-person witnesses. This kind of truth is not objectively verifiable as fact; it requires our assent, as witnesses and potential witnesses, and it engages us actively in the effort to define what really happened in a particular place, what really happens in the world at large.

The human dimension is what can make the difference between art and news. Art has, above all, an individual perspective, a sense that it has been shaped by a human mind to be taken in by a human mind. This does not mean that only individually shaped things can be art. Found objects can be art; collaborative efforts like films or theater productions can be art. What makes them art is our sense that an individual sensibility is speaking to us through them, in a way that undifferentiated reality cannot. I once saw a production of *King Lear* directed by a Japanese theater artist named Tadashi Suzuki, with all the parts played by kimono-clad men (even Goneril and Regan, even Cordelia) and large segments of dialogue slashed from the play; and this particular production struck me as truer to the individual sensibility of the play than any other performance I've ever seen. The vision which shaped this production was so powerful that we in the audience could feel it coming through in every line, every gesture. It was a shaping intelligence that came from somewhere offstage: we couldn't see it, but we nonetheless knew it was there. This authority—whether it was Shakespeare's or Suzuki's or, as I believe, some combination of the two—was the consoling strength that made Lear's tragedy bearable. It reassured us that while there may not be a God, there is at any rate an artist.

A videotape of an execution that had an individual sensibility would be a very different thing from the news footage KQED proposed to produce. But then, it is not at all clear that anyone *could* produce the kind of uninflected, unemotional videotape KQED was proposing. One of the great ironies of *KQED v. Vasquez* was that KQED, in this age of post-Newtonian perspective, should have built its case so heavily on an idea that the rest of us—philosophers, literary critics, visual artists, and quantum physicists alike—had long since come to doubt: the idea of the "neutral witness."

The primary exponent of that neutrality, in the context of the *KQED v. Vasquez* trial, was Michael Schwarz. It was he who believed that a videotape camera could capture an event without "filtering" it through an individual's viewpoint. At one point in his testimony, he explained how he planned to use the camera technically in order to render the undiluted truth. "Let me try a way to put it: to capture the event, and without— well, what we call a lockdown shot," he began, leaping from the unstated problem ("without" interpretation, "without"

filtering, "without" human distortion) to the proposed solution—"a lockdown shot," with its uncanny mimicry of prison
terminology. "I would essentially want that person to show me
a picture of what I would see if I was there," Schwarz continued,

> by starting with a picture that was a fairly fixed shot of
> the person being executed, and then doing nothing while
> the execution was happening to modify that image. I
> would not want the camera to contribute to what was
> being seen in the frame ... It would be almost the way a
> surveillance camera would work, where you just have
> your shot, and then whatever happens, happens. But you
> don't zoom in or zoom out, which could create editorial
> effect that I would want to avoid.

Michael Schwarz apparently doesn't watch the sort of
TV *I* watch: the one-hour murder series and two-hour murder
pilots and made-for-TV murder movies. If he did, he would
know that the surveillance camera has become such a ubiqui-
tous plot device as virtually to signal a forthcoming murder.
But leave this aside. Leave aside, as well, the role of the surveillance camera in *1984*, and thence its popularization as the
far-from-innocent demon of modern society. I will even leave
aside the strangely formulated paradox, "I would not want the
camera to contribute to what was being seen in the frame,"
where the very notion of a "frame" shows what, among other
things, the camera is necessarily contributing. For now, all I
want to examine is the central notion in his statement: the idea
that a locked-down camera, with no zooms or pans or jump-
cuts or other special techniques, can avoid by its very stillness
the creation of "editorial effect."

When a prose writer strives for the objectivity of a surveillance camera, the result—as George Orwell, Christopher
Isherwood, and Samuel Beckett variously demonstrate—is
that clarity and precision become the distinguishing features
of the style, to such a noticeable extent that they create an

especially powerful authorial presence. In Orwell's descrip-
tions of an elephant being shot in Burma or a fellow soldier
preparing for battle in Spain or even himself starving in Paris,
the language of affected affectlessness defines the piece as vintage Orwell, as singularly smacking of his own personality.
Isherwood's snapshots of Berlin are composed in such lumi-
nously clean, delicately inflected sentences that no subsequent
writer has managed to capture or imitate their particularity;
even the autobiographical Isherwood of the later years seems
to be providing an intrusively heavy-handed gloss when he
retells the stories he has earlier conveyed through his camera-
like fiction. And when Beckett, in *The Lost Ones*, describes a
community of unidentified beings purely in terms of their
physical characteristics and surroundings, the very neutrality
of the descriptive voice, its emphasis on measurement and
repetition and objectifying phrasing, is what makes us feel
pity for the creatures. By simulating an unfeeling recorder in
his prose, Beckett calls on us to fill in the emotional vacuum,
to sympathize with the beings who are the victims of such
merciless dissection.

Because we expect language, and especially literary language, to express feeling, an affectless style is a noticeable
style. The situation with film is somewhat different, and it's
possible that in the early years of movies or television, audiences could be persuaded to take an unmoving camera as a
direct rendering of reality. It's more likely, however, that they
would be oblivious to zooms and pans, which, after all, imitate
our natural freedom to step closer or farther away, to move
our heads and look around. A lockdown shot, on the other
hand, would be liable to make itself felt, if only viscerally. Like
the unblinking camera in Hitchcock's *Rope*, which, through a
highly conscious manipulation of technique, appeared to
convey the entire action of the movie in a single take, a lockdown shot of an execution might well create in the viewer a
feeling of claustrophobia. It might, as its name implies, make

us feel visually trapped, and therefore make us more likely to
sympathize with that other victim of imprisonment, the condemned man.

Nor is the affectation of objectivity a stance free of editorial effect. Frederick Wiseman, among others, has taught us
this. If a camera is simply *there,* and things take place in front
of it, they seem more real, more true, than if the cameraman
elaborates with close-ups and wide-angles and other obvious
devices. The absence of a statement is itself a statement. It
says: "Believe what I am showing you as if you were watching
it in person. I did not select this material, I did not go after it, I
did not edit it in any way. These sights were thrust upon me in
exactly this form." The bare style also says: "I am not an artist,
molding reality according to my own prejudices and illusions.
I am a scientist, an investigator, a sociological note-taker." The
fact that all these statements are fictions, or at any rate
modifications of the truth, does not make them any the less
importantly persuasive. No film style is without its connotations; the connotations of the lockdown shot may be Factu-
ality, or Control, or Voyeurism, or Victimization, or Oppres-
sion, but whatever they are—and they may even conflict with
one another—they cannot be eliminated to make way for
some kind of neutral rendering.

This was demonstrated particularly well by a piece of
film that was made widely available during the course of
*KQED v. Vasquez:* the official San Quentin footage of the gas
chamber. During the trial and its corresponding publicity,
snippets of this tape appeared on every television program
that aired the issue. If you had seen the original tape, you
could recognize its reappearances in the greenish-tinged
vision of the gas chamber itself, the frontal view of the imprisoning chair, the slamming-to and locking-up of the heavy door
sealing off the chamber. This was the sole available piece of
film about the San Quentin gas chamber, and media people

could obtain it only by applying directly to the San Quentin authorities (or else borrowing it from other media people).

One would expect the officially released film of the empty gas chamber to present a neutral picture, if anything would. The prison authorities were presumably not interested in disseminating inflammatory or horrific footage, and the film does maintain a locked camera position for each shot, much in the manner recommended by Michael Schwarz. But the effect is far from uninflected. Like Beckett's scientific-sounding incantations, like Kafka's circular traps, and most of all like Errol Morris's slightly varied "reenactments" in *The Thin Blue Line*, this segment of gas chamber film induces a slowly growing horror partly by virtue of its very repetitiveness. (The film is totally unattributed—there is no indication of who made it, or even when it was made—but as I watched it unfold, I enjoyed imagining that it had been shot anonymously by Errol Morris himself, when he was a young criminology student at UC Berkeley.)

Released to the media on a cassette that also includes footage labeled "DEATH ROW," the gas chamber film, which begins with the label "GAS CHAMBER" in yellow block letters, follows immediately on the Death Row segment and resembles it in format. Though it contains no condemned prisoners, the second segment echoes with the presence of those who are absent from it—the trapped, dehumanized, fragmentedly-shot men who appear in the preceding segment. It literally echoes as well: a major part of the eeriness of "Gas Chamber" is created by its use of sound. Before we see anything except the outside of the gas chamber building (a concrete-adobe structure with a green door), we hear the sounds—keys jingling, a heavy door slamming, and the slow, heavy footsteps of a guard walking. These are the only sounds on the soundtrack, and they are repeated over and over again, echoing loudly in the empty chamber. After we hear them for the first time, we are shown the gas chamber itself, a green octagonal room with a pyramid-like top, windows in four contiguous faces, and a circular railing separating it from the viewing area. We get very little sense, throughout the film, of what this viewing area is like; the focus is entirely on the death chamber itself. The camera gives us various still or slowly moving shots of the chamber, from one side, from the other, and finally from the "back," where the door into the chamber is located.

Our first view of the two seats that are built to hold the condemned prisoners comes through the open door of the chamber, which the guard then closes heavily (sound of slamming) and seals with a circular, captain's-wheel type of lock. Only then, *after* seeing the door closed, do we see it opened by the guard in a reverse series of gestures. As the door opens again, we get a close-up of the twirling lock and then a close-up of the two seats with their restraining straps. This sequence, that of the door opening, is repeated several times. Then the guard goes in to check the straps, or to simulate checking the straps, and comes back out again, locking the door. After that we get a very long, unmoving take of one of the seats, shot from below; only subsequently do we get a straightforward frontal shot of the same seat. The camera then shows us a black telephone—rotary, not pushbutton—outside the death chamber itself, with a sign on it saying "Governor's Office." This, evidently, is the hot line for last-minute reprieves. The final scene in the film is taken from inside the gas chamber, and it shows the heavy door shutting on us, locking us in and blocking out our last view of the potentially life-saving phone.

The last scene is only the most extreme of the ways in which the movie creates in us a feeling of entrapment. I was going to say "a Kafkaesque feeling of entrapment," but in Kafka at least the guards are human, particular, engaged ("You are insatiable," the guard teases in the "Before the Law" parable), whereas here the guard is a silent adjunct of the death machine itself. The repetitive, echoing sounds—keys, heavy doors, guard footsteps—all suggest imprisonment. The slow or unmoving camera, meaninglessly repeating episodes (meaninglessly from the point of view of any narrative, though the slightly varied repetition no doubt helps TV editors select the exact angle they want), makes us feel trapped in the mind of a slow-witted maniac. The restraining chairs, which are the first and only referent to the potential victim's body, are not introduced until some distance into the film, as if to turn up the level of our already heightened anxiety. And the first view of those chairs is through an open door which then slams closed, not (as logic would dictate) a normally locked door which then swings open.

Overall, the various elements in this film, up to and including the final scene, emphasize a movement toward closing, away from opening. This is even true, coincidentally, of the captain's-wheel lock itself, which spins clockwise to lock, counterclockwise to open—as if the forward movement of time would inevitably bring closure, entrapment, sealing-in. (This feature is coincidental in that locks are normally designed this way, but the camera's repeated focus on it may be more than coincidence.) These elements ask us to identify with the potential victim of the gas chamber, make us feel locked in the same clockwise-moving system that will eventually close off the condemned man's life. Yet we are also the executioners, for that long, initially inexplicable shot of the restraining chair *from below* is taken from the position of the gas pellets that will eventually do the killing.

The absence of an actual victim in some ways makes the San Quentin gas chamber footage more threatening. "It could be anyone," the empty chamber suggests, "even you." Something similar is accomplished through the vague sketchiness that characterizes Howard Brodie's drawings of Aaron Mitchell's 1967 execution. "These are very rough sketches," Brodie testified, because "I didn't want anything in here unless they were things that were precisely in my memory." If accuracy was the motive, then a certain generalized Everyman quality is part of the result. All one can be sure of, from the drawings, is that Mitchell was a bearded man; one can barely even tell he was black. A photograph would have portrayed him as a distinct, separate individual, a "not me." In Brodie's drawings, he could be anybody, even, or especially, Jesus Christ.

"I *am* Jesus Christ," Brodie scribbled on one of his preliminary sketches, with the verb underlined; the sentence is accompanied by the notation, "His last words:" In court, during Howard Brodie's testimony, Bill Turner read aloud the words and then asked, "Why did you write that down?"

"There is no doubt in my mind that that is what he said," Brodie answered. "They were the only four words I heard. And I really was astonished when he said, 'I am Jesus Christ.'"

Other witnesses to the execution, as Turner proceeded to point out, had heard slightly different statements: "Oh, my, Jesus Christ," "Somebody help me," "I am Jesus Christ — look what they have done to me." One of the witnesses — someone connected with the prison authorities — remembered no last words at all. But Howard Brodie was insistent that these were Mitchell's last words. "They had been etched in my mind," he said.

"An execution is not a complex verbal event," said state's attorney Karl Mayer, requesting (unsuccessfully) a dismissal of the case midway through the trial. "The testimony is that there was not — there were only a few words spoken during the Mitchell execution: 'I am Jesus Christ.' A reporter does not need a notepad to remember that statement."

Though the judge did not grant the dismissal, he himself seemed sympathetic to the idea that an execution was not a "complex verbal event," or at any rate not an event requiring multiple perspectives and interpretations. "Now, tell me," he asked Robert Jewett Gore, the plaintiff's witness testifying in his capacity as Governor Deukmejian's press secretary, "other than public relations, is there anything practical served by having more than one reporter as a witness?"

Gore replied by pointing out that "everyone likes to have their own witness. We could fill up the execution chamber with reporters and the media still wouldn't be happy . . . But one single pool reporter would work, yes."

"Except for the artist," Judge Schnacke followed up, "they're all doing the same thing, they're all going in there and sit and look and then come back out and report on what they'd seen."

What Mayer and Schnacke seemed to forget, in their search for practicality and simplicity, is that different witnesses are likely to convey different things. Take, for instance, the reports on the Aaron Mitchell execution published in the *San Francisco Examiner* and the *Oakland Tribune* on April 12, 1967. The *Examiner,* then known as a conservative paper, began its story:

> Aaron C. Mitchell, screaming and groaning to the end, became the first person to be executed in California's green-walled gas chamber in more than four years today.
> The 37-year-old itinerant Negro cotton-picker from Alabama died in a final burst of incoherence after a series of last-minute appeals by opponents of capital punishment failed.

Distanced from the paper's largely white audience by the census-like description of his age, race, and occupation, Mitchell almost seems in this account to have died of his own screams, his "final burst of incoherence" substituting for the firing squad of a traditional execution.

In contrast, the *Oakland Tribune* described Mitchell primarily as a victim:

Aaron Mitchell was forcibly carried into the San Quentin gas chamber today.

He fell limply into the chair, struggled briefly against his guards and snapped his head around to stare in wide-eyed terror at the witnesses.

He choked out hysterically his final, anguished words: "I am Jesus Christ—look what they have done to me." Then the hydrocyanic gas fumes spewed forth from a pan under his chair.

What marks the *Tribune* story, among other things, is its personal, individual perspective. Unlike the *Examiner* story, it is signed: by "Dave Lamb, Tribune Staff Writer." While the *Examiner* does mention those debated last words—it reports only "I am Jesus Christ"—they are not in the leading paragraph; Lamb, on the other hand, uses them to shape his opening. Like Howard Brodie's sketches, Lamb's tale is a modern version of a crucifixion. (Were it not for the corroboration of the other witnesses I might suspect that Brodie, as an artist, would have *had* to hear Mitchell's last words as "I am Jesus Christ," whatever the man actually said. For in the world of artistic renderings, of paintings and frescoes and mosaics and sculptures, one execution has been portrayed with far more frequency than any other.)

The *San Francisco Examiner* was not always guilty of such cold-blooded impersonality. On December 3, 1938, one A. D. Hyman wrote a signed piece for the *Examiner* describing in detail the first gas chamber execution to take place in California. The article is a model of tonal control and authorial sensibility—both qualities singularly lacking in the *Examiner* report on the killing of Mitchell. "California's new death-factory went into capacity production yesterday and turned out two of the neatest corpses San Quentin's executioners have ever seen," Hyman began his piece, continuing:

> It took Albert Kessell and Robert Lee Cannon, young convicts who had committed murder in an attempt to

escape Folsom prison and, by an adroit adaptation of the hydrocyanic process, it killed them before the eyes of 45 unenthusiastic witnesses.

The finished product was two men seated peacefully side by side, with heads bowed as in reverence; two men who might have been at prayer, except that they were newly dead, and their skin was blue and their distended lower lips were not pleasant to see.

The by-products were undisguised feelings of revulsion ... and widespread suspicion that the State's new lethal gas chamber is a chamber of horror.

The superficially cool way in which Hyman carries through with the "death-factory" metaphor verges on the Swiftian, and the other major figure of speech—the reference to bodies "with heads bowed as in reverence," "who might have been at prayer"—aims to stir the same spiritual feelings that Lamb is reaching for in his allusion to Mitchell's "I am Jesus Christ." The argument in favor of capital punishment is often voiced as "an eye for an eye." What these reporters do is quietly suggest that there is another, less vindictive moral code that is meant to govern our behavior toward our fellow sinners.

As his opening suggests, and as Hyman goes on to demonstrate later in the article (he imagines, for instance, what the older, more hardened con might be saying to the younger, frightened kid behind the glass wall of the gas chamber), a human witness can tell you things that a video camera cannot. One might say that the writer is adding an "interpretive element"; one might equally well say that the video camera is leaving out normal human perceptions. The response of other people, those "45 unenthusiastic witnesses," is partly what creates and shapes our feelings about an event, but a video camera, if its "eye" were trained fixedly on the execution itself, would be able to tell us nothing of those responses. At its best, news reporting has always given us the reactions of others to the significant event itself. Commenting on television's images of major public events, such as the *Challenger* explosion or JFK's funeral, Richard Wightman Fox has noted: "We remember both our own original experience of seeing (which often included watching others who, standing in for us, witnessed the event in person) and many of our subsequent reflections on and conversations about what we all saw ... Watching—and watching others watching—is not always a passive exercise. It can be a participatory ritual of profound dimensions." The reactions of other audience members *are* part of the news story. In offering to give up the right to show such reactions—and, in that sense, the right to shape our response to the story, to "editorialize" as all news coverage must and does, if only by selection—KQED was giving up an important part of its role. The phrase "the tools of the press's trade" was crucial to KQED's claim that it had the right to bring a camera into the execution chamber; but a camera person who has signed away the right to record reaction shots is not using a fully functioning tool of the trade. Alone in our livingrooms, watching the transmitted execution in isolation, we would each experience it as a death entirely without social context. In this way a man's murder might well become exactly what A. D. Hyman ironically foresaw, a "finished product" of a new technological "process."

The last words of the condemned man are not the only things that make an execution a complex verbal event. The need to describe it makes it so. No medium is sufficient to convey everything, and even an individual witness may need to use different media to convey different aspects of the event. Howard Brodie, for instance, created several different "renderings" of the Aaron Mitchell execution, of which I've seen three: his sketches, the transcript of his courtroom testimony about the event, and a videotape recording of Brodie describing the event. (This last was part of the KQED film *Appealing Death.*) All three versions clearly come from the same sensibility, and all three contain emotion. ("Contain," in this context, can have a double meaning: possessing emotion, and also keeping it held in.) But the nature and extent of the emotion will vary not only from medium to medium but also according to who is responding. Because Brodie is an artist, many people find his sketches the most compelling version; because I am essentially a reader and writer, I respond most deeply to the transcript of his testimony, whose very sketchiness allows me, as the rough visual sketch allows him, to read reality into bare truth; and I can imagine there are people — inveterate TV newswatchers, for instance — who would find the videotape his most accessible and moving testimony. None of these renderings can have its effect outside of a context, and none excludes the need for the others.

Horrific news photos or obscenely violent pieces of silent news footage can disgust or terrify us when we first see them. But unless we associate them with some kind of narrative — either historical or personal, preferably both — their power to move us may drain away with time; they may cease to upset us in the same way. If they do continue to stir us, it may be either because we know the history that surrounds them, as with photos of Auschwitz survivors or videotape of execution-style killings in Vietnam; or because we associate them with a private personal narrative, perhaps the feelings we remember having the first time we saw them. In my own case, the photograph of the student killed by the National Guard at Kent State in 1970, with the young woman kneeling over him in grief and horror, has both these qualities: I remember the moment I first saw it, at dawn in the newsroom of my college newspaper, when it had just come in over the wires; and I have watched, in the two decades since then, how this photograph and the event it commemorates have come to take their place in our national history. In such circumstances, *we* become the author who lends words and feelings to an event that is otherwise portrayed wordlessly.

With a skilled written rendering of a violent event, this work is done for us: the horror and disgust are continually reignited by the author's words. The voice that mediates between us and a murder—shielding us, tempering it, making it into a story—also makes us unable to forget or ignore the murder. The authorial voice keeps the death alive for us. You can see how this works by comparing the first newspaper accounts of an electrocution in America, written in 1890, with the first (and only) photograph of an American electrocution published in a newspaper.

The photo caused an uproar when it appeared on the front page of the January 13, 1928, edition of the New York *Daily News*. Engaged in a marketing war (and hence a competitive sex-and-violence fest) with the other tabloids in New York, the *Daily News* sent a photographer named Tom Howard to Sing-Sing to record the execution of Ruth Snyder, who had been convicted of strangling her husband. Howard sneaked the camera into the execution chamber by hiding it under baggy trousers; the photograph was thus shot from ankle level. This low-angle perspective (which, through movies ranging from *Psycho* to *Henry: Portrait of a Serial Killer,* has become familiar to us as a threatening viewpoint) is the most ominous thing about the photo. One searches in vain, in the fuzzy, impersonal, virtually faceless rendering of a woman strapped to a wooden chair, for the indications that a murder is *at that moment* taking place. It is our knowledge of what the photo portrays, and not anything in the picture itself, that makes it horrifying.

In contrast, consider the specific verbal material contained in the newspaper accounts of William Kemmler's execution in 1890.° Since Kemmler's was to be the first state-induced electrocution in America, it became the biggest New York news story of its season. The daily journalists were cavalierly jolly and glib as they waited the days and then the weeks that elapsed before the electrocution was finally carried out.

---

°For the summary of these reports, I am indebted to Arthur Lubow's *The Reporter Who Would Be King.*

"Humanity and the interests of the afternoon press demanded that the good news be no longer held back," joked one of the *Evening Sun* reporters about a stay of execution. But in the event they sobered up, and the reports of the death itself are both moving and horrifying. The newspaper reporters have kept alive for us Kemmler's own words, his own characteristic way of putting things. The condemned man becomes a particular individual with a particular relation to his guards—submissive, friendly, even helpful. "Joe, you forgot to strap the other arm," he says as they bind him into the electric chair, and later he insists they readjust the rubber cap holding the sponges that will electrocute him: "Oh, you'd better press that down further. Press that down. . . . Well, I want to do the best I can," Kemmler explains. "I can't do any better than that."

It is this poor creature, Dostoyevskian in his pathos ("If I had known about that Saviour story, I never would have killed her," said the simpleminded and previously illiterate Kemmler after his jailhouse Bible education), whom we then see electrocuted. "Those who were looking at the strapped-down man saw a sudden twitch pass over the body," wrote the *Evening Sun* reporter, emphasizing, as the written testimony generally does, the presence of horrified spectators; "the limbs seemed to shrink up about an inch or so, and there was dreadful contortion of the body. The mouth worked convulsively, saliva spattered out, and it seemed as if the writhing form would tear itself away from the binding straps." This is what "being there" was like—this specific, ongoing, dehumanizing pain—this, and not the fuzzy image snapped out of time in a photo.

The fact that words are often evocative in a way visual images are not can be of use even to a filmmaker. That is, films too—like executions, like murders—are "complex verbal events," and the filmmaker can at times choose to elevate the verbal over the visual. Errol Morris does this at the climactic moment of *The Thin Blue Line*, in his final interview with David

Harris, where he essentially gets Harris to admit to having committed the murder with which Randall Adams was charged. This is the only moment in the movie when someone speaks and does not appear onscreen at all during the entire speech; it is the only speech supplemented by printed subtitles; and it is the only moment at which we also hear the filmmaker's interviewing voice. The visuals for this scene are stark and bare: they consist only of a tape recorder, its cogs turning as we watch the confession emanate from it. The dialogue, too, is stark, direct, but also loaded with unspoken meaning.

"Would you say Randall Adams was a pretty unlucky fellow?" we hear Errol Morris's voice asking, his words repeated in the type that simultaneously appears on the screen.

"Heard of the proverbial scapegoat?" David answers.

"Is he innocent?"

"Did you ask him?"

"Well, he's always said he's innocent."

"There you go." Here David pauses. "Didn't believe him, huh? Criminals always lie."

"Well, what do you think about whether or not he's innocent?"

"I'm sure he is."

"How can you be sure?"

"'Cause I'm the one that knows."

The richness of this scene comes partly from its doubleness, from the sense that David Harris is finally telling us the truth even as he's asserting that "criminals always lie" (this assertion too, in Greek paradox fashion, being a lie). But another kind of richness comes from the scene's unusual singleness, its having eliminated one of the two normal elements in film to focus all its energy on the other. I use words like "choose" and "eliminate" and "focus" as if they represented directorial intention, whereas Errol Morris himself claims the scene *had* to be done this way: the camera he brought to his final interview with Harris failed to work, and he was left with only the backup audiotape. However serendipitous its origins, the scene has meaning and power for us largely by virtue of its insistence on spoken, verbal truth. In *The Thin Blue Line,* that kind of truth seems particularly valuable when set against the eleven different "reenactments" of the crime, all of which are starkly visual and without dialogue (though some take place against background narrations).

Photography, which has often been used to capture moments of violence and death, nonetheless bears a strange relation to murder. Photography focuses on surfaces, murder stems from and speaks to hidden depths; photography celebrates distance and removal, murder condemns the failure to interfere; photography is commemorative, murder seeks oblivion; photography freezes time, making a moment last forever, whereas murder creates irrevocable change.

Paul Theroux's *Chicago Loop* is mainly a novel about murder, but it is also, in two specific places, an essay on photography—one of the best essays ever written on the photographs of Robert Mapplethorpe. The novel, through the perceptions of its main character, Parker, who is himself the murderer, takes two different and opposing views of the Mapplethorpe photos. The first and longer view occurs as Parker and his wife stroll through the Mapplethorpe exhibition in Chicago:

> Parker squinted and kept walking. He did not want to stop and examine these pictures. They were of bald black men hugging bald white men, and they all had smooth buttocks and thick cocks ... There were photographs of flowers, too: big white blossoms with thick perfect petals, and large stark vegetables. Parker thought: The flowers have no odor, the vegetables have no taste ...
>
> Three panels showed a young man urinating in an arc into the mouth of a man kneeling before him ... They passed another showing a man's whipped genitals, just that, wet and wounded, and it reminded Parker of a small animal that had been run over in the road: burst and

bloody and flayed from the beating of heavy traffic, all those wheels.

The description goes on, accurately and mercilessly, for about two pages. Then Parker's wife says reprovingly to him, "It's easy to make jokes about pictures that take so many risks."

"Not as easy as you think, darling," Parker answers her, in what sounds to me exactly like Paul Theroux's own authorial voice. "I mean, sure these images are stark. They're totally reductive, and he's removed all context. So what you have is a kind of icon, and it's not obscene, because it doesn't touch on any other reality."

This is very much Theroux, but it is also very much Parker: part of what makes *Chicago Loop* a powerful murder story is that its murderer, like Mailer's Gilmore, shares so many of his author's qualities. To bring a murderer to life requires projection of one's own feelings into him. That's apparently true of photos of well, or at any rate of Mapplethorpe's photos, for it's only at the end of the novel, when he has come to think of himself as a victim, that Parker can find anything to love in these too-lovely pictures of unloveliness:

> Out of curiosity, and because he had nothing else to do, Parker returned to the exhibition and saw the men in leather and the nudes and the slave collars and the bloody genitals and the swollen flesh, and it seemed to him now that the photographs had a dignity and a directness that he had not seen before. They had pathos, they had humor, they did not seem freakish; some seemed to Parker tragic.

What Parker eventually brings to the photos is what they are not capable of suggesting in themselves: the passage of time. The most moving words in this quotation, I think, are "it seemed to him now"—it is those words, as much as Theroux's direct assertions, which lend dignity, pathos, and humor to the photographs. For these are human qualities, and only something that acknowledges the passage of time can partake of the human. To say these final responses to Mapplethorpe are Parker's projections is not to reduce or invalidate them in any way, for photographs like Mapplethorpe's (perhaps *any* photographs) can come to life only if they are given the context of the viewer's feelings, are made to touch on the viewer's reality (to borrow Theroux's, or Parker's, terms). Theroux's final Mapplethorpe affirmation is connected to his earlier Mapplethorpe critique: in this way, too, the novel makes a loop.

A photographer who wrote his own verbal counterpoint—and who, in his photographs, directly addressed the subject of murder—was the brilliant photojournalist Weegee. In his 1945 book about New York, *Naked City*, there is a whole section entitled "Murders." It turns out, however, that only five of the ten pictures in this section actually show dead bodies, and none of the pictures—to Weegee's apparent regret—catches a murder in progress. ("Some day I'll follow one of these guys with a 'pearl gray hat,' have my camera all set and get the actual killing . . . could be," he muses in the opening notes.) For Weegee, murder in New York is always about spectatorship.

"Balcony Seats at a Murder" is the title of one photo, in which the zigzag of a fire escape runs down the side of a Little Italy tenement, visually leading from the heads that peer out of every available window to the cops standing over a dead body below. This is one of the few Weegee photographs in which you might be able to deduce the circumstances had he not stated them. The others are more opaque. "Murder in Hell's Kitchen," for instance, shows only the spectators at the windows; they could be looking down at anything (*we* are looking *up* at them), though their intent, uniformly focused expressions suggest that it is something serious, if not unusual or shocking. "Gee!" is the only caption to a crowd of people, mainly poorly dressed boys, who are staring, pointing, and peering over each other's shoulders at some unidentified

"Balcony Seats at a Murder"

"Gee!"

point of interest located behind us and slightly to our right. As in "Murder in Hell's Kitchen," we—the picture-taker and hence the picture-viewer—are closer to the murder site than the spectators are, but we are not quite there, and our backs are turned to it. Located on the page facing "Gee!" is "Crime and Punishment," a photograph of a policeman kneeling over a male dead body, its "pearl gray" hat upended on the sidewalk beside it, while two other cops form a visual arch over the kneeling man. The caption tells us: "This happened at eight o'clock on a Sunday night. . . . People were rushing to the movies . . . there was a good double feature at Loew's Delancey Street . . . one being a gangster picture."

Weegee's tone is so cynical and hardboiled, and so counter to the elements in the picture that might be called spiritual (the kneeling, the arch), as to seem self-parodic. "This is what you expect a hardened newspaperman to feel about murder, isn't it?" he suggests, and then implies: "This is what *you* feel about murder, or you wouldn't be relishing these pictures in that ghoulish fashion." We are, clearly enough, the reflected images of the spectators he's so interested in. We are the consumers, the purchasers, on whose behalf *Time* magazine issued him a check with the notation "Two Murders: $35.00." (This check stub is the opening picture in the "Murders" section.) Our own lurid desires, and not just the sordid events, are what make New York a "naked city," exposing its private secrets to Weegee's lens.

The eeriest and most horrifying photo in the "Murders" section, to my mind, is one of those in which no dead person appears. It has no title, just a caption: "A woman relative cried . . . but neighborhood dead-end kids enjoyed the show when a small-time racketeer was shot and killed . . ." Even without Weegee's words, we would sense something feverish and cannibalistic about the spectators in the photo. Pressed up against us in a jumbled crowd, and set against a hulking black building and a strangely lit up night sky, they resemble

"A woman relative cried . . . but neighborhood kids enjoyed the show when a small-time racketeer was shot and killed . . ."

nothing so much as a collection of humanoid zombies from *Invasion of the Body Snatchers*. Several mouths are open, with prominently visible teeth; one face, at least, seems to sport a savage grin. The heavy-set crying woman, whose expression looks more like physical pain than sorrow, has her eyes closed, but everyone else is open-eyed, though their glances go in different directions—one with eyes cast down, another looking directly to the side, and several peering over our right shoulder, at what we take to be the murder scene. A girl located on the right side of the photo has her eyes so wide open that she appears to be visually devouring the corpse: her animation and evident pleasure correspond to the manic grin of the boy in the upper left. But between them, toward the lower-left side of the frame, comes a face that has an entirely different expression—an intelligent face with slightly knitted brows, narrowed eyes, and a thoughtful tilt of the head. This girl *could* be looking at the crime scene, but she could also be looking at us. She is nearer to us than anyone else in the picture—in terms of physical location, and also in terms of projected sensibility, for we *want* to feel we are like her, intelligently and seriously considering murder. What Weegee reminds us, by giving us this woman as one of our mirrors, is that even our most thoughtful spectatorship implicates us in the crowd's bloodthirsty curiosity.

Turgenev tells us the same thing in a different way in his extraordinary account of witnessing an execution. "The Execution of Tropmann," written in 1870, details the death by guillotine of a notorious murderer, a man whose cruel and bloody destruction of an entire family made him a celebrated villain in the French daily press. Turgenev, dining with a friend in Paris, receives "quite an unexpected invitation" to attend the beheading. The vacillation that characterizes his acceptance is only the first and least of many doubts, self-accusations, and painful realizations that will color the entire essay. "As a punishment of myself," he says, "—and as a lesson to others—I should now like to tell everything I saw." Through Turgenev's steady gaze—steady not as a camera would be, unmovingly, but with a steadiness infused with all the flinching of a decent moral disgust—we see how the witness to an execution takes on the emotions not only of the victim but also of the executioner.

As he and his companions are walking toward the site of the execution ("jauntily—as though on a shooting expedition"), Turgenev is actually mistaken for the executioner by the assembled crowd. "A lovely beginning!" he thinks darkly to himself. He is aware that both he and the enthusiastic masses (who are permitted a less intimate view of the execution than the few august guests) are all intended, by their presence, to certify the death in some way, to represent the "public" against whom Tropmann has committed his crimes, and by whom he has been convicted. But in the face of the actual execution, Turgenev can feel no such meaning to his presence. Nor can he justify it even in his capacity as an author, a student of human emotions. "As for me, there was one thing I was sure of, namely that I had no right to be where I was, that no psychological or philosophic considerations excused me," he says of the seemingly endless "irksome and wearisome" hours spent waiting through the night for the dawn execution. And after the killing takes place, "not one of us, *absolutely no one looked like a man who realized that he had been present at the performance of an act of social justice:* everyone tried to turn away in spirit and, as it were, shake off the responsibility for this murder" (his italics). If the ostensible purpose of Turgenev's essay is to satisfy our curiosity and also lend us some moral "benefit," its deeper purposes are connected with the infliction of pain: the pain of empathy and the pain of guilty responsibility, inflicted both on us and on himself.

Like Weegee, Turgenev understands the guilty side of spectatorship, the way in which turning the death into a "show" calls into play the sleaze factor. He sees and does not deny his own connection with the mass of spectators, that "overjoyed crowd which had at last caught sight of what it had been waiting for." (The vagueness of the unspecified object in this clause is typical of Turgenev's way of presenting the execution: he amplifies the horror by making it unmentionable. "Then something suddenly descended with a hollow growl and stopped with an abrupt thud," he says of the actual dropping of the guillotine blade.) What he shares with the crowd is his role as a theatrical spectator; what distinguishes him is his shame at that role. At one point in the essay he makes this condition explicit. "On my way back to the prison governor's apartment," he writes, describing part of the waiting period, "I passed the guillotine and saw on its platform the executioner surrounded by a small crowd of inquisitive people. He was carrying out a 'rehearsal' for them." Turgenev goes on to exculpate *and* implicate himself:

> I did not stop to watch this "rehearsal," that is to say, I did not climb on to the platform: the feeling of some unknown transgression committed by myself, of some secret shame, was growing stronger and stronger inside me. . . . It is perhaps to this feeling that I must ascribe the fact that the horses, harnessed to the vans and calmly chewing the oats in their nosebags, seemed to me at that moment to be the only innocent creatures among us.

Animals may be innocent here (though they are given that innocence only through the perceptions of a shamed human: "seemed to *me*"), but later even the nonhuman world comes to seem voracious, guilty, responsible for the murder. "Suddenly the two halves of the gate, like some immense mouth of an animal, opened up slowly before us," Turgenev says of Tropmann's final entrance; and the sound of the guillotine blade falling is "Just as though a huge animal had retched."

Even Turgenev's attitude toward Tropmann himself is molded by his perception of the execution as a performance.

Watching the preparations, as the condemned man is stripped naked and then dressed, Turgenev notes that

> at the sight of that composure, that simplicity and, as it were, modesty—all the feelings in me—the feelings of disgust for a pitiless murderer, a monster who cut the throats of little children while they were crying, *Maman! Maman!*, the feeling of compassion, finally, for a man whom death was about to swallow up, disappeared and dissolved in—a feeling of astonishment. What was sustaining Tropmann? Was it the fact that though he did not show off, he did "cut a figure" before *spectators*, gave us his last performance?

As the actual moment of death approaches, all else gives way to the ritual, the spectacle. Tropmann becomes neither the hated murderer nor the pitied victim, but simply the primary actor in the performance, the centerpiece of the theatrical event. This, in turn, makes him a creature of mystery for Turgenev, who, unsuccessfully trying to imagine what was going on inside Tropmann's mind, can only concede it "was a secret he took to the grave with him."

Some of Turgenev's sentiments are echoed in a modern account of an execution written by a New Orleans reporter named Jonathan Eig, who witnessed a 1990 death by electrocution at the Louisiana State Penitentiary. (Eig's eyewitness account is reproduced in *The Angolite*, an extremely informative magazine put out by inmates of the Angola, Louisiana, prison.) Eig, too, is impressed by what he *doesn't* learn from watching an execution. "After leaving the prison, and upon reflection," he remarks, "it was curious to me that I, a reporter, witnessed an execution yet had so little knowledge of what actually happened." Like Turgenev, if less subtly and self-implicatingly, Eig attributes this partly to the theatrical, ritualized nature of the event. "I think an explanation for my lack of inquisitiveness lies in the fact that the whole process of witnessing an execution is so organized and orderly," he says. "It is like a solemn procession that just goes forward and once I was wrapped up in the procession, I had little chance to make careful inquiry into what was going on."

But if Turgenev locates in the event's theatrical nature the source of his strong feelings (of shame, of astonishment), Eig reacts in the opposite way. "The orderliness also serves to make the execution unreal. It creates a distance," he says. "It makes it difficult to understand that a life is being ended. If there is anything gruesome about electrocution, I was shielded from it. I witnessed a sanitized version of death, through a window, as a spectator — as if it were a performance put on for the benefit of the audience."

As in many ways it is. The problem is that *this* performance, *this* exemplary moral tale of justice wrought, is also a real event, and the villain who dies before the audience's expectant gaze (expectant even if anguished, as in Turgenev's case) is not just acting. Theatrical spectatorship implies a certain paralysis, a certain recognition of one's inability to alter predetermined events. This can be frustrating even to audiences of actual plays, as the old tales of backwoodsmen rushing onstage to save Desdemona from Othello suggest. In the real theater, that level of frustration is a morally acceptable and even functional one: it helps the characters come to life for us. Eig's account suggests that the theater of murder, the witnessed execution, may have the opposite effect. By impressing on its audience members their helplessness in the face of events, it forces them, out of moral self-protectiveness, to view the death as unreal — either that or suffer irrevocable shame, as Turgenev does. Whether the theatrical mode suggests paralysis as the appropriate response, or paralysis causes spectators to think of the event as mere theater, is not clear; but there does seem to be a connection between the two.

Even Lord Byron (or perhaps I should say, given his grandstanding way of life, *especially* Lord Byron) remarked on this connection between paralysis and spectatorship in his account of an execution in Rome. His whole description, contained in a letter to a friend, emphasizes the ceremonial, theatrical qualities of the event. The final sentence of his report then comments on the effect of seeing three men guillotined in quick succession: "The first turned me quite hot and thirsty, and made me shake so that I could hardly hold the opera-glass (I was close, but was determined to see, as one should see every thing, once, with attention); the second and third (which shows how dreadfully soon things grow indifferent), I am ashamed to say, had no effect on me as a horror, though I would have saved them if I could."* Byron's shame is of a very different sort from Turgenev's — it doesn't, for one thing, seem to bother him much — and there is something icily cavalier about the way he admits that the men's lives are worth more than his instructive experience. But it is in the chilling admission of that loss of feeling, in that teetering disequilibrium between horror and acceptance, that Byron makes his most profoundly moral point. Would one say that sort of thing about Desdemona? About King Lear? I don't think so. To acknowledge in this cool manner that one would have saved them if one could, *regardless* of the emotions aroused in one, is to recognize the difference between murder and theater.

*I owe the discovery of this passage to Leonard Michaels, who used the last eight words as the title for one of his books.

# 8

## Enter a Murderer

It is a difference, however, that murder and theater do their best to overcome. Aristotle, our first and most rigorous theater critic, defined tragedy as "a representation of an action that is worth serious attention, complete in itself, and of some amplitude." Of the elements that made up tragedy, he insisted, "the most important is the plot, the ordering of the incidents; for tragedy is a representation, not of men, but of action and life, of happiness and unhappiness . . . it is their characters, indeed, that make men what they are, but it is by reason of their actions that they are happy or the reverse . . . Thus the incidents and the plot are the end aimed at in tragedy, and as always, the end is everything."

Murder stories are by definition plot-based; in them, literally, "the end is everything." The examples of tragic plots that suggested themselves to Aristotle's mind all involved murder, usually by close family members: "the murder of Clytemnestra by Orestes, for instance, and that of Eriphyle by Alcmaeon . . . The deed may be done by characters acting consciously and in full knowledge of the facts, as . . . when for instance Euripides made Medea kill her children. Or they may do it without realizing the horror of the deed until later, when they discover the truth; this is what Sophocles did with Oedipus." Aristotle particularly deplored the plot in which a murder is promised but not delivered, in which the potential

188

murderer "is on the point of acting but fails to do so, for this merely shocks us, and, since no suffering is involved, it is not tragic." In describing tragic theater, Aristotle acknowledged the importance of spectacle — "spectacle is an essential part of tragedy" — but also pointed out that spectacle is tragic only when it is used to produce pity and fear, the two central emotions of tragedy. "Those who employ spectacle to produce an effect, not of fear, but of something merely monstrous, have nothing to do with tragedy," he remarked, in a comment that might well have been employed by either side in *KQED v. Vasquez.*

An execution offers our only predictable opportunity to witness the real-life version of the spectacle of murder. In this respect, the execution is an inherently theatrical event. This does not, however, differentiate it from the rest of life. "A very small part of acting is that which takes place on the stage!" T. S. Eliot announced, with uncharacteristic exuberance, in his essay "'Rhetoric' and Poetic Drama." This idea and its extensions are the basis of Erving Goffman's book *The Presentation of Self in Everyday Life,* first published in 1959. An imaginative and observant anthropologist of contemporary British and American behavior, Goffman remarked in his preface that "the perspective employed in this report is that of the theatrical performance; the principles derived are dramaturgical ones." Like Freud's use of the same phrase in his *Psychopathology of Everyday Life,* Goffman's title and his whole premise are meant to shake us up; the idea is interesting mainly because we tend to think that theatricality, like psychopathology, is something that does *not* intrude on everyday life. We associate theatricality with artificiality, and insist that someone is behaving "theatrically" if we feel he is exaggerating or amplifying or otherwise tinkering with his behavior to create an inflated effect. Following Aristotle, we think of theater as something shaped, purified, made meaningful by an author. "The essential," said T. S. Eliot in another essay, "The

Possibility of a Poetic Drama," "is to get upon the stage this precise statement of life which is at the same time a point of view, a world—a world which the author's mind has subjected to a complete process of simplification." By "simplification" Eliot meant something quite complicated: not simplemindedness, not even perfect clarity, but the absolute intensity, the singleness of vision, that we find in the old Greek tragedies.

One of the reasons we try to view a real murder as theater—a grand tragedy, a significant event, at the very least an authorially constructed plot—is to remove some of the terrifying randomness from it. A mundane murder is not only inexplicable; it is inexplicable in a very unsatisfying way. By lifting the murderer himself out of the realm of the ordinary, we give the plot some grandeur, enable it to inspire us with some degree of terror and pity. If the questions surrounding the murder remain unanswerable, they are at any rate unanswerable in a large way, like the question "Does God exist?" or "Is the true nature of man good or evil?" Unlike "How did he dispose of the murder weapon?" and "Can we believe her alibi?" these larger questions can be satisfying even if unanswered; in a way, their unanswerability *is* their answer. So, faced with a situation that has no straightforward answers to the mundane questions, our tendency is to raise the discussion onto this higher, tragic plane.

Elizabeth Hardwick, in *The Simple Truth*, has one of her characters mock another for exactly this kind of theatricalizing attitude. "You seem to think of this boy as having committed a sort of ritual murder," Anita's friend March says to her, "like the horde killing off the father in primitive times. For such an act there is no punishment that can be found in law books. The act exists on another level, a mythical, magical level. It has to be; it's the very nature of man to act in such a way and he cannot come to his own maturity in any other fashion."

Anita denies this characterization heatedly ("I don't think anything of the sort!") and so would any of us in her place. But this doesn't mean that we don't adopt some form of the "mythical, magical" thinking March describes. It's easy to mock in its simpleminded, reductive form—that's the nature of simpleminded reduction—but anyone who ever views a real murderer as the lead actor in a tragedy is guilty of this kind of thinking. Intelligent people do it all the time; indeed, their intelligence, in the form of their literary sensibility, is partly what makes them do it.

When Janet Malcolm first meets Jeffrey MacDonald, the convicted murderer of *Fatal Vision* fame, she notices the grace with which he deals with being handcuffed and then uncuffed. "Meeting a visitor under these circumstances would not seem to offer much scope for a soigné entrance," she comments in *The Journalist and the Murderer,* "but MacDonald somehow managed to get through the humiliating ritual as if he were an actor swiftly shedding his costume before greeting friends in the green room, rather than a prisoner coming out of solitary confinement for a few hours." Mailer's Gary Gilmore is also a consummate actor, as reported by several of the other characters in *The Executioner's Song.* "It was as if each of his personalities took a turn," thinks one of Gilmore's lawyers, listening to a tape Gary made for Nicole, "and Ron thought it was like an actor putting on one mask, taking it off, putting on another for a new voice." Larry Schiller has a different take on Gilmore's theatrical abilities, as displayed during a legal hearing: "Schiller was now twice impressed with Gilmore as an actor. He did not rise to this occasion like a great ham actor, but chose to be oblivious to it. Merely there to express his idea. Gilmore spoke in the absolute confidence of the idea, spoke in the same quiet tone he might have employed if talking to only one man. So it became the kind of acting that makes you forget you are in a theatre."

The marvelous irony of that last sentence turns on the idea of having to "forget you are in a theatre" when in fact you are not in a theater. But in a murder trial the courtroom *becomes* a theater. This is particularly true of well-publicized murder trials like Gary Gilmore's or Ted Bundy's. "What did he see in the intermission—you had to call it an 'intermission' rather than a recess, they were creating such TV theatre—but this fellow Schiller sitting in one of the chairs that belonged to the Attorney General's staff," Mailer has Earl Dorius thinking. Ann Rule, in *The Stranger Beside Me*, brings this figure of speech to the surface: "The trials and hearings of Ted Bundy had become akin to a Broadway play, its long run ended, replaced by a road company. Only the star remained in the lead role, surrounded by a new cast." Later in the book, analyzing the TV mini-series *The Deliberate Stranger*—filmed with Mark Harmon in the Bundy role, and broadcast while Ted was still alive on Death Row—Rule intelligently points to the way the trial actually converted Ted into a lead actor, a star. "Ted Bundy had begun his 20s as the man I knew, the socially inept man, the man who felt he didn't fit into a world of wealth and success," she says. "It was the latter-day infamous Ted who was smooth and charismatic. Infamy became Ted. Only as his crimes made black headlines did he become the Ted Bundy portrayed by Mark Harmon."

It doesn't take a writer of Elizabeth Hardwick's wry intelligence, Norman Mailer's unruly brilliance, or Ann Rule's impressive competence to perceive and use the theatrical metaphor in regard to a murder. Daily news reporters do it all the time—or they used to, before journalism decided its role was one of impersonal objectivity. That's the vocabulary Weegee was borrowing in his caption references to "balcony seats" and "enjoying the show," the hardboiled tabloid language that was common among his fellow journalists.

If such phrases seemed appropriate to a street murder, how much more so to an execution: a plotted, nearly scripted

murder to which seats actually *could* be obtained in advance.
Reporting on the double execution of Richard Eldon Hawk
and John Lininger in 1941, the *San Francisco News* began its
front-page story by announcing:

> San Quentin's lethal chamber—where Death frequent-
> ly is starred in single features on Fridays—presented its
> first double bill today. A rat poison killer and a holdup
> murderer, with nerves strengthened by a sort of Damon
> and Pythias friendship and hope of "a better world
> beyond," shared honors with the star for a few awesome
> moments in the steel-and-glass cage. Then they pitched
> forward as far as the bonds that held them to twin chairs
> permitted, gasped—and the drama was over.

The mixture of metaphors here, and the way the nameless journalist manages to keep that unruly mixture just barely
under his control, are nearly guffaw-inspiring. Death is "the
star," and the executed murderers are his back-up players—
but they are also Damon and Pythias (a pairing picked up in
the "twin" chairs and, less directly, in the words "the bonds
that held them"), and they are a "double bill" as well. The
author seems unable, or unwilling, to choose between the language of movies and the language of the theater, and there is
even a hint of the circus in that reference to the steel-and-glass
"cage." "Drama in Prison Gas Chamber," trumpets the inside
headline, and what *kind* of drama doesn't seem to matter, so
long as it's something with "spectators" (as the witnesses are
called in this news story).

Yet spectatorship is far from identical in the theater and
the movies, though the dramatic metaphors applied to murder
tend to gloss over the differences. Mailer blurs the two categories in the phrase "TV theatre"; Ann Rule alludes to a
Broadway show and then to a TV mini-series as if the two are
interchangeable; and the *San Francisco News* reporter can't
decide whether he's watching a Friday afternoon double bill
or a Greek tragedy. Perhaps it seems petty of me to complain

that people aren't differentiating between theater and film when what I should apparently be complaining about is their far more significant refusal to distinguish theatrical event from real life. But I think the two refusals are connected. How theater differs from film, and how each in turn differs from reality in its less artful, less mediated forms, are distinctions which can, if looked into, tell us something about our desire to witness murder.

The central fact about theater is that it places us in the presence of fictional characters. In that element of fiction, it differs from reality; and in that element of presence, it differs from film. A dramatic piece may exist on the page as a series of words, a printed text, but as a theatrical event it exists only at the moment (in some cases, quite an extended moment) during which we witness it. It is a different event each time it is performed. Unlike film, it disappears into thin air, never to be repeated in exactly the same way. This ephemerality accounts for the thrill, the beauty of theater, and it is also what connects theater with mortality. Murder is an ideal topic for theater because the form is itself about being in the imminent presence of death. The Elizabethan name for actors — "shadows" — reflects this fact, linking them with the shades of the underworld as well as with the flickering figures who are, according to Plato, all we can know of life. The characters portrayed by theater actors are by definition illusory or fictional, but the actors themselves are bodily present to us, verifiably real, and the two creatures, actor and character, are impossible to separate for the duration of the play's performance.

Theater on a stage, with an audience, is necessarily artificial. It has been shaped by an artist's mind — a writer's, a director's — and actors have had to learn lines or present characters that are not identical with themselves. Film, on the other hand, needn't be artificial in this sense; it can be straightforwardly real, as with documentary or news footage.

Yet film can also be *less* real than theater. Film has a greater
affinity with dream than theater does: it can slide easily from
external to internal states, portray distorted viewpoints as if
they were embodied realities, fail to distinguish between the
real and the imagined. Anything shown on a theatrical stage is
generally assumed to be there — *is* there, if we can see it. Anything in a film could be imaginary, an individual character's
projection or hallucination.

Let me explain what I mean using an example from *Macbeth*. On the stage, a director has to decide whether Banquo's
ghost is "real" or not — whether he should be played by a real
actor (in which case we in the audience see the ghost, as Macbeth does, confirming his hallucination), or produced by some
kind of optical trick (in which case we share the viewpoint of
Lady Macbeth and the other dinner guests: the ghost is not
really there). Henry Irving, the great nineteenth-century
actor/director, made different choices at different times in his
career: in 1877 he created a transparent silhouette of a man,
in 1888 he used a real actor, and in 1895 he represented
Banquo's ghost simply with a shaft of light. Roman Polanski,
filming *Macbeth* in 1971, did not have to make such choices.
He could put the actor playing Banquo in the chair (complete
with disfiguring wounds and unraveling flesh) and *still* have
him be a potential hallucination — just as the floating dagger
was in the earlier scene. The film director does not have to
choose between illusion and embodiment: he can have both at
once, in a much more fluid manner than theater can. In a way,
this means that the film director loses the essential paradox of
the scene, and thereby loses its motivating tension, its central
theatrical point. A theater director can insist that a ghost is
purely imaginary even if played by a live actor; but that actor
has presence, has weight, is made of the same stuff as the
other people on the stage who are being presented to us as real
and alive. Film doesn't ask us to believe in ghosts or shadows.
Its actors are all, literally, "projections." Theater asks us

simultaneously to believe and disbelieve in what we are seeing. Ghosts are only the most extreme example; *everyone* on stage is both really there and not there at all.

Stanley Cavell makes this point toward the end of his essay on *King Lear*. "What is the state of mind in which we find events in a theater neither credible nor incredible?" he begins, and goes on to refer to "the usual joke" about "the Southern yokel who rushes to the stage to save Desdemona from the black man." Cavell then asks:

> What is the joke? That he doesn't know how to behave in a theater? ... But what mistake has the yokel in the theater made, and what is *our* way? He thinks someone is strangling someone. — But that is true; Othello is strangling Desdemona. ... You can say there are two women, Mrs. Siddons and Desdemona, both of whom are mortal, but only one of whom is dying in front of our eyes. But what you have produced is two names. Not all the pointing in the world to *that* woman will distinguish the one woman from the other.

Cavell concludes this hypothetical disagreement by remarking that "the intentions with which we go to the theater are equally incomprehensible. You go," he argues with his made-up opponent, "according to what has so far come out, in order to find that Mrs. Siddons is not dead; I go to watch Desdemona die. I don't particularly enjoy the comparison, for while I do not share your tastes they seem harmless enough, where mine are very suspect."

If we get at what makes Cavell's tastes "suspect," we may be able to tell ourselves something about the connection between murder and theater. It's not just that Cavell (or any theatergoer) coldheartedly enjoys watching someone die: "enjoyment" is not the right word for our reception of Shakespeare's tragedies. Is it that we want to be moved to tears without risking our own life, our own heart? Is it that we masochistically like to put ourselves in situations where we are powerless to prevent oncoming disasters? Do we need to be reminded, through the vicarious thrill of fear, that we are still alive while others have died? None of these feelings is unique to the theater. All would be aroused, in some form or other, if we were to witness an execution.

But unlike those at executions, the deaths in a theater are not real. Is this what makes our emotional response to them suspect? Brecht thought so. He objected to naturalistic theater on the grounds that it enabled people to vent their emotions in a socially useless way; he objected, that is, to Aristotle's "catharsis." Brecht wanted a theater of the rational mind, not one of the bleeding heart. He wanted to do away with thoughtless empathy, with our cleverly manipulated ability to feel through a fictional character. In *The Messingkauf Dialogues* he suggests as much, and then has one character ask: "Does getting rid of empathy mean getting rid of every emotional element?"

"No, no," answers Brecht's Philosopher. "Neither the public nor the actor must be stopped from taking part emotionally . . . Only one out of many possible sources of emotion needs to be left unused, or at least treated as a subsidiary source — empathy." I take this to be an echo of what T. S. Eliot meant when he said in "'Rhetoric' and Poetic Drama":

> A speech in a play should never appear to be intended to move us as it might conceivably move other characters in the play, for it is essential that we should preserve our position of spectators, and observe always from the outside though with complete understanding . . . when a character *in* a play makes a direct appeal to us, we are either the victims of our own sentiment, or we are in the presence of a vicious rhetoric.

Near the beginning of *The Messingkauf Dialogues*, Brecht's Philosopher presents himself in a theater, insisting that he is there to learn about life. "What interests me about your theatre," he says, "is the fact that you apply your art and your

whole apparatus to imitating incidents that take place between people, with the result that one feels in the presence of
real life. As I'm interested in the way people live together I'm
interested in your imitation of it too."

"I get it," responds the Dramaturg. "You want to find out
about the world. We show you what takes place there."

"You haven't got it entirely, I think," says the Philosopher. "Your remark lacks a certain uneasiness."

The source of Brecht's "uneasiness" is near to that of
Cavell's "suspect" feeling: both originate in the exploration of
motive in regard to theater attendance. Once theater ceases to
be religious ritual, with people gathered into each other's
presence for an explicit reason, the question of motive produces unease. As long as theater *is* ritual, the answer is
obvious: we are all there for the same reason, to be in the presence of God, or God's manifestations (including, in some rituals, human sacrifice). But a theater separated from religion is
a theater of individual motive, and each person's reasons for
seeking that kind of stimulation are hidden from the others.
Kafka's petitioner in the "Before the Law" parable is in this
sense a modern man at the theater: the door through which he
might pass to be in the presence of something transcendent is
a door for him alone. We are no longer in this together, as we
were in a house of worship. In a secular theater, our access to
transcendence — to illusory reality, to belief that is not credible — is largely personal. The men and women in the seats
around us are there for their own individual, hidden reasons.
We cannot be sure of what they are thinking or feeling. They
are all "suspect."

This description in many ways belies the actual feeling of
being in a theater. Part of what theater gives us — at its best,
and at its audience's best — is a sense of community, a feeling
of shared if unspoken response. This feeling of shared existence does not just apply to the members of the audience; it
links the audience to the people on stage as well. For the dura-

tion of the play, we share the same universe as fictional characters. Our spectatorship brings them to life, and they in turn
create a world for us. Even with tragedies, this process is fes-
tive; even death-dealing theater has a life-giving side. This is
different from the spectatorship of film. If a film were shown
in Bishop Berkeley's empty forest, it would exist just as much,
or just as little, as a falling tree. But if a play is performed
without an audience, there is a very definite sense in which it
doesn't, as a play, take place; in that case, it is just a rehearsal.
We in the theater are under contract to the actors as much as
they are to us. We all share a set of unspoken agreements, a set
of conventions. This, in part, is why Cavell's yokel is making a
profound mistake: he is killing Desdemona himself, driving
her away from the arena of the stage by violating the conventions that allow her, for the duration of the play, to live.

So theater is centrally and inherently about both suspicion and belief: the suspicion that the people around us are not
what they may seem (not, that is, "like us") and the belief that
the people on stage are. A play like *Macbeth* takes this as its
subject, in addition to or as part of its subject of premeditated
murder. One of the things we may be suspicious *of* is that
other people might want to kill us; one of the things we normally take on faith is that they will not. The question of
murder, and of our vulnerability to one another's murderous
desires, is intimately tied to our assessments of what people
really are, and whether they are telling us the truth, and
whether we can believe them or believe *in* them. When those
people are actors, the answers must always be double-edged.

"I' th' name of truth," Banquo asks the Weird Sisters,
"Are ye fantastical, or that indeed / Which outwardly ye
show?" Ghosts are a special case, of course; even more than
with actors, their presence is debatable. Yet in this play
everyone and everything begin to have that debatable quality:
"nothing is / But what is not," as Macbeth mutters to himself a
short time later. It's not just that existence comes to seem mere

empty theater—that, as Macbeth beautifully and sorrowfully puts it, "Life's but a walking shadow, a poor player / That struts and frets his hour upon the stage / And then is heard no more." You might be tempted to write that off as the conclusion of a grief-stricken, beaten man (Macbeth, surrounded by a foreign army, has just been told his wife is dead by her own hand); but in this play even the winners, the heroes, are always acting, always on stage. When Macduff goes to sound out Malcolm about taking over as king, Malcolm first gives him a long song and dance about what a vicious, lascivious, avaricious son-of-a-bitch he is. Only when Macduff reels back in horror does Malcolm admit he was just testing him:

> I am yet
> Unknown to woman, never was forsworn,
> Scarcely have coveted what was mine own,
> At no time broke my faith, would not betray
> The devil to his fellow, and delight
> No less in truth than life. My first false speaking
> Was this upon myself.

The emphasis on truth-telling in the list of Malcolm's virtues—there are no fewer than three different ways of saying he doesn't lie, in this list of six—only makes us notice the more what the final remark admits: that he has just been lying quite skillfully about himself. "Criminals always lie," jokes David Harris with Errol Morris as he's finally telling him the truth, and something of that vertiginous circularity colors Malcolm's statement here.

Even at the moments of greatest emotional pitch, Shakespeare is willing to have the characters remind us they're in a play. One of the most heartrending moments in *Macbeth* is when Macduff learns his family has been murdered:

MACDUFF: My children too?
ROSS: Wife, children, servants, all
    That could be found.

MACDUFF: And I must be from thence!
  My wife killed too?
ROSS: I have said.

Macduff's next words are still uncomprehending:

He has no children. All my pretty ones?
Did you say all? O hell-kite! All?

The pathos in this scene is particularly intense because it clings so closely to the format of humor. The man who, unable to take in a single piece of information, needs to be told it over and over again—this is a comic routine, borrowed and modified here for the purposes of intensifying the cruelty. Antonin Artaud, who coined the term "Theater of Cruelty," understood extremely well this permeable borderline between tragedy and comedy. "In order to understand the powerful, total, definitive, absolute originality . . . of films like *Animal Crackers* and, at times . . . , *Monkey Business*," he said about two early Marx Brothers movies, "you would have to add to humor the notion of something disquieting and tragic, a fatality (neither happy nor unhappy, difficult to formulate) which would hover over it like the cast of an appalling malady upon an exquisitely beautiful profile." What Shakespeare has done in Macduff's grief scene is to reverse that motion, converting the Elizabethan equivalent of Marx Brothers shtick into deeply felt tragedy.

Then, on top of that, he has Macduff stress his own theatrical unreality. Recovering from his brief emotional collapse, and responding to Malcolm's urging that he "Let grief / Convert to anger," Macduff announces:

O, I could play the woman with mine eyes,
And braggart with my tongue! But, gentle heavens,
Cut short all intermission; front to front
Bring thou this fiend of Scotland and myself;
Within my sword's length set him.

I would not be so sure of "intermission" if I did not have "play" to back it up, but here it seems to me obvious that, on at least some level, the intermission Macduff is referring to is the kind that interrupts the action of a play. (The *OED* gives the date 1563 as the first use of the term in this sense, and it is still the most common meaning in America, though in England "interval" is now used instead.)

Nothing reminds you that you are watching a play as strongly as an intermission—that artificial break in the action, arranged for the convenience of the spectators, which marks the drama as theatrical, intentional, shaped, and unreal. Nothing could be so designed to puncture the verisimilitude of a theatrical moment as a reference to the intermission. (As Earl Dorius said, "you had to call it an 'intermission' rather than a recess, they were creating such TV theatre.") Yet when Macduff talks about playacting and intermissions at this moment of high drama, it doesn't make us feel any less strongly about him. We don't say, "Oh, well, of course, he's just a theatrical character. No need to feel bad about *his* wife and kids." We acknowledge the theatrical element—in him, and in the play as a whole—and go on feeling as strongly as before. More strongly, in a way, because we are additionally moved by his ability to rise up out of his fictional universe and point to his own role in our theatergoing world.

"The really fine rhetoric of Shakespeare occurs in situations where a character in the play *sees himself* in a dramatic light," T. S. Eliot pointed out, and went on to remark that "in actual life, in many of those situations in actual life which we enjoy consciously and keenly, we are at times aware of ourselves in this way." So a person who sees himself as performing in a play needn't, by virtue of that alone, strike us as unrealistic. Part of the nature of living in social reality is that we often feel we are performing a role. In *The Presentation of Self in Everyday Life,* Goffman demonstrated in detail how our ordinary behavior resembles the theater, with people as actors or masks, different performances as "truth" or "reality" for different audiences, backstage access versus frontal presentation, and all the other implicit conventions that govern the relationships between audiences and performers. That each of us at various moments can play either audience or performer (or both) is part of Goffman's insight.

Goffman's ideas are particularly applicable to events that are both undeniably real and blatantly theatrical, such as the proceedings of the criminal justice system. Remarking on the "type of scene" that occurs when confrontation is allowed to break out, Goffman observes: "Criminal trials have institutionalized this kind of open discord, as has the last chapter of murder mysteries, where an individual who has theretofore maintained a convincing pose of innocence is confronted in the presence of others with undeniable expressive evidence that his pose is only a pose." The leap from courtroom to murder mystery is instructive: it suggests that the two exist on a continuum of ritual, which incidentally happens to extend from the sphere of the actual into the realm of the fictional. Goffman comes even closer to the nub of *KQED v. Vasquez* when he says, "Whether it is a funeral, a wedding, a bridge party, a one-day sale, a hanging, or a picnic, the director may tend to see the performance in terms of whether or not it went 'smoothly,' 'effectively,' and 'without a hitch,' and whether or not all possible disruptive contingencies were prepared for in advance." Warden Vasquez explicitly addressed this issue when, as the "director" of Robert Alton Harris's execution, he insisted he wanted it to be "carried out with tactfulness and precision." Implicitly, he was also objecting to the alternative "performance" that might be framed from the same material by another director: that is, the television cameraman.

Vasquez's choice of the word "tactfulness" is eerily appropriate here, for "tact" is exactly the word Goffman uses to describe the curious relation between audiences and performers in real-life settings. Tact is what the audience uses to

protect the performers from its own spectatorship. "Audiences are motivated to act tactfully because of an immediate
identification with the performers," Goffman mentions, "or
because of a desire to avoid a scene, or to ingratiate themselves with the performers for purposes of exploitation." An
audience's tact, especially when exercised to protect inexperi-
enced or unskilled performers, may extend so far that "these
tactful actions on the part of the audience can become more
elaborate than is the performance for which they are a
response." Tact is the audience's way of acknowledging its
own presence in front of the performers ("front to front," as
Macduff says); it is a way of making that presence into a role
*in* the performance. Tact of this kind inevitably disappears
when an in-person performance is converted into something
on film or, in the case of *KQED v. Vasquez,* something on television. An event that previously required one's collaboration — or at the very least, if we are to believe Turgenev, one's
participatory shame — now has no role for its audience at all.
In a televised execution, the audience is not only mute and
paralyzed, but invisible.

Part of what actual, bodily present witnesses to an execution provide for the dying man is the impression that he is surrounded by human eyes. It is an impression that ricochets
back on the witnesses themselves, whose stares are returned
by the victim. "I was astonished to see him slowly rise and
coincidentally happen to stare out the window into which I
looked. And so I had this vivid impression of him," Howard
Brodie says of Aaron Mitchell's slow death by cyanide. Dave
Lamb, the reporter from the *Oakland Tribune,* observed the
same phenomenon: that of Aaron Mitchell snapping his head
around "to stare in wide-eyed terror at the eyewitnesses." The
witnesses to an execution are there to be seen as well as to see,
and the "tact" in their role — to the extent they are allowed to
exercise any — lies in their reversal of that predetermined witnessing. An execution, like all such live performances, makes

use of what Goffman calls "a basic social coin, with awe on one side and shame on the other." But when the execution is transferred to film, that coin loses all its currency. The witnessing audience becomes instead a non-existent presence, an invisible crowd of spectators who yield up nothing on behalf of the performer. Tact gives way to voyeurism.

Writing about Frederick Wiseman's documentary technique, Bill Nichols praises Wiseman for his "tactlessness," his willingness to pierce through "institutional rhetoric," while simultaneously acknowledging that "this lack of tact also pulls Wiseman's cinema toward the realm of voyeurism." If Goffman is right, though, then his variety of tact, the kind that mediates between live actor and audience, cannot ever exist on film. Wiseman's documentary about the Bridgewater Correctional Facility not only confronts that fact; it is centrally *about* that fact. The legal charge against *Titicut Follies* —a charge finally overturned only in 1991, more than twenty years after the film was made—was that it invaded the privacy of the inmates. The implication behind this charge was that Wiseman conducted his invasion carelessly, or recklessly, or ignorantly, without considering the feelings of the men involved. But when you actually see *Titicut Follies*, you realize that the invasion of these particular men's privacy is one of the primary subjects of the movie; and it is a subject handled, by this beginning filmmaker, with the delicacy and complexity we have now come to expect from the mature Wiseman.

One of the subsidiary charges against *Titicut Follies* was that it showed "full frontal nudity." In doing so, the Commonwealth of Massachusetts suggested, Wiseman was exploiting the incapacitated inmates, exposing them to leering gazes, using their nakedness to titillate. But the nudity was not something imposed or inserted by Wiseman; it was the standard dress for a large number of the inmates at Bridgewater. The nudity in *Titicut Follies* is disturbingly casual, routine, uninflected, because the men themselves, like animals in a stable, were routinely kept naked in their cells and herded naked to their showers. If this nudity is an embarrassment to us — and the intervening passage of time, with the increasing use of nudity in commercial films and even on television, has made it less of one — that embarrassment is aesthetically and ethically functional, for it makes us feel, on behalf of these institutionalized men, the shame of which their institution has attempted to deprive them.

Nor are we coincidental recipients of the shame. Our role as witnesses has made us deserve it, just as Turgenev's presence at Tropmann's execution made *him* deserve it. Yet because we are not bodily present, our witnessing is even more culpable than Turgenev's, or Howard Brodie's, or Dave Lamb's. We cannot return the gaze of the person at whom we stare. This is the nature of our "invasion of privacy"; this is the voyeurism built into documentary film. Wiseman's understanding of this fact, his acknowledgment of his and our voyeuristic invasion of these men's lives, is made clearest in the film's framing device, the "Titicut Follies" themselves. The Follies were a theatrical performance, a kind of comic-vaudeville show, put on jointly by staff and inmates every year at Bridgewater. Wiseman uses footage from this performance — a performance in which the sick and the well, the incarcerated and the free, are hard to tell apart — to open and close his documentary film. Watching these sequences as if from the position of the Bridgewater audience, one is made to understand an essential difference between theater and film: the fact that our presence is live and complicitous and acknowledged in the former, hidden and unacknowledged and, yes, voyeuristic in the latter. As viewers of a documentary film, we inevitably commit the sin of allowing someone else to be exposed without being exposed ourselves. We are present through the eye of the camera, but in reality we are safely absent; in the face of the inmates' nakedness, we are fully clothed.

I have said that this quality distinguishes film from theater. But Antonin Artaud, drawing up the list of complaints that would lead him to call for a new Theater of Cruelty, saw voyeurism as one of the central problems of the naturalistic theater. Writing in 1938 in *The Theater and Its Double,* he remarked that "as long as the theater limits itself to showing us intimate scenes from the lives of a few puppets, transforming the public into Peeping Toms, it is no wonder the elite abandon it and the great public looks to the movies, the music hall or the circus for violent satisfactions, whose intentions do not deceive them." If Brecht objected to the theater's desire to coerce us into feeling, Artaud objected to the theater's incapacity to make us feel sufficiently. "The misdeeds of the psychological theater descended from Racine have unaccustomed us to that immediate and violent action which the theater should possess," said Artaud. Nor did he feel that the relatively new film technology was a proper substitute: "Movies in their turn, murdering us with second-hand reproductions which, filtered through machines, cannot *unite with* our sensibility, have maintained us for ten years in an ineffectual torpor, in which all our faculties appear to be foundering." The end result, Artaud complained, is that "the public is no longer shown anything but the mirror of itself."

It seems to me that it took the advent of film — in particular naturalistic film, film with sound — to highlight for theorists like Artaud and Brecht the shortcomings of the naturalistic theater. If one wanted to be voyeuristic, apathetic, and unstimulated, then one could do it with a vengeance using the new technology. Why rely, then, on the tired old forms of psychological theater for a weak version of the same thing? If film was an alienated, distancing, audience-divorcing form, then why not make the new theater *self-consciously* so? And so Brecht invented his "alienation effect." If movies were "murdering us" with "violent satisfactions," why not enable theater to do it even more intensely? This is the impulse behind Artaud's Theater of Cruelty—not, as he put it, about "the cruelty we can exercise upon each other by hacking at each other's bodies . . . but the much more terrible and necessary cruelty which things can exercise against us. We are not free. And the sky can still fall on our heads." (I hear echoes here of Paul Bowles's sensibility: "Let it come down.") Movies, I think, helped give Brecht and Artaud their ideas about new possibilities in theater; film, defining its own relationship to audiences, opened up a new and different relationship for theater.

The influence worked both ways. If theater, after Brecht and Artaud, began to draw on the ways in which it was uniquely "live," then film in turn focused on its own deadness, its own capacity for secondhand, relayed experience. "Peeping Toms . . . murdering us with second-hand reproductions . . . no longer shown anything but the mirror of itself": Artaud's phrases could be a summary of Michael Powell's classic thriller *Peeping Tom*, in which a camera-carrying murderer shows his victims, as their final sight, their own deaths in a mirror. It is this horror of theirs which he catches on film for his own peculiar satisfaction, and as we sit in the darkness of the movie theater watching our own horrors and satisfactions mirrored on the screen, we are not in the best position to fault him.

The relationship between the sadistic moviemaker and the voyeuristic filmgoer becomes a central subject of the murder thriller from Powell onward. This tendency cuts across genres, from the low-budget naturalism of *Henry: Portrait of a Serial Killer* to the high-tech outlandishness of David Cronenberg's *Videodrome*. In *Henry*, the eponymous murderer and his disgusting sidekick Otis videotape their murders as they commit them, and the most distressing scene of the film—the slaughter of a whole family—is shown to us in this secondhand form, as a home movie of death. In *Videodrome*, the James Woods character is driven into homicidal madness by the manipulative sex-and-death films he plays for himself on his videotape machine. You can rent this movie and watch it alone on your own VCR, as I did, in which case you will discover that its most frightening as well as most compelling quality is its self-enclosed circularity, combined with its unbroken continuity with our own world. We too are in that loop. *Peeping Tom, Henry,* and *Videodrome* are the film equivalents of Artaud's Theater of Cruelty. They take as their subject not only the seemingly predetermined cruelties of everyday life—the sense in which "we are not free," as Artaud says—but also the coldness of the rendering medium. They are about our own distance from the events that purportedly horrify us.

The distancing effect of film has begun to influence even our perspective on real life. "It's like you're in a movie all the time," said my student Crip, the self-confessed murderer, speaking about life on the Oakland streets. By which he meant *You're always performing for an imagined but unseen audience* and also *Nothing seems real.* A recent documentary, Jenny Livingston's *Paris Is Burning,* takes this street perspective as its subject matter. The transvestite characters in Livingston's film are always looking for "realness," and finding it only in the most elaborate disguises and charades. Like Crip, they contend daily with urban violence and hopelessness, and they too derive their conceptions of reality from movies and television. In *The Executioner's Song,* Gary Gilmore says about the second murder he committed, "I felt like I was watching a movie or, you know, somebody else was perhaps doing this, and I was watching them doing it . . ." The self-conscious distance of movies has become the self-distanced movie of life, and the murderer has become both protagonist and audience: "he *sees himself* in a dramatic light," but also (to borrow another Eliot phrase) manages to preserve his position as spectator "and observe always from the outside."

Our own capacity for sympathy, our ability to be moved, seems to be dependent partly on the acting ability of the victim. "If they want to kill me," said Robert Alton Harris in the KQED documentary *Appealing Death*, "then it's just like them going to a show, a movie, and say, 'Hey, let's watch this. This is something new. Let's try it.'" (Harris said this before the proposal to televise his death even came up; he was just talking about the execution itself.) Yet the noteworthy thing about Robert Alton Harris, in this respect, was that he had *not* mastered the skill of presenting an "appealing" death. Unlike Gary Gilmore, Harris was generally felt to have an ineffective stage manner, and his proposed execution—especially if televised in the cool manner promised by KQED—seemed unlikely to reach the heights of tragedy that Gilmore's death became in Mailer's hands. This is not to say that Harris would be any the less dead when the execution was over; only that we would feel less about him.

Our tendency to notice our own feelings in such a situation may be one of our more reprehensible qualities. Dostoyevsky criticized Turgenev's account of Tropmann's execution by saying that all Turgenev could see was the tear in his own eye. This may not be fair, but it is instructive. The more "thoughtful" and "self-conscious" we are, the more likely we are to evaluate not only our own feelings, but the performance that gives rise to them—a performance which we measure in terms of the feelings it produces in us. So even condemned murderers, like Gilmore and Tropmann, get reviewed as actors by the master-novelists who chronicle their deaths. At its most real, an execution is still a form of theater—as was pointedly demonstrated by the five actors from the Curran Theater in San Francisco who requested, and received, permission to attend an execution at San Quentin in February 1935. All we really know is that their names appear on the witness list, along with their theatrical affiliation; but one assumes they were there to pick up a few tips on how to die a believable death.

Being primarily interested in our own response to murder may be a sign of decadent self-indulgence on our part, but it is a version of self-indulgence that can lead to moral conclusions—the conclusion, for instance, that perhaps executions ought not to be televised. The most persuasive reason I can think of not to televise executions, like the most persuasive reason not to have executions, has to do with the effect on us: the witnesses, bystanders, and tacit permitters. I'm not speaking of the specific emotional effect on each of us—repulsion, sick gratification, or whatever—nor of the larger social or political effect on our collective behavior. I'm thinking of what it would mean about us, the audience, if we allowed someone's actual murder to become our Theater of Cruelty, our self-reflective murder film. No social outcome, however beneficial, would warrant this tactic; no end could justify this means.

I may sound coldblooded when I say that the reason not to *have* executions is their effect on us. I mean the reason at a minimum, in the abstract, regardless of how we may feel about a particular murderer and his crime. This is what I take Brecht to mean when he insists on the removal of empathy as a preliminary to drawing moral conclusions. I can imagine, though I have never felt myself, that somebody might deserve to die for his crimes; what I cannot imagine is that another person should deserve to kill him. We are not in a position to administer death from on high, "to decide who is to live and who is not to live," as Sonia Marmeladov put it to Raskolnikov. This problem has practical effects—the discriminatory difference between execution rates for blacks and whites, for instance, or the occasional incidents of a convicted "wrong man" like Randall Adams—but the practical issue is connected to a theological one or, if you prefer a less freighted term, an ethical one. There may be a right to execution, but we do not have it.

Because we have no right to execute, we also have no right to use execution, even as morally instructive theater intended to defeat execution itself. Televising an execution is not, finally, comparable to Wiseman's invading the privacy of the Bridgewater inmates, which can be aesthetically and morally justified as making a point *about* the invasion of privacy. Such justifications need to be made in terms of our willingness to implicate ourselves, "ourselves" in this case including both artist and audience. But we do not have enough self available to risk, to implicate, in a theater of actual murder. Art that puts us at moral risk must draw on what we actually have to lose, if it is not to be false or sophistical or merely sentimental. We do not have enough to cover an execution; we cannot afford to risk what that kind of theater would cost us.

# 9

# The Changeling

Even a theater of fictional murder is not an innocent theater. The point, or one of the points, of the murder story is that there can be no innocence in circumstances that give rise to murderous impulses—even if the impulses are aroused in mere bystanders, witnesses, observers; even if the murder is not real.

Theatricality itself, according to Antonin Artaud, has affinities with murder, affinities most evident in the violent emotions employed by the actor and brought out in the audience. But they are affinities defined in part by their differences. "Compared with the murderer's fury which exhausts itself," Artaud wrote, "that of the tragic actor remains enclosed within a perfect circle. The murderer's fury has accomplished an act, discharges itself, and loses contact with the force that inspired it but can no longer sustain it. That of the actor has taken a form that negates itself to just the degree it frees itself and dissolves into universality."

"Morbid, lurid, barbaric, bloodlust": the words that California attorney general John Van De Kamp used to describe the prospect of televising executions would not have struck Artaud as negative terms. On the contrary, Artaud wanted to invent a new theater specifically to bring the stage's murderous, life-giving impulses—"this carnage," he called it approvingly—back to the modern audience. He blamed the

inheritance of Renaissance theater for the decline in the audience's emotional involvement. "It is because we have been
accustomed for four hundred years, that is since the Renaissance, to a purely descriptive and narrative theater—story-
telling psychology; it is because every possible ingenuity has
been exerted in bringing to life on the stage plausible but
detached beings, with the spectacle on one side, the public on
the other"—it is for these reasons, Artaud argued, that the
modern theater is moribund. "Shakespeare and his imitators
have gradually insinuated the idea of art for art's sake, with
art on one side and life on the other," he complained.

We have by now become used to the idea that each gener-
ation of artists has to kill its forebears in order to feel it is
achieving something new and purposeful; but Artaud's characterization does unfair violence to "Shakespeare and his imitators." This is not a matter of defending the author of *Macbeth*, who needs no defense. My impulse to combat Artaud
comes from a self-serving desire to see us as continuous with
the great works of the past—not as excluded from them, but
as their living, life-giving, perpetual audience. One of the
ways in which the tragic actor's role "negates itself" (to borrow Artaud's term) is by bringing old deaths to life. The
murder on stage, far from exhausting itself, takes place over
and over again, eternally, each time the play is performed
before an audience. Fictional film may have some of the same
effects—we start, each time we see a murder movie, with the
idea that these characters are again alive for us—but I don't
think this is equally true of documentary footage. A videotape
of Robert Alton Harris's execution would have a ghostly tone
from its outset: we would realize, even as we saw the living
man strapped into the gas chamber chair, that this person was
already dead, and repeated watchings of the tape would only
increase our sense of his deadness. Like photography—"the
inventory of mortality," as Susan Sontag calls it—documentary footage has a memorial quality even as it's being filmed; it

reminds us of the closing down of life's possibilities, not their open-endedness. In contrast, murder on stage is a true-life version of reincarnation, Artaud's "perfect circle." In this version, we the audience are the life-giving gods.

Thomas Middleton and William Rowley said as much in the epilogue to *The Changeling,* one of the great murder plays of the Jacobean era. In the final lines of the play, Alsemero—who, in quick succession, has learned that his new wife, Beatrice Joanna, is an adulteress and a murderess, and has then seen her die before his eyes—turns to the audience and says:

> All we can do to comfort one another,
> To stay a brother's sorrow for a brother,
> To dry a child from the kind father's eyes,
> Is to no purpose; it rather multiplies:
> Your only smiles have power to cause relive
> The dead again, or in their rooms to give
> Brother a new brother, father a child;
> If these appear, all griefs are reconcil'd.

Artaud objected to a theater which had decayed into entertainment or amusement, to "poetry as a charm which exists only to distract our leisure." Middleton and Rowley seem far more sanguine about the efficacy of "your only smiles"—a formulation which suggests, not just that only *we* can "cause relive / The dead again," but also that our amusement, rather than any more serious involvement in the play, can do the trick. The authors of *The Changeling* realize, though, that if we bring the dead to life—including the murderous Beatrice Joanna and her pawn and lover, De Flores—we also bring to life the chain of events that leads again to their murders and suicides. Our power is enormous but not unlimited: we can reincarnate only what already existed, exactly as before. This emphasis on the fixity of events seems ironic in a play called *The Changeling,* where all things, from the moon, the wind, and the pleasures of sex to a loyal servant's honesty, a beautiful woman's virtue, and a madman's sanity, are described as being utterly changeable and impermanent.

Like *Macbeth*, Middleton and Rowley's play is partly about the inherent connections between acting and other forms of suspicious behavior.

> I'll be your pander now; rehearse again
> Your scene of lust, that you may be perfect
> When you shall come to act it to the black audience
> Where howls and gnashings shall be music to you,

says Alsemero to De Flores upon discovering his crimes. *The Changeling* is also, like Wiseman's *Titicut Follies*, about the connections between theater and madness, for it features a scene in which the fake fool Antonio, the official "changeling" of the title, is forced to perform with his fellow asylum inmates for the benefit of the local aristocracy. Both of these elements of the play invite us to wonder about our own role as the play's audience. Are we the hellish crowd whose "howls and gnashings" spur De Flores and Beatrice Joanna on? Are we the thoughtless pleasure-seekers who derive amusement from the antics of pathetic madmen? Alsemero's final address to us suggests, behind its polite and conventional praise, that as the audience whose presence created the arena for the play's action, we may be partly responsible for the unfolding horrors we've witnessed.

It is important not to overstate our responsibility here. Being part of an audience may give us some degree of responsibility for the actions that take place before our eyes, but it is nothing compared to the responsibility we bear for a state-imposed execution, whether or not we witness it. We may, at Alsemero's urging, *feel* responsible for the deaths in *The Changeling;* we *are* responsible for the deaths of executed prisoners. This point was brought out nicely in the film version of *In Cold Blood*, where one newsman asks, on the occasion of Perry Smith's execution, "What's the name of the executioner?" and another answers, "We the People." The humor of this joke lies in its discomfort, or vice versa. Fictional murder, by lifting some of the actual responsibility and its attendant discomfort from our shoulders, leaves us more open to bearing the feelings of responsibility. It is this readiness of ours that Alsemero's final speech takes advantage of.

*The Changeling* itself is reincarnated—given an updated, modern, contemporarily believable rendition—in a powerful and mysterious novel called *Scorpio Rising*, the final work of a Texas writer named R. G. Vliet, who died of cancer only days after completing the manuscript in 1984. The biographical facts matter because they so strongly color the novel. *Scorpio Rising* speaks from a point just this side of death—sometimes, it seems, just the other side. "Right now I'm in my decay phase," sardonically comments the novel's narrator, Rudy Castleberry, taking a skeptical tone toward the forecast for his astrological sign, Scorpio—"the sign of 'change, growth and decay, creation and destruction.'" The remark sounds a lot less skeptical and a lot more sardonic if we view it as coming from the cancer-riddled author. The dead haunt this novel, which repeatedly asks, in one way or another, where they've gone. Of a young woman visiting her mother's grave, the novel says: "She turned away from her mother, wherever she was, in the shadow of the ground or in a whisking air of angels' wings ..." The author himself has a ghostly presence in the novel we hold in our hands: he speaks to us, literally, from beyond the grave. His uncannily intimate voice is proof, even for skeptics, that there is some kind of life after death. This novel about cyclical reincarnation is itself an example of reincarnation: of a recently dead novelist, and also of two Jacobean playwrights. Middleton and Rowley as well as Vliet come to life in *Scorpio Rising*, which in that very specific sense has the "power to cause relive the dead again."

If this power is due in large part to voice, it is due in even larger part to structure. The novel is a "perfect circle": you can't really absorb all the hints and implications of the first half without having read the second half. The second half of the novel (which, unlike the first, is not told in Rudy's voice) deals with his Castleberry ancestors and their turn-of-the-century lives. It is this second half which borrows heavily — some might say "steals" — from *The Changeling*. The central murder plot of that play is reproduced exactly, but the action has been translated to early-twentieth-century Texas. Beatrice Joanna has become Victoria Ann Castleberry, her murdered fiancé has changed from Alonzo de Piracquo to Carson Gilstrap, her new beloved is Earl Leroy St. Clair in place of Alsemero, and the strange, obsessed, loyal, repellent man who is her partner in murder and fornication is no longer De Flores but Junior Luckett. Otherwise, the stories are strikingly similar: even the language and the small gestures are identical in places. Both stories culminate in the murder, at the young lady's behest, of Alonzo/Carson by De Flores/Junior; the murderer's insistence on Beatrice/Victoria's maidenhead as his payment; the increasingly lustful couplings between the criminal twosome; their eventual discovery by her father, her new fiancé, and the dead man's brother; and, finally, the sinners' deaths. In *The Changeling* this ending brings a sense of completion, however temporary, to the plot. But when you reach the end of *Scorpio Rising* — which, having begun with Rudy in 1976, ends, without returning to Rudy, in 1904 — your overwhelming impulse is to turn back to the first page of the book. ("So there's beginning and perfection too," says Alsemero in the speech that opens *The Changeling*, alluding to the classical perfection of the circle.) There you'll find, as Rudy's first lines: "I'm going to run the home movie again. Unlike the Egyptian mummy, I ain't pressed for time." The joke captures the beautiful doubleness of this work: if Rudy isn't in any hurry, as the idiom would have it, he is nevertheless, like the mummy, preserved for all time, pressed between the leaves of this book—a different kind of reincarnation from the one the Egyptians believed in, but a cyclical form of existence nonetheless.

*Scorpio Rising* is a novel that could not have existed before the movies, from which it learned something new about the possibilities of cyclical narration. Even before movies, a book could always be reread. But a narrative art form which takes place in time, like the theater or the opera, and yet which can be rerun exactly, like a written text—a narrative which, in that sense, is both linear and cyclical—came into being only with the movies. Film crosses the boundary between communal and private time, demands that you accede to the public schedule but also gives you the opportunity to make up missed moments on your own. Early in the novel, Rudy recalls the movie theater of his childhood in Alto Springs, Texas: "They show two shows a week and on Sunday nights a Mexican movie. If you're late, and you're the last one in, Dorr will start the movie over: at the exact same place you came in the film stops, the lights come up and it's time to go home." This is the structure Rudy has borrowed for his own "home movie"; this is the linear-but-circular pattern Vliet has seized on to tell his murder story, because, as Rudy says, "the shock waves of an old violence in a Texas town don't go away until the story's been told over and over. And maybe not even then."

One thing books and movies have in common is that they don't alter in reruns. In this, they resemble the actual past. However much we think it over, the past remains the same, and its events—and their effect on us, its present inheritors—are unavoidably fixed. Yet if *Scorpio Rising* focuses obsessively on such determinism, it is also a novel about how we in the present can create or re-create the past. This is a truth that extends beyond the world of Vliet's novel. Norman Mailer made use of it when re-creating Gary Gilmore's death, and even that re-creation has not remained fixed. The present's ability to change the past is what makes *The Executioner's Song* a different novel now, after thirteen years of increasingly routine executions, from what it was when it first came out, shortly after the Supreme Court had lifted its ban on capital punishment. It is also what might alter the nature of an execution videotape, however fixed in film it was. Think, for example, about what it would be like to watch such a videotape *after* executions had been permanently abolished. The recorded event itself would remain the same, but its meaning would have been altered by subsequent events.

"Beneath the stars, upon yon meteor / Ever hung my fate 'mongst things corruptible" is the line of Beatrice Joanna's that Vliet chooses for his epigraph, the one explicit sign he gives us that *The Changeling* has shaped this novel. Even the line itself cuts both ways: she blames her actions on fate, but it is a fate with human and not godlike causes, changeable like a meteor, not fixed like the stars. Beatrice Joanna's history is both predetermined and her own fault. The effort to recast an old play as a contemporary novel has a similar tension: Vliet is stuck, by choice, with a preexisting plot, but he gives it new life, and even new suspense. Part of his achievement is that *Scorpio Rising* has a painful, freshly compelling quality each time you reread it. Like Rudy, you find yourself working through the tragedy once again, hoping each time that it won't happen.

Rudy is a victim of the past (his misshapen body and his hopeless love of beautiful women have, he thinks, been inherited from his grandfather, Junior Luckett), but he is also its author. The second half of the book can, if you choose, be taken as a delirious dream of Rudy's — or, if not that, then a literal intrusion of himself into his past, whereby he becomes his own grandfather. That we *can* invent our own grandparents is suggested by an earlier scene in the novel, where Rudy comments on a family photo displayed by his friend Lita: "It's

interesting to see what Lita's grandma and great-grandma-
and-pa were like. Lita picked out the picture from a box of
them at Goodwill's."

"Who *is* this man? Where-all does he come from?" won-
ders Victoria Ann, who is in many ways Lita's prior incarnation, about the repulsive, doggishly attentive Junior Luckett,
who is Rudy's. The novel's structure tells us that he comes
from nowhere: he is a backward projection from the future, or
a dreamer's invention. Yet "invention" cannot be the right
term for a creature borrowed so wholly from Middleton and
Rowley's play, and Vliet acknowledges as much when he has
Victoria Ann dream her first sinful dream. The sin she commits in it is plagiarism. "Victoria Ann had turned in a book-
length report, expecting praise. She had copied out a whole
book to pass off as her own. She wept and said she had
written the paper her ownself." She has this dream the night
after commissioning Junior Luckett, though not in so many
words, to kill off Carson Gilstrap. Plagiarism is being used
(by Vliet, by the dream) as the stand-in for murder; but the
acceptable version of plagiarism — that is, literary allusion — is
the means by which Vliet lends life to *The Changeling*'s antique
characters, gives them currency and renewed existence. The
answer to the question "Where-all does he come from?" is
"The author's imagination" — Middleton and Rowley's, if you
wish, rather than Vliet's or Rudy's, but I'd say they all begin to
blur together. If this plagiarism is life-giving, it is also death-
dealing, for the main character Vliet recreates is the murderer.

Though Vliet is unusual in making it the center of his
plot, the question "Where does the murderer come from?" lies
at the heart of most murder stories. The murderer is always in
some way a changeling figure, a creature who appears to come
from nothing human. How did he get this way? we always
ask, and it never seems fair, or sufficient, to blame his parents
or his environment. As in *Scorpio Rising*, the answer invokes an

author's imagination—even when the murderer is real. A murder becomes a murder "story" when the murderer becomes, at least in part, the invention of an author.[*]

Often the process of inventing a murderer includes protection, affection, and even a kind of nurturing encouragement. Unlike Dr. Frankenstein, who rudely abandoned his creature at birth, most present-day creators of monsters are rather good parents to their "hideous progeny." They bring these frightening figures to life and then work to keep them alive—on the page if not out of the gas chamber. Ann Rule directly addresses these feelings of parenthood in a dream she describes in *The Stranger Beside Me*. Appearing approximately two hundred pages into the book, the dream, which occurred shortly after Ted Bundy was initially convicted, reveals her first feelings of misgiving about her own role in relation to Ted:

> I found myself in a large parking lot, with cars backing out and racing away. One of the cars ran over an infant, injuring it terribly, and I grabbed it up, knowing it was up to me to save it. I had to get to a hospital, but no one would help. I carried the baby, wrapped almost completely in a gray blanket, into a car rental agency. They had plenty of cars, but they looked at the baby in my arms and refused to rent me one.

Eventually she uses a child's toy wagon to pull the baby to an emergency room. There, the nurses refuse to admit the infant, saying, "Let it die. It will do no one any good to treat it." At the end of the dream, when everyone has turned away and refused to help, Rule looks down at the bundle in her arms: "It was not an innocent baby; it was a demon. Even as I held it, it sunk its teeth into my hand and bit me."

---

[*]Very occasionally, the murderer's two creators—his parent and his author—are one and the same, as exemplified in Lionel Dahmer's recent decision to do a book about his son Jeffrey, a decision headlined in *Publishers Weekly* as "Dahmer's Dad Strikes a Deal."

Ann Rule explains the dream as "all too clear. Had I been trying to save a monster, trying to protect something or someone who was too dangerous and evil to survive?" She focuses, that is, on the element of protection in her personal relation to Ted Bundy. What she neglects is her position as the murderer's author—a job she had already taken on, remember, *before* she knew her friend Ted was the culprit. As author, she is saving Ted in a different way: not saving the person she knows from execution, but preserving the murderer forever between the pages of a book. Bundy is "pressed for time," as Rudy Castleberry would say, given life-after-death through the murder story Ann Rule has carefully wrapped around him. In this respect, she is not just a bystander who happens to have found an injured baby; she is the changeling's mother.

Rule's dream explicitly offers us the image of the murderer who has surreptitiously taken the place of an innocent baby. But isn't that the claim always made, and often compellingly, in regard to murderers? They all started off as innocent children, sometimes children who were themselves abused or victimized. Such were the claims made for Robert Alton Harris in a clemency hearing before Governor Pete Wilson. But while acknowledging that Harris "suffered monstrous child abuse," Wilson nonetheless drew an impermeable line between innocent child and guilty adult. "As great as is my compassion for Robert Harris the child," the governor announced, "I cannot excuse or forgive the choice made by Robert Harris the man." The implication was that some severe disjunction had taken place; the child was no longer father to the man.

A similar kind of radical disjunction appears in *A Mother in History,* Jean Stafford's bizarre and blackly hilarious account of three days spent in the company of Lee Harvey Oswald's mother in 1965. "How many boys at age thirteen that play hooky from school would come home from school

and tell his mother that he did so?" Marguerite Oswald asks
rhetorically, defending Lee's youthful integrity. She goes on to
argue for the strong family values embodied in all the Oswald
boys: "They didn't cuss—of course, I don't say they didn't on
the outside, but they didn't in front of me . . . I wanted to be
sure that no boy of mine would come into my home drunk.
And I can truthfully say not one of them ever entered my
home stinko." Such character testimonials, while possibly
true, are singularly inappropriate to the consideration of Lee
Harvey Oswald's guilt. Would we think better of him if we
saw him as a sober, clean-spoken assassin? Marguerite
Oswald's odd statements and Stafford's masterly presentation
of those statements cause us to question the very idea of establishing the "character" of a murderer.

I have already suggested that the victim's inherent sweet-
ness or innocence has little bearing on the severity of the
crime; but I am now making the even more extreme assertion
that even the murderer's character is largely irrelevant, except
insofar as it bears directly on his reasons and motives for committing the murder. Our usual standards for judging human
worth are useless in the face of the enormity of murder; normally admirable qualities like sobriety or honesty or gen-
erosity or intelligence or artistic talent do not weigh in the balance against the single catastrophic act. This does not mean
that the murderer's only character is his character as a murderer. On the contrary: we would not be aware of the irrele-
vance of his peripheral virtues if they did not stand out in contrast to his character as a murderer. William Hazlitt makes
this point in his essay "On Cant and Hypocrisy," where he
says:

> Some people have expected to see his crimes written in
> the face of a murderer, and have been disappointed
> because they did not, as if this impeached the distinction
> between virtue and vice. Not at all. The circumstance
> only showed that the man was other things, and had

other feelings besides those of a murderer. If he had
nothing else—if he had fed on nothing else—if he had
dreamt of nothing else but schemes of murder, his features would have expressed nothing else: but this perfection in vice is not to be expected from the contradictory
and mixed nature of our motives.

To which I would simply add that among all the contradictory
"motives," the only ones we ought to consider, in arriving at
either a legal or an ethical accounting, are the ones that led
directly or indirectly to the murder. The others are of interest
to us as readers, writers, news collectors, citizens, fellow
human beings. But they should not affect the severity or le-
niency of our official judgment.

This is not to say that character, and the shaping
influences of home and family, cannot be seen as causal elements in the murder itself, in which case they *do* weigh in the
balance in our assignment of blame. *A Mother in History* offers a
case in point. If Stafford's rendition even approaches reality,
Marguerite Oswald's craziness can certainly be seen as a contributing factor to John F. Kennedy's death, for a child who
was subjected to this degree of nuttiness on a daily basis could
not be expected to come away with an undistorted view of
reality. Yet children *do* survive such childhoods; not every
child of a Marguerite-like mother grows up to be an assassin.
So even in the most extenuating circumstances, we allow for a
disjunction between deterministic childhood and adult moral
responsibility, between the parent's effect and the child's
behavior. We do not, in such cases, view the murderer purely
as a victim.

It is to Stafford's credit that she does not view the mother
as a pure monster, either. Or, if she views Marguerite as a
monster, it is one to whose monstrosities she finds herself
unusually susceptible. *A Mother in History* gives us, even more
specifically than Ann Rule's book about Ted Bundy, a sense of
the connection between a murderer's mother and a murder-

story author. Perhaps this connection is particularly strong when the author is a woman—even a woman who, like Stafford, has never had a child. Something of this underlying female link is both proposed and mocked in a passage that comes near the beginning of *A Mother in History*, a passage in which Stafford sets the peculiarly engaging tone that will pervade this off-putting book:

> Accustomed as she was to public speaking, Mrs. Oswald did not seem to be addressing me specifically but, rather, a large congregation; this was to be her manner with me on each of the three occasions I saw her. Taking advantage of my anonymity in this quiet crowd and of the fact that her back was turned, I looked around the room in the snoopy way women do when they are in other women's houses, and tried to think what sort of occupant I would assign to it if I did not already know who she was.

Jean Stafford's funniness is sharp and purposeful where Marguerite Oswald's is unintentional. But that extreme distinction begins to blur around the edges when Stafford's journalistic job is reduced to looking around "in the snoopy way women do ... in other women's houses," a phrase that also reduces the journalist to another version of her subject. This blurring of their personalities increases throughout the little book, so that twenty pages on Stafford admits, "I was surprised each time she used the royal or tutorial 'we,' and only the most tenuous hold on reality kept me from glancing from left to right to see who besides me was attending the lecture." Here the author jokes about her tenuous hold (which was more, at any rate, than Mrs. Oswald had), but by the beginning of the third day she reports with some seriousness: "My impulse was to eliminate the day by taking a sleeping pill, but I was committed; I must go with Mrs. Oswald to her son's grave." In this book about craziness and political convictions, "committed" carries a great deal of weight here. It stands for the feel of the whole sentence, the whole book—for the way in which Jean Stafford's firm but highly idiosyncratic grasp on reality makes us see Marguerite as she is, as both a distorted, extreme version of Jean (or of any woman) and as someone entirely alien.

The complicity of the author and the mother—both seeking to perpetuate the son's myth, both furthering their own reputations by doing so—reaches an explicit climax around the middle of the book. In a statement that, as Stafford puts it, was "designed to cause the blood of her interlocutor to run cold with embarrassment and to immobilize the tongue," Mrs. Oswald confesses to her sufferings at the hands of journalists. Stafford responds not to Mrs. Oswald, but to us: "I was guilty, I had contributed my galling bit to this treasure house of anguish and humiliation, but so had everybody else on earth." Even in 1965, the question of exactly who was guilty and how far the guilt extended was central to any examination of Lee Harvey Oswald. Marguerite presciently summarized the essential feeling of Oliver Stone's 1991 movie *JFK* when she said to Stafford, "Now the only thing I'm *sure* of is that *I* had nothing to do with the assassination. I'm not sure about anybody else. And because I am looking for the truth, everyone is under suspicion in a way." Presciently, but crazily: her claim to total innocence is part of her craziness, just as Jean Stafford's admission of shared guilt demonstrates her sanity. And yet Stafford's portrait of the murderer's mother is complicated enough to make us feel that there is also something lucid in Marguerite's claim, and something nutty in Jean's.

In part because of the gender difference and in part because Mailer stays fully hidden in his book, the murderauthor's identification with the murderer's mother takes a different form in *The Executioner's Song*. But the identification is nonetheless there. No figure in Mailer's true-life novel is portrayed more sympathetically than Bessie Gilmore, Gary's mother. Among other reasons, this may be because she actually was a warm and open and decent woman who deserved sympathy for the tragedies in her life, of which Gary was only one. So it would seem, at any rate, from Mikal Gilmore's recent memoir, which supports and substantiates Mailer's portrayal of Bessie. According to her son Mikal, Bessie was a lifelong opponent of capital punishment. He remembers that during his childhood she would repeatedly ask her sons to join her in writing letters to the Oregon governor pleading that death sentences be commuted; she would explain to Gary, Mikal, and the others that "these were the only killings we *knew* were going to occur and the only killings we could prevent." That this statement should have been made by the mother of the late twentieth century's most famous executed murderer, years before he committed murder and was executed, may seem unbelievably ironic; but then, such ironies underlie most interesting murder stories, including, if not especially, Mailer's.

One of the ironies that Mailer is particularly intrigued by is that he and Gary Gilmore's mother—both, he would argue, attractive, intelligent, morally responsible people—should nevertheless have given birth to a monster. Having each created this monster (though in very different ways), Norman Mailer and Bessie Gilmore were then faced with the problem of continuing to love him while seriously taking his moral measure. Moreover, both had to listen to Gary's explicit pleas for death and decide whether to give him life against his will. In the end, they reached opposite conclusions. Bessie refused to back the ACLU lawsuit to save Gary from execution because, despite her longstanding hatred of capital punishment, she respected Gary's right to choose death over life imprisonment. Mailer, in contrast, took Gary's professed hatred of publicity as an ambivalent, nonbinding stance, something along the lines of Kafka's instructions to Max Brod ordering that his manuscripts be burned after his death, a request that was perhaps meant to be ignored. Mailer chose to publicize Gary's life and death, and thereby chose to give him a particularly useless and painful immortality: "life imprisonment" as a literary character within the pages of *The Executioner's Song.* He made a choice opposite to Bessie's, but, as is usual in Mailer's self-divided work, he presents the two decisions so that his opponent's seems more persuasive, more commendable than his own. Bessie Gilmore was a mother who was willing to allow her changeling son to die; Norman Mailer is the kind of parent who insists, above all, that his literary progeny must live.

It is a position in which he was not entirely without Gary Gilmore's support. Mailer tells us as much in the final encounter between Gilmore and Mailer's stand-in, Larry Schiller. Schiller approaches Gary to shake hands just before the execution: "It was as if he was saying good-bye to a man who was going to step into a cannon and be fired to the moon, or dropped in an iron chamber to the bottom of the sea, a veritable Houdini." (One of those facts about Gary that Mailer would have had to invent if it weren't true—but it *was* true, according to Mikal—is that the Gilmore boys believed themselves to be directly if illegitimately descended from the famous escape artist.) "He grasped both of Gilmore's hands and it didn't matter if the man was a murderer, he could just as well have been a saint," Mailer/Schiller continues, "for either at this moment seemed equally beyond Schiller's way of measure—and he said, he heard it come out of him, 'I don't know what I'm here for.'"

Mailer's next paragraph picks up the Houdini reference, highlights the odd relation between a condemned man and his self-appointed author, and eerily echoes the final moment of Ann Rule's dream:

> Gilmore replied, "You're going to help me escape." Schiller looked at him sitting in the chair and said, "I'll do it the best way that's humanly possible," and was think-

ing by that, he would treat it all in the most honest way, and Gilmore smiled back at him with that funny tight grin of his, just a little expression in the upper lip, as if he alone knew the meaning of what had just been said, and then the grin broadened into that thin-lipped smile he showed on occasion, evil as a jackal, subtly jeering, the last facial expression Schiller would have to remember of Gilmore.

Like Rule's dream-infant, Gilmore ends by biting the hand that chronicles him. Schiller obviously interprets the plea about escape, not as a literal request or even a joke about such a request, but as a transcendent wish for a life in print — a life beyond the grave, like R. G. Vliet's or Junior Luckett's. His answer to this wish is to hand Gilmore over to Mailer, a great writer who will "treat it all in the most honest way." But is "honest" the right word with which to praise a true-life *novel?* It is always a touchy word in murder stories: "honest Iago," "honest De Flores." We suspect it instantly. Only by explicitly announcing himself as dishonest, as Mailer does with his claim to fiction, can the author of a murder story begin to win our trust.

One effect of the changeling syndrome is that the author of a murder story, in giving birth to his own version of the murderer, takes on certain elements of criminality himself. Ann Rule's dream makes this apparent, and so does Janet Malcolm's elucidation of the MacDonald/McGinniss case. The author, in the process of creating his murder book, comes to value that book excessively — comes to view its conception and gestation as requiring and deserving protection, to an extent that even frees him from the normal ethical principles governing human behavior. "A book is a living thing," Malcolm quotes Joseph Wambaugh saying in defense of McGinniss. "When you get to the point where you have this entire investment in it, then this book is as much alive as anyone you've ever known—sometimes more so—and you have a moral obligation to protect that life, not to let it die aborning. If I have to tell an untruth to a sociopathic criminal to protect this living thing, to let it be born, then that's where my moral obligation lies." Elsewhere in *The Journalist and the Murderer,* another person says of McGinniss, in a letter written to Mac-Donald before *Fatal Vision* was completed: "I think he is having a struggle with the book. I guess all good writers have labor pains." (This in a letter to a man who had been condemned for stabbing his pregnant wife.)

Janet Malcolm's book is not just about the criminality of giving birth to a murderer; it is about the criminality of confusing living and inanimate things, real people and fictional characters. This is a crime (the kind of crime, like being a sleaze, "which the law, as such, is not designed to deal with") in which Malcolm, by her own admission, engages. She tells us toward the end of her book that "once I began writing this chronicle, I lost my desire to correspond with MacDonald. He had (once again) become a character in a text, and his existence as a real person grew dim for me (as it had grown dim for McGinniss, until MacDonald's lawsuit brought it back into glaring incandescence)." The fact that Malcolm is not entirely in control of her subject and its implications should not diminish for us the importance of what she reveals. All of these true-life murder stories—Rule's, Stafford's, Mailer's, Malcolm's, McGinniss's—involve a drastic confusion on the part of the authors. They (a "they" that includes me) give birth to a "living thing" that is just words on a page, while a real person dies, or at best languishes in jail, in order to provide the raw material for the literary character they fashion. Nor are their readers innocent bystanders to this process. The book becomes a living thing only by virtue of people's willingness to take it up and read it; the author converts a person into a character for her readers' amusement and edification. "Your only smiles have power to cause relive/The dead again": Middleton and Rowley are right to accuse the audience of being crucial participants in the cycle of rebirth and death.

Of course, there is a very real sense in which all this business about the criminal implication of author and reader is nonsense, especially in regard to a real murder. To imagine killing somebody is not the same as actually killing somebody. To think about dropping the cyanide pellets or pulling the switch—even to will that these things be done, but without communicating or effecting that wish—is not the same as carrying out an execution. This is why a televised execution would be doomed to failure as moral instruction. We would not, as Howard Brodie has asserted, feel that "we" were responsible for the killing. At the moment of execution, all communal spirit would dissolve, and to save our own souls and sensibilities we would each disown the death (as Turgenev did, for instance, choosing personal shame over any sense of public, communal, political responsibility). And we would be right to do so. Else all boundaries would be in danger of dissolution, with action and feeling blurred together as one. There has to be a difference between wishing (or watching) someone executed, and actually committing murder; without such a distinction, there can't even be gradations of guilt or innocence.

But in fictional murder, the difference between feeling or thinking and doing is not so vast. The murder itself is imaginary, imagined. Therefore the author's act of imagination, and in turn the reader's, can be said to be no less reprehensible than the murderer's nonexistent, purely fictional act. More reprehensible, perhaps, if we deem author and reader to be possessed of more independent will than a created character, who can only do what he is ordered to do.

This is one of the central insights offered by *The Changeling*, and by the twentieth-century novel it gave rise to.

Beatrice Joanna (or Victoria Ann) was the author of the murder plot, and De Flores (or Junior Luckett) merely the character she invented to carry it out. Like all authors of murder stories, she both hated and loved her creature, with a love that fed intensely on her own prior feeling of repulsion. She seized upon him because he was close at hand at the opportune moment and could quickly accomplish what she wished; in that sense, she thought their connection was both timely and temporary. But she was soon to learn—as have all murder-story authors, from Poe and Dostoyevsky to Norman Mailer and Ann Rule—that the tie couldn't be broken so easily: she and her monster were to be joined in an immortal bond, extending at the very least beyond both of their deaths.

# 10

.......................................................................................

# The Big Clock

Murder stories hinge on the tension between endlessness and finality. By this I do not just mean the matter of individual mortality, though I mean that too: the life that seems
all-encompassing, limitless, world-defining to its possessor,
who cannot conceive of the universe continuing without that
life; and the sharp conclusion brought to this life by murder or
execution. But the exposition of such a life and such a death
also carries with it other tensions between open-endedness
and termination. The very techniques on which the telling of a
murder tale relies—foreshadowing, delay, irony, surprise, a
sense of determinism, the theatrical immortalization of the
main character—are techniques that play with the notion of
time.

In murder stories, time speeds up or stands still. The
crime itself, often committed in a moment of passion or psy-
chosis or at the very least self-forgetfulness, has a temporal
quality of its own. It often seems to be outside time, from the
murderer's point of view. Following this brief and unexpected
event, there is a peculiar but predictable race against time—
the detectives' effort to catch the murderer before the trail has
gone completely cold. Then comes the long-drawn-out grind-
ing of the judicial machine: the trial date set far in advance
(and often put off several times); the creakingly detailed slow-
ness of the trial itself; the further delay for sentencing and, in

234

some cases, execution—this last generally coming years after the initial crime, so that the executed man is virtually a different person from the younger self who committed the crime. Even the consequences of murder can vary with time, depending, for instance, on whether you happen to commit the crime or go on trial before or after the precise moment when the state you are in legalizes capital punishment. By the time of the trial, and even more so by the time of an execution, the murder itself has dwindled into the past. And that past, because of the prospect of capital punishment, has an odd, disjunctive relationship to any possible future—even grammatically, as Stendhal's hero in *The Red and the Black* discovers as he awaits his own execution: "Ah, I am in the condemned cell. That is right. Count Altamira has told me that before his execution Danton said in his loud voice: 'It is singular how the verb guillotine cannot be conjugated in all the tenses.' You can say 'I shall be guillotined,' 'Thou wilt be guillotined,' but not, 'I have been guillotined.'"

The murder story inherent in *KQED v. Vasquez* had its own paradoxical relation to time. There was, first of all, the dual time scheme in regard to Robert Alton Harris's execution: on the one hand, the series of stays, appeals, and execution dates that determined if or when he would die; and, on the other hand, the trial about media coverage of his death, which ran on an entirely parallel and unconnected track. It was possible (though the laggardly pace of appeal procedures made it unlikely) that the courts could rush ahead and determine to put Harris to death before the issue of media coverage had been resolved, in which case the outcome of *KQED* would be moot in regard to this particular execution. Within the *KQED* trial itself, the issue of timing came up in regard to "live" versus prerecorded broadcasting of an execution, the difference between a murder taking place in real time—in our time, as we watched—and a televised report of such a murder. Even a taped recording of an execution would have a special temporal quality not found in eyewitness reports, as George Osterkamp noted in his testimony: "You have this tape that is running, often in real time when you can go back and see what happened," minute by minute and second by second, so you wouldn't have to rely on anyone's assertion about what time the cyanide pellets were dropped, or how long it took the prisoner to die, or whatever. The fact that the execution *could* be filmed by prearrangement was also due to a time factor. Only a scheduled murder could be captured in this way, preserved and broadcast under predetermined, legally agreed upon conditions. And only at a scheduled murder could the press be banned: there are no limits—other than good taste, observed more in the breach than otherwise—on the opportunely taped murders a network can broadcast.

At moments in the *KQED* trial, one was also reminded of the temporal elements in videotape itself: the way the timing of a filmed scene (for instance, the official San Quentin gas chamber footage, with its crawling pace and incessant repetitions) strongly influences its emotional content. Time—even "real" time, unedited time—is a seemingly objective, impersonal factor that film has learned to use with immense and powerful subjectivity. Time, or timeliness, is also videotape's strongest claim to importance. To film an execution for television, according to some of the plaintiff's witnesses, was both to present it as news and to preserve it for posterity: a topical, current, immediate function combined with a long-term historical value. Perhaps in response to this dual sensibility, the trial itself was both retrospective and futuristic, drawing on Howard Brodie's memories of 1967 and Raymond Procunier's testimony about past executions even as it tried to posit the kind of world we would inhabit if people were able to watch scheduled murders on TV. To witness the trial as I did, with this book in mind, was to inhabit at least two time schemes at once: the day-to-day, temporarily inflamed topicality of the media-fanned event, and the much more enduring meaning that the trial might be seen to have in context, long after it was over. Like a sketch artist at an execution or a photographer at the scene of a crime, I had to situate myself between the two positions, the presently experienced and the retrospectively considered, "being there" and "rendering reality."

If one is to create a judicial or documentary or literary murder story that attempts to offer some kind of explanation, the murder itself—once a momentary event, fleeting and filled with simultaneous impulses—must be laboriously and retrospectively reconstructed. Hindsight lends greater importance to events that came before the murder, so that the past seems to open up like a widening tunnel, larger near its origins, narrowing to the moment of the crime. A murder takes place in forward-moving time (piercingly and irrevocably forward-moving, in that it can't be undone), but the story about a murder glances backward. Thus time in murder stories is both linear and circular, suspense-filled and progressive but also looping back to its own origins ("So there's beginning and perfection too"). Like the Egyptian mummy, the participants in a murder story are "pressed for time": speeded up, racing against the clock to reach, or avert, their fated conclusions, but also preserved for all eternity in the silent stasis of a tale. The hands of the big clock—the image reappearing again and again, in books and movies, documentary and fiction—move around the impersonal clock face, describing with their very motion the paradox of linear circularity, of endlessness that approaches a terminal moment.

That recognizable clock—you've seen it countless times, with its bluntly legible numbers and impassive black-on-white face and creeping hands ticking off the tally-marked minutes—has become such a murder-story cliché that Errol Morris can use it in *The Thin Blue Line* the same way he uses the numerous reenactments of the crime or the clips from old cop-and-gangster movies: as a signal about the fictional nature of his documentary enterprise. It is the same clock that appears, repeatedly and heavyhandedly, in movies like the 1958 *I Want To Live* or television episodes like Hitchcock's "Cell 227"—both fictional accounts (though *I Want To Live* was based on real events) of an innocent person wrongly condemned to execution. In *I Want To Live*, which features Susan Hayward as the unlucky Barbara Graham, the clock is so omnipresent during the final pre-execution moments that it becomes a main character in the movie; and when Hayward at one point says, "Fifteen minutes!" (referring to the time she has left to live), there are actually fifteen minutes of real time left until the movie ends. In both *I Want To Live* and "Cell 227" the clock is a serious, oppressive, suspense-inducing device (though complicatedly so in the Hitchcock episode, which manifests that program's usual wry sense of humor). In Morris's film the device is used ironically, humorously; and yet because *The Thin Blue Line* is a documentary, and Randall Adams really did suffer the abuses of "doing time"—first under threat of execution, and then at the expense of eleven wrongfully lost years—the implied comment is upsetting and sad as well as comic.

Though the big clock is a visual image, it has received its fullest rendition not in a movie, but in Kenneth Fearing's novel of that name. *The Big Clock*, which was originally published in 1946 (and which was then made into a movie—quite a good one—a year or two later), is not exactly a murder mystery, for we learn the identity of the killer at the moment of the killing. Nor is it a standard novel of detection, for here the detective's primary aim is to steer the search *away* from the suspect. This is because the detective and the suspect are identical.

They are combined in the person of George Stroud, editor of the monthly publication *Crimeways*, a journalistic cog in the giant New York corporate machine owned by Earl Janoth. Janoth has killed his girlfriend Pauline in a fit of passion, and he knows that there is only one man—a shadowy figure he noticed outside her apartment building—who can put him at the scene of the crime. So, on the advice of his righthand man, the coolly ruthless Steve Hagen, Janoth puts his *Crimeways* expert in charge of finding the unknown man. Stroud, who had been having a secret affair with Pauline up to the moment of her death, knows that he will be quietly eliminated once Janoth and Hagen identify him as the witness. If he goes to the police, on the other hand, he risks losing his wife Georgette and daughter Georgia—as well as being framed for the murder himself. So he must put together an investigative team and simulate a manhunt even as he tries to make himself unfindable. The chief clues to his identity, and the things that almost get him caught, are his habit of hanging out in bars and his passion for the paintings of an artist named Louise Patterson.

Written in a hardboiled, semi-comic, but strangely moving style, *The Big Clock* has a tonal affinity with Weegee's "naked city" photographs, which were taken at about the same time the novel was written. Fearing's novel also forecasts, explicitly but also delicately, the merging of sleuth, murderer, and victim that was later to characterize such films as *The Silence of the Lambs* and *Manhunter.* As Stroud's team pieces together a portrait that is increasingly and unpleasantly recognizable as him, we come to see that *The Big Clock,* in a way that seems emblematic of all murder stories, is literally about the search for one's own identity. The nature of Stroud's task is reflected in an early scene of the novel, when we watch him talking to himself in a mirror—discovering who he is from the outside, as Joe McGinniss and Tom Ripley do with the aid of *their* mirrors. Stroud's double-natured self (his double life that includes adultery, and his double role as detective and suspect) also gets a symbolic rendering in the highly formal works of Louise Patterson—one of which, hanging prominently on his office wall, is described as "the profiles of two faces, showing only the brow, eyes, nose, lips, and chin of each. They confronted each other, distinctly Pattersonian."

This image becomes a reality late in the novel, when Stroud and Patterson face off in his office. She is one of the few people capable of identifying him as the mystery man, and yet she chooses not to. "For the fraction of a second we looked at each other with complete realization," runs Patterson's narrative. "I knew who he was, and he knew that I knew." (Like the fragmented but interpretable portrait of the suspect, the novel itself is composed of various narrative viewpoints — mainly Stroud's, but with chapters by Janoth, Hagen, Georgette Stroud, Louise Patterson, and even one of Stroud's punctiliously incompetent investigators.) Patterson "knows" Stroud not just on a superficial level, as a suspect whom she recognizes, but deeply, because they are both eccentrics, both square pegs unable to fit into the round holes of New York corporate life — "the big clock," as Stroud keeps calling the grindingly impersonal machine that surrounds him.

In its emphasis on Patterson's feeling about her own paintings, *The Big Clock* introduces a new version of the artist's relation to the changeling she creates. In this case the changeling creation is not a murderer, but a potential murder victim. Repeatedly in this novel, Stroud and then Patterson refer to the kind of people who "murder" artworks. "The big clock didn't like pictures, much. I did," Stroud muses at one point. "... There were lots of good pictures that were prevented from being painted at all. If they couldn't be aborted, or lost, then somebody like me was despatched to destroy them." Stroud then adds, referring to Janoth's hit man: "Just as Billy would be sent to destroy me." The word "abort" is not used idly here. Nor is it coincidence that the artist in this novel is a woman. Patterson, who is portrayed as the mother of numerous children, exhibits her most protective maternal tendencies toward her own paintings. "I looked at him through a haze of rage. He was another picture-burner," she says of one Janoth employee. "... Another one of those decent, respectable maniacs who'd like nothing better than to take a butcher knife and slash canvases, slop them with paint, burn them." What she likes about Stroud, what protects him from her capacity to give him away, is that she knows he values her work.

The reason a painting can be murdered is that it is unique and irreplaceable, like a person. This is not true of a book. A book can die a short death and then be resuscitated—perhaps even under a new name (as was Fearing's *The Big Clock*, recently reissued under the comparatively inane title *No Way Out* to coincide with its faint remake as a movie). And if a book is replicable and hence discardable, how much more so a monthly commercial magazine, a piece of pulp designed to be read by faceless masses who are presumed to dislike anything original or unique. Fearing's novel is in part about such magazines and the machine-like people who produce them—like Steve Hagen, "a hard, dark little man whose soul had been hit by lightning, which he'd liked. His mother was a bank vault, and his father an International Business Machine." In this inhuman world, researchers come up with ideas like the Funded Individuals project, one of Janoth's *Futureways* notions, whereby specific people become million-dollar investment opportunities, and all murder supposedly ceases because no one wants to destroy a good investment. To men like Janoth and Hagen, people are infinitely replicable. This perception is echoed and mocked in a joke practiced by George Stroud's unique little family—George, Georgette, and Georgia—each member of which calls the other two "George."

The big clock of Fearing's title is both the press of time—the relentless search for the suspect, against which Stroud struggles like an animal caught in the pincers of a closing trap—and the press itself. ("Toni knew why they called them the press. They almost squeezed her to death," Mailer has one of Gary Gilmore's relatives thinking about the media people swarming around the execution.) The press is never very far from any big story about murder, and one needn't work for *Crimeways* to be employed in the pursuit of blood. Weegee was a member of the working press; so were Dave Lamb, who chronicled Aaron Mitchell's execution, and Howard Brodie, who sketched it. The whole *KQED* case was explicitly about the way the press insists on following a murder, this time in the form of an execution.

"As the hangman said to the condemned man, 'No noose is good noose,'" jokes a Preston Sturges character in *Christmas in July.* No news *is* good news on an execution story: the press often shows its worst side on such occasions. Decades before *KQED v. Vasquez* reached the courtroom, many of the problems raised by the lawsuit were anticipated in the movie *His Girl Friday.* This version of the Hecht-MacArthur play, directed by Howard Hawks during the Weegee/*Big Clock* era, comments repeatedly on the bloodthirstiness of reporters. Most people remember that the film stars Cary Grant and Rosalind Russell as editor Walter Burns and reporter Hildy Johnson, with Ralph Bellamy as the unfortunate third party in their relationship; but few viewers recall that this bleak romantic comedy is set against the backdrop of an impending execution, with much of the action occurring in a press room that directly overlooks the prison yard where the execution is scheduled to take place.

"They ain't human," says the condemned man's girlfriend as she listens to the assembled reporters joking about the gallows.

"I know," answers Rosalind Russell; "they're newspapermen."

*His Girl Friday* also contains its own version of Janoth's Funded Individuals idea, his corporate humans-as-investment-opportunities project, in its reference to Ralph Bellamy's profession of insurance salesman. "Of course we don't help you much when you're alive, but afterwards—that's when it counts," Bellamy bumblingly salespitches to Cary Grant, his rival for Russell.

"I don't get it," Grant deadpans in response. Personally effective as a retort, Grant's answer nonetheless begs the question of how much his own profession as newsman resembles Bellamy's as insurance man: they both try to calculate the odds on exactly when someone is going to die, and figure out what kind of profit can be made.

Where *His Girl Friday* only implies the link between the various forms of corporate money-making, *The Big Clock* makes it explicit. Fearing's novel works if you imagine Janoth's corporation to be any large publishing empire, but it derives an added piquancy from the obvious resemblance between this multi-magazine organization and Time, Inc. Even the *Crimeways* notion is not purely Fearing's invention; it was *Time*, remember, that issued the check for "Two Murders: $35.00" to Weegee.

*Time* is a fascinating name for a weekly magazine, when you come to think of it: nothing could sound more solid and enduring, and yet timeliness of the sort it practices is almost by definition evanescence. Like journalists working under deadline, the investigative squad seeking Stroud's identity are working against the clock—a clock that can be stopped only by the big machine itself, when it swallows its own tail (Janoth's empire is eventually acquired by another corporation) and decides that the search is yesterday's news. With an irony that fits not only the novel itself but the whole murder-story genre, Stroud's unexpected salvation comes from the impersonal whims of the very machine he's been fighting and fleeing. "Its arms and levers and steel springs were wound up and poised in search of some other person in the same blind, impersonal way it had been reaching for me on the night before," Stroud tells us at the end of the novel. "And it had missed me, somehow. That time. But I had no doubt it would get around to me again."

The threat, the fear, is never really over in these murder stories, and the best ones acknowledge that fact. Even murder mysteries, with their cartoon-like victims, raise anxieties that their neat solutions can't entirely quell. Before Hollywood sequels even existed to be exploited, good murder stories left their endings open, with a veiled threat of fear's return. This tradition is as old as Mary Shelley's *Frankenstein* (where the monster disappears into the distance, lost to our sight and only presumably dead), and as new as *The Silence of the Lambs* (where the last scene is of Hannibal Lecter marching off to make a meal of his psychiatrist). It accounts, in part, for the false consolation we feel at the end of *Crime and Punishment:* it's not just that Sonia and God are insufficiently good to redeem and comfort Raskolnikov, but that *nothing* seems powerful enough to banish the terrible anxieties of the preceding five hundred pages. What Hitchcock tells us explicitly at the end of *North by Northwest*—that the doomed lovers dangling over Mount Rushmore can be saved only by a directorial sleight of hand, a jumpcut to a train's sleeping berth—is implied in most good murder stories. The big clock keeps ticking even after the official action ends, and the *memento mori* of a murder, once invoked, cannot be so easily returned to oblivion.

True-life murder stories have the same open-endedness as fictional ones, only more so. Look, for instance, at the battling epilogues in Joe McGinniss's *Fatal Vision* and Janet Malcolm's *The Journalist and the Murderer,* each designed to counter the charges raised by the other. Had they words enough and time, the two murder chroniclers could continue attacking each other anew in each fresh edition. Even working on his own, McGinniss was unable to close the book on this case: the 1989 paperback of *Fatal Vision* contains both a 1985 afterword and a 1989 (post-Malcolm) epilogue. Ann Rule's *The Stranger Beside Me* follows the same pattern, with a first afterword composed six years after the book's initial 1980 publication, and a further update (bravely, or perhaps foolishly, titled "The Last Chapter") appended in 1989. Rule at least acknowledges the problem, pointing out in her 1986 afterword: "In my naiveté in 1980, I ended *The Stranger Beside Me* by suggesting that the Ted Bundy story was at last over. It was not. I vastly underestimated Ted's ability to regenerate in both spirit and body, to pit his will and mind continually against the justice system. Nor was I able to extricate Ted from my mind simply by putting him and my feelings about him on paper." It's the last sentence that conveys the real story. Even after his execution, Ted is somehow capable of "regenerating" in the minds of his author, her readers, and the public at large. These changelings never die.[*]

On a more mundane level, the series of epilogues can be attributed simply to the glacial pace of the American criminal justice system. Murder authors can't finish their books because a conviction isn't the end of the story; the appeal process can take years, even decades. Mailer's book is in some ways an exception: Gary Gilmore, who rejected his chance to appeal, got his execution over in time for the initial publication date. Yet even in that instance the story didn't die with Gary. It revived itself first in the movie of the book, which both Gilmore and Mailer foresaw, and subsequently in Mikal Gilmore's recently published memoir of his brother, which may bring about, in turn, its own additional movie. Until it reaches the Supreme Court, and sometimes not even then, no legal version of a murder story can be said to have reached its conclusion. This is why the end of my story about *KQED v. Vasquez* can only be open-ended, at best.

On June 7, 1991, Judge Schnacke delivered his verdict in the case. During the hearing, which started shortly before noon in the Federal Courthouse in San Francisco, Howard

---

[*]In Bundy's case, this trend is made explicit in a novel published in the fall of 1992 by Pocket Books, a mass-market paperback house. *The Stranger Returns*, written by Michael R. Perry, is described in the publicity materials as "The Terrifying Novel of Serial Killer Ted Bundy and his Second Rampage of Death." His electrocution in 1989 is dismissed with the phrase, "Now Bundy has the perfect alibi."

Brodie sat in the press box, sketching the judge as he spoke. The trial had long since become a media event, and the courtroom was filled with representatives from newspapers, radio, and television (though without their cameras and tape recorders, their "tools of the trade," which appeared only later, in the press room, at KQED's post-trial press conference). The judge began the hearing by announcing that he had been exhaustively briefed by both sides already, but that he would hear oral arguments if they insisted. William Bennett Turner, who had prepared a closing argument on KQED's behalf, offered Judge Schnacke the choice of listening to it or not; the judge said he'd rather not.

He then proceeded to rule, briefly, on what he termed the two "moot" issues — that is, the exclusion of all press from the execution chamber and the prohibition on pencil and paper. Schnacke labeled these moot because he felt the warden hadn't really intended to enforce those restrictions; the state hadn't even tried to justify them legally during the trial. They were meant, Schnacke believed, as mere irritants in response to the lawsuit. Nonetheless, he bothered to rule against them. "I can see no valid reason presented why the long and traditional practice of admitting the press shouldn't be continued," the judge said. "Whether the press has an actual *right* may be questionable ... but it would be irrational, unreasonable, and capricious to bar the press at this point." On that basic First Amendment issue, therefore, KQED could be said to have won its case.

On the rest of the points, however — the points that had caused the plaintiff to bring the suit in the first place — the television station was not so successful. Schnacke ruled in favor of the existing method of selecting press witnesses, remarking that "the method used by the state appears to be a perfectly sensible one," and adding that "a rational attempt has been made to provide as broad an access as appropriate for all segments of the media." So in response to KQED's charge that the media selection process was unfair and susceptible to political maneuvering, the judge decided in favor of the defendant. More important—at least from the point of view of the assembled carrion birds—he also sided with the defense on the issue of cameras in the execution chamber. "The press has a right of access to whatever the public has a right to, but no *special* access," he asserted. "A great many reasons have been advanced for excluding cameras"—and Schnacke then went on to agree with all of them: the fear on the part of prison personnel of having their identities publicly revealed; the rigorous security arrangements that needed to be left entirely up to the professional judgment of the warden; the potentially inflammatory effect of execution photographs or videotapes on the prison population; even the risk that a heavy object such as a television camera might break the glass of the gas chamber. (This last assertion had, earlier in the trial, been derided by the judge himself as the Myth of the Suicidal Cameraman.) In short, the judge came down in favor of all the security arguments broached by the defense, and ignored all the KQED attempts to counter those arguments. Nonetheless, he concluded his oral verdict on June 7 by congratulating Bill Turner for doing "an excellent job" on KQED's behalf, making it clear he felt the case was destined for the Supreme Court. "I assume this is merely the first step on the way to achieving your goals," he said to the plaintiff's attorney. "Unfortunately, you stumbled a bit on your first step."

But the case was to go no further. KQED—evidently worn out by internal differences on its board, as well as tired of fielding the complaints of irate members—decided not to mount an appeal. The state, also, decided not to appeal the decision about mandatory press attendance with pencils and paper; apparently, as Judge Schnacke had surmised, these prohibitions had been instituted only for the purposes of the lawsuit. The case, however, has not died forever. Even as the judge was preparing to deliver his verdict, Bill Turner received a call from an attorney in Arizona who was thinking of bringing a similar suit there. Somewhere, in the next few months or years, someone else will file this kind of case again; and someday, I suspect, a television station *will* be permitted to broadcast an American execution. The only way of averting this prospect is to stop executing people; and that, I am afraid, will not happen soon. I write these words in the hope that the big clock will overtake and devour them—in the hope that the future will prove me wrong.

When I began writing this book, shortly after the end of the *KQED v. Vasquez* trial in 1991, Robert Alton Harris was still sitting on Death Row in San Quentin. He had been sitting there since 1979, when he was convicted of the 1978 murders of Michael Baker and John Mayeski, and in some ways it seemed as if he would be sitting there forever. No one had been executed in California since Aaron Mitchell's death in 1967. Outside of a few traditionally conservative states, no one had been executed in America since the Supreme Court ban on capital punishment was lifted in 1976. It was possible to feel that all those death-penalty laws in northern, western, and midwestern states were symbolic genuflections to the voting public's vengeful feelings, with no danger of leading to actual deaths. And this illusion (for it was indeed an illusion) freed me to write about the *KQED* case without focusing on the man whose execution would or would not be televised. Robert Alton Harris had become, for me, an abstraction, an invisible presence, a nonplayer in the courtroom drama I was watching.

This willful inattention to reality came to an abrupt end in the spring of 1992, when Harris became the first person in twenty-five years to be executed in California—the first condemned prisoner whose death, in my own state, made a memorable impression on me, though I was born here forty years ago and thus lived through the killings of Caryl Chessman,

Barbara Graham, Aaron Mitchell, and many others. Perhaps in part because I was writing this book, Harris's death had a profound effect on me. It filled me with anxiety and sadness, so that for days I was able to think of nothing else and for months was unable to write about it. Such tribulations are minor, of course, compared to what happened to Robert Alton Harris. But then, that is part of the terrible irony of the death penalty: we take personally something that is not actually happening to us, so that even the suffering—the one thing left to the condemned man, the one thing we have not deprived him of—becomes our own rather than, or as much as, his.

I was not the only person in California to react in this way. Newspapers reported widespread emotional distress among the population at large. "The fact is there's a new reality in California, and the ruminations and obsessions with it are an attempt to cope with it," said Dr. Samuel Gerson, a Berkeley-based psychologist quoted in the *San Francisco Chronicle* two days after the execution. "Some people will have nightmares," he continued, "—images they can't get out of their minds—and that imagery stays until the reality settles in." Another psychologist, Gerald Davidson, concurred: "People dwell on what it means for people to be put deliberately to death, and it frightens them. They keep reliving it in their minds."

These "images" of the execution afflicted us even though we didn't actually see it—a problem the newspapers self-righteously blamed on television. "Visions of the Harris execution stayed in the mind, fed by the kind of obsessive instant replay even the NFL no longer permits," the same *Chronicle* article asserted (resorting, as if unavoidably, to Judge Schnacke's favored sports analogy). The article then went on to quote a Los Angeles psychiatrist, Dr. Calvin Frederick, who complained about the death watch, "The media overworked it, particularly TV ... There was a panel discussion afterward about whether he jerked or twitched, whether he lowered his head or moved it to the right, whether his left finger moved. It got to be very gruesome in terms of the detail they kept going over and over and over." But these details didn't come to us only through television. The newspapers were filled with them in the days leading up to and following the execution. Even TV could only give us in abbreviated form what the newspapers gave us at length: the verbal reports of eyewitnesses. The images that plagued and frightened us were made up entirely of words.

What the coverage of Robert Alton Harris's death demonstrated, among other things, was what David Bruck intelligently and passionately pointed out on the *Nightline* episode about televising executions: that the actual moment of the killing, the "thirty seconds or sixty seconds or two minutes that the public would see" on TV, is not the whole death penalty. "The death penalty is the process of waiting for death for years and then measured by the calendar and then finally by the clock," said Bruck. "The death penalty is going to the families ..." Robert Alton Harris's death, and the way that death was reported to us in the papers, made it possible to understand what Bruck was talking about.

The media coverage began during the weeks preceding the execution, when Harris's representatives were working on two different fronts to save him. On the one hand, they made a clemency appeal to Governor Pete Wilson. (This course, however, offered little hope, since Wilson, who had been elected on a pro-death-penalty platform, had also been mayor of San Diego at the time the two teenagers, Baker and Mayeski, were murdered there. Given this background, he was possibly the least likely politician in California to grant clemency for Harris.) On the other hand, Harris's lawyers worked through the federal courts to stay Harris's execution—first on the grounds that new material applying to the case had arisen since his conviction, and second on the grounds that gas chamber executions constituted torture, or "cruel and unusual punishment."

The material that came out about Robert Harris's childhood in the course of the clemency appeal was hair-raising. Undisputed testimony showed that he had suffered repeated physical and psychological abuse from both his parents. Born to an alcoholic mother and a violent, drunken father, he may well have been the victim of Fetal Alcohol Syndrome: he did not learn to walk until he was nineteen months old, he had problems with physical coordination and with speech, and he did badly in school from the very beginning. Whatever congenital problems may have existed were certainly exacerbated by the treatment he received at home. All the Harris children were terrified of their father, who, when drunk, would load his guns, yell that they had thirty minutes to hide, and then go hunting for them. But Robert apparently suffered the most direct abuse. According to his older sister Barbara, Robert was about two when his father hit him so hard he knocked him out of his high chair. "Robbie was in convulsions, and there was blood coming out of his mouth, his nose, his ears," his sister reported. "Father started strangling Robbie with a table cloth, and he was choking him, and he said, 'Oh, lookie, Evelyn, your baby is bleeding to death.'"

Evelyn, the mother, was no saint either. After the family had broken up, Robert was working with his mother as a migrant laborer when one day she told him he wasn't working hard enough and he should "hit the road." (Harris himself described this in a 1989 interview.) When he was out on the highway, his few possessions packed in a bag, he sat down and waited for her to come and get him. But when Evelyn and her boyfriend appeared in the car, "my mom just beeped the horn and waved at me and kept going," Harris said. From that time on Robert Harris was on his own. He was eleven years old.

The effect of all this information was not to save Harris's life. "Mr. Harris' childhood was a living nightmare. He suffered monstrous child abuse. But . . . Harris was not deprived of the capacity to premeditate, to plan or to understand the consequences of his actions," Governor Wilson announced in his predictable denial of clemency. "As great as is my compassion for Robert Harris the child, I cannot excuse or forgive the choice made by Robert Harris the man." But what the child-abuse material *did* succeed in doing was to create a particular portrait of a previously unknown man scheduled for execution. It made us realize that a pathetic individual was about to be killed — it aroused, that is, our theatrical sympathies, our un-Brechtian empathies — and as a result hundreds of letters pleading for clemency (mine among them) were received by Wilson's office. As such material will, the childhood stories also set in motion a sentimental response to Harris's death, a tendency on the part of certain bystanders to view him as an innocent victim.

This tendency came through most clearly in Larry Bensky's report on the execution for the East Bay *Express,* Berkeley's left-wing weekly. Bensky admitted that "by all accounts, Robert Alton Harris was not innocent of the crimes for which he was killed," but this admission weighed for nothing in Bensky's calculus. "His innocence," Bensky went on, "if such it can be called, was of another, weightier kind — the innocence of a person condemned to his fate by a society which, hideously wounded in itself, had nothing to provide a hurting child in desperate need. The conclusion is inescapable: since his community could not sustain Robert Alton Harris, it chose to kill him instead."

Such rhetoric strikes me as both dangerous and offensive. As I've suggested already, the executed murderer doesn't have to be an *innocent* victim to be a victim; we needn't convert him into a wounded hero to feel shame and guilt at having murdered him. The obvious deniability of Bensky's assertions — especially his "inescapable" conclusion — makes it easier for the skeptical reader to react in favor of the death penalty. If we need only save those killers to whom we are willing to grant "innocence . . . of another, weightier kind," most Death Row inmates may have to be sacrificed. In making his case for Robert Alton Harris as a particularly pathetic victim, the *Express* reporter clumsily veers over the boundary between sentiment and sentimentality. "He learned to knit and to paint pictures of quiet, isolated places. He sculpted animals from toilet paper, and tried to keep a mouse as a death row pet," Bensky says of this pitiable figure, whom he finally describes as "a remorseful man with powerful thoughts and visions."

One objection to this is D. W. Winnicott's: that there is a grave danger in adopting "a sentimental attitude toward crime" because "in sentimentality there is repressed or unconscious hate" and "sooner or later the hate turns up." Another, related objection is that of Brecht, or of T. S. Eliot, who suggested that when we submit to such theatrical manipulation of our feelings, "we are either the victims of our own sentiment, or we are in the presence of a vicious rhetoric." Bensky's claims make us see exactly where the viciousness in such a rhetoric lies, for they imply that the execution of a banal, unappealing criminal (which, by most accounts, Robert Harris *was*) would not warrant our concern in the way that the death of a "man with powerful thoughts and visions" does.

Brecht's and Eliot's dramaturgical ideas apply to Robert Harris's death because, like all planned and publicly announced executions, his became a kind of theater. "Deathwatch resembles macabre media circus," trumpeted the *Oakland Tribune* on the day of the execution, in the headline to an article that began: "SAN QUENTIN. The tiny Main Street leading up to the gates of the prison here took on the eerie feel of an open-air carnival yesterday—with death as the main event." The antique theatricality of the reporter's language (which echoed almost exactly the coverage of executions in the 1930s and 1940s) perhaps helped to generate Robert

Harris's own view of his role as a kind of dying folk hero. At any rate, that's the impression he seemed to be trying to create in his carefully crafted last words, which, as reported to the media by Warden Daniel Vasquez, took the form of a two-line piece of doggerel: "You can be a king or a street sweeper, but everyone dances with the Grim Reaper." And Harris's remark in turn heightened the melodrama of the media coverage of his death. The first and most detailed newspaper report following the execution — Larry D. Hatfield's eyewitness account in that afternoon's *San Francisco Examiner* — began with these sentences:

> Everyone, said Robert Alton Harris, eventually has to dance with the Grim Reaper, but Harris had to offer himself twice before the Reaper would take him in its deadly arms.
>
> Harris' death in San Quentin's gas chamber was both banal and macabre; at times, the night seemed so theatrical as to be surreal; at others, too brutal to be real.

What Hatfield was referring to was the jarring sequence of stays and stay-liftings that resulted from the second prong of the attempt to save Harris's life: the legal efforts to prove that gas chamber execution constituted torture. On the Sunday before Harris's scheduled Tuesday-morning execution (as it happens, Easter Sunday), the *San Francisco Examiner*'s banner headline proclaimed, "Harris Gets Reprieve." The basis of this reprieve was U.S. District Court Judge Marilyn Patel's decision that, given the evidence presented by Harris's lawyers, a gas chamber execution *might* violate the Constitution's ban on cruel and unusual punishment. She had issued a stay forbidding all gas chamber executions for ten days, pending the presentation of additional evidence and a possible further stay. Her decision was issued on Saturday, April 18. If it remained in effect, it would spare Robert Alton Harris for forty days or more, since the existing warrant for his death required that he be executed sometime on Tuesday, April 21 (Warden Vasquez had, with characteristic assiduousness, named 12:01 A.M. as the scheduled time), and it would take at least forty days for the state to obtain a new warrant.

But Patel's stay was lifted on Monday by a three-judge panel of the U.S. District Court, and plans went forward for Harris's execution at just after midnight that night. In the course of that Monday, however, a judge from the U.S. Court of Appeals issued another stay that succeeded in delaying preparations for the execution—until, that is, the stay was overturned by the U.S. Supreme Court at nearly midnight. In the course of that Monday night and Tuesday morning, federal judges from the Court of Appeals in San Francisco proceeded to issue three further stays, and each time the stay was overturned immediately by the U.S. Supreme Court. Finally, the Supreme Court (possibly in violation of the Constitution) issued a ban on all further stays in the Robert Alton Harris case, and at 6:01 A.M. the execution was carried out. The series of on-again, off-again reports by the media meant that most of us went to bed on Monday night wondering if Robert Harris had been spared, and woke up Tuesday morning to read an enormous "HARRIS WINS DELAY" headline in our *San Francisco Chronicle*s. I was ridiculously relieved at seeing the paper; only later, when I spoke to friends who had turned on their TV sets early that morning, did I learn that Robert Alton Harris was already dead by the time I read about his temporary salvation.

For Harris himself, and for those who had assembled to watch him die, the roller-coaster effect was even more intense. Kevin Leary, who reported on the execution for the *Chronicle*, gave this eyewitness account:

> Harris was first strapped in Chair B, one of two in the chamber, at 3:49 A.M. Two minutes after the door had been closed, as the sound of liquid was heard pumping

into the vat below the chair, there was a single telephone ring. It was a call from the U.S. Court of Appeals Judge Harry Pregerson with the fourth stay of the night.

Harris didn't know about the call at the time, and as he sat there, he seemed embarrassed that he was unable to die. He gave a thumbs-up sign, looked under his chair, raised his eyebrows, then shrugged several times as if to say, "What's wrong?" and at one point said, "Let's pull it," referring to the lever that releases the cyanide.

But at 4:01 A.M., he was hauled from the chamber by four guards to wait out another brief reprieve. The observers were hustled out of the death room. Harris seemed perplexed as he was unstrapped from the chair and escorted back to the death-watch cell by the four guards.

Other witnesses reported that when Harris reappeared two hours later for his actual execution, he seemed broken: "He was a different Robert Harris than we saw a couple of hours ago," said a reporter from a San Diego radio station. As Leary pointed out, "It was almost as if Harris was forced to endure the ordeal of his execution twice." For the *San Francisco Chronicle* reporter—a lifelong backer of capital punishment—this meant that Harris's slow death was really a form of torture. "Whatever your feelings about the death penalty—and I don't oppose it, or didn't—the brutal, clumsy way Harris was snuffed was an obscene business," Leary concluded. Later he told a reporter from another paper, "I think this is the last execution I'm going to cover."

The particular conditions of Harris's death may have exaggerated the usual cruelty of an execution. "All that play with his emotions ... they killed him before he really died," said an unnamed citizen, in one of the on-the-street interviews conducted by the local CBS news the evening after the execution. Most of the people I spoke to, even those who thought they had supported the death penalty, seemed to agree. But no execution is completely routine, and people who witness executions—in particular, people like reporters—gradually start to see torture in all of them. This came through in an account by Gale Cook published in the *San Francisco Examiner* two days before Harris's death. In the course of his long journalistic career, Cook had witnessed five executions, and in this article he was describing what it had been like to be a "detached" observer covering the execution of Barbara Graham:

> Back in the office . . . as I began to write, I realized that I was emotionally involved after all. Graham had been subjected to deep humiliation and torment. This had nothing to do with her guilt or her innocence. Those inhumane, last-minute delays had made her die a thousand deaths instead of one.
>
> And so I became undetached in the lead sentence of the story.
>
> "Barbara Graham was tortured to death by the sovereign state of California yesterday," I wrote.
>
> That sentence lasted only through the first edition of the paper. Then a properly detached editor changed "tortured" to "put."

Cook concluded his article by commenting, "As for the death penalty, I voted for it in Proposition 7 in 1978. But now? Well, detachment isn't that easy anymore."

As David Bruck suggested, it's not just the moment itself that constitutes the death penalty—it's all those horrible moments leading up to the execution as well. With a scheduled death that has even an infinitesimal chance of being averted, the experience for both onlookers and participants is one of excruciating tension: tension between the certainty that the condemned man will die and the feeble, remote possibility that he may not. David Magris, a former Death Row inmate who now leads the Northern California Coalition Against the Death Penalty, described the tension well when he explained why he would not be joining in the demonstration outside the prison on execution night. "It's like a physically nauseous feeling," he said of the experience of waiting for the death. "It's like reading a book that you've already figured out. You feel emotionally whacked."

For both sides in the capital punishment dispute, there is a terrible desire for an end to the tension that surrounds an execution. "What's done is done," remarked an opponent of the death penalty who had stood vigil outside San Quentin until Harris was killed. "I think we've made our point." The families of Harris's victims, Michael Baker and John Mayeski, were more explicit about their anxiety to close the book. "We want to put this behind us," they kept saying as their argument against clemency, in favor of execution. "We need to have some kind of closure to end our grief."

"What is all this closure business?" argued a friend of mine who opposed the execution. "How is Harris's death going to make them any more able to live with their children's deaths?" But I understood exactly what they meant. The Bakers and Mayeskis wanted Robert Alton Harris to die; I wanted him to live. But either way the execution would let us off the hook. It would enable us to stop taunting ourselves with the question, "Will he die?" because the question would be answered, finally and completely, by his death. The victims' families would be deprived of their wish for him to die, and I would be deprived of my wish for him to live; we would both be freed from the desire that had held us suspended.

For one of the family members, the execution brought a different sort of closure as well. When he was strapped into the gas chamber chair for the last time, Robert Harris craned his neck to look around at the witnesses. He searched the roomful of observers and then met the eyes of Steve Baker, Michael's father, a San Diego police detective who had actively sought Harris's execution. Harris held Baker's gaze with his own, and then mouthed the words, "I'm sorry." Baker nodded stiffly in response, and Harris then looked away, as if satisfied. "My nod was acknowledgment but it was not forgiveness," Baker stated afterwards. But he also admitted that he had been surprised by Harris's silent apology. Whatever their motives, the two men had managed to acknowledge each other in a way that would not have been possible if television had been their intermediary.

The issues raised in *KQED v. Vasquez* resurfaced during the days preceding Harris's execution in two distinct ways. One had to do with which journalists got invited to witness the execution. A couple of weeks before the scheduled death date, a group of editors gathered together to protest the selection of media witnesses, a process that they felt shortchanged newspapers by dramatically reducing the number of slots available to them. The number of places available to media witnesses of all kinds, print as well as broadcast, had been reduced from forty at Mitchell's execution to seventeen at Harris's; of these, only seven would go to newspapers. In particular, the *San Francisco Examiner* felt that, as the major afternoon newspaper in the region of the execution, the one best placed to bring out an extensive report immediately following the death, it deserved to have an eyewitness at the proceedings. The *Examiner* brought a lawsuit in the Superior Court of Marin County (the county in which San Quentin is located), and Judge Beverly Savitt ruled in the newspaper's favor, thereby allowing Larry Hatfield to be present at the execution.

The other and perhaps more significant way in which *KQED* peripherally reappeared was in regard to the videotaping of the execution. When Judge Marilyn Patel initially ordered a stay of execution based on the cruel and unusual punishment grounds, she did so in response to declarations submitted by the ACLU that amounted to thousands of pages of statements, by over a hundred witnesses, about the cruel effects of gas chamber deaths. But the state, in opposing this stay, suggested that such eyewitness accounts were unreliable. (Note that this was the opposite argument to the one the state

mounted in *KQED v. Vasquez,* where it was the television station which argued that eyewitness accounts were insufficient,
and the state which felt they were perfectly adequate.) In
response, Judge Patel ordered that the execution of Robert
Alton Harris be videotaped—and it was. This videotape now
exists in the possession of the U.S. District Court, for use in
any future cases involving the constitutionality of a gas
chamber execution. Thus far the videotape has not been
released to the public in any way, though the media are
already rubbing their hands. "We are definitely interested in
getting hold of the tape," said Al Corral, managing editor of
Eyewitness News at KPIX-TV, the local affiliate of CBS.
"Obviously, it would be worth showing, although we would
still have to discuss whether we would do it."

But to date the media and the public depend on the eyewitness accounts of reporters who were actually present at the
execution. For the public's purposes—instilling in our minds
gruesome details we can't get rid of, stimulating nightmares
and depression, making us feel we actually saw Robert Alton
Harris look bewildered and confused and finally broken—the
accounts of reporters seem more than sufficient. These accounts manage to answer questions that a videotape might not
even be capable of asking, as the *Examiner*'s Larry Hatfield
points out in the conclusion to his eyewitness story about the
execution:

> Later, at a briefing for our colleagues who weren't
> there, we were asked if now, having seen it, did we think
> death in the gas chamber was cruel and unusual punish-
> ment.
>
> No one really had an answer for that—probably
> because most of us felt that the correct question would be
> did we think *execution* was a cruel and unusual punish-
> ment.
>
> Nobody asked that question that way and we didn't
> answer it.

But most of us, after the night's events, probably have an opinion.

An opinion is a singularly human thing: no machine can express one, no videotape camera can formulate one (though a videotape, in the proper hands, can *convey* one). It is in the nature of occasions like executions to demand the formulation of opinions. And it is also in their nature to refuse fixed, easy, solid, logically demonstrable answers. In this respect, execution stories partake of the characteristics of that larger category to which they belong — that is, murder stories.

At the conclusion of any murder story, there is an inevitable feeling of let-down. The end brings superficial answers and explanations, but all the underlying, anxiety-producing questions such as "Why do people murder each other?" and "Why are we interested when they do?" remain unanswerable. Murder stories leave us, in the end, back at their own beginnings. This circularity is why the murder story can be so satisfying, so "perfect"; it is also why, even at its best, it remains naggingly unsatisfying. All murder stories — including this one — stimulate the hunger they purport to feed, offering us a few morsels but leaving us, finally, with our own unappeasable ravenousness.

# Notes

Notes are keyed by page number.

## 1. *What Draws Us*

1    *The Republic of Plato*, trans. Allan Bloom (New York: Basic Books, 1968), Book X:605b-c, p. 289.

1    Marcia Pally's *Sense and Censorship: The Vanity of Bonfires* (published in 1991 by Americans for Constitutional Freedom and the Freedom to Read Foundation) summarizes the scientific evidence demonstrating that there is no proven causal link between pornography and sexual violence. Pally's study is cited in Ronald Dworkin, "The Coming Battles over Free Speech," *New York Review of Books*, June 11, 1992, p. 61.

9    Joel Black, *The Aesthetics of Murder: A Study in Romantic Literature and Contemporary Culture* (Baltimore: Johns Hopkins University Press, 1991), pp. 3, 5, 6.

10    T. S. Eliot, from an essay in *The Criterion* (1923), quoted in Christopher Ricks, *Keats and Embarrassment* (London: Oxford University Press, 1976), p. 96.

11    Eugene Taylor was not Crip's real name; I have changed it to protect his privacy.

14    Quoted from a story on Chris Noth in the "Arts and Leisure" section, *New York Times*, March 1, 1992.

17    Walter Benjamin, "The Storyteller," in *Illuminations* (London: Collins/Fontana Books, 1973), p. 101.

19    Richard Wright, *Native Son* (New York: Harper and Row, 1989), pp. 224–225.

19    Ann Rule, *The Stranger Beside Me* (New York: New American Library, 1989), pp. 16, 394.

21    Ibid., p. 59.

## 2. *KQED v. Daniel B. Vasquez*

*31-32*     Chief Justice Burger quoted in Plaintiff's Trial Brief, *KQED, Inc. v. Daniel B. Vasquez,* March 25, 1991, p. 13.

*33*     All quotations of statements made in court are either taken directly from the official transcript or drawn from my own notes. The same is true of all quotations from television programs or films. No further citations will be given for such quotations.

*33*     Plaintiff's Post-Trial Brief, June 7, 1991, footnote on p. 24.

*36*     Henry Fielding, *An Enquiry . . . ,* 1751, quoted in Thomas W. Laqueur, "Crowds, Carnival and the State in English Executions, 1604–1868," in *The First Modern Society: Essays in English History in Honour of Lawrence Stone,* ed. A. L. Beier, David Cannadine, and James M. Rosenheim (Cambridge: Cambridge University Press, 1989), p. 330.

*36-37*     House of Commons Member Knatchbull-Hugessen, 1868, quoted in Laqueur, p. 353. Laqueur's comment about the increasing bureaucratization of morality was made to me in conversation on May 7, 1991.

*37-38*     *The Presidential Papers of Norman Mailer* (New York: Bantam Books, 1964), p. 11.

*39*     Cameron Harper quoted by Charles L. Howe in "Arizona Killer Dies in Gas Chamber," *San Francisco Chronicle,* April 7, 1992.

*40*     Letter from William Bennett Turner, March 6, 1992.

*41*     Plaintiff's Trial Brief, p. 23.

*42*     Bill Nichols quoted in Carolyn Anderson and Thomas W. Benson, *Documentary Dilemmas: Frederick Wiseman's Titicut Follies* (Carbondale: Southern Illinois University Press, 1991), p. 38.

*43-44*     *Presidential Papers of Norman Mailer,* p. 11.

*44*     D. W. Winnicott, *Deprivation and Delinquency* (London: Tavistock Publications, 1984), pp. 202–203, 114.

## 3. *The Killer Inside Us*

*52*     Carol Clover's *Men, Women, and Chainsaws* (Princeton: Princeton University Press, 1992) supports my common-sense assertion. Clover extensively documents the ways in which male audience members identify with female characters in horror movies, showing that gender boundaries are more permeable than most film theorists have supposed.

53 Thomas Harris, *Red Dragon* (New York: Dell, 1990), p. 18.

54 "The Tell-Tale Heart," in *Great Short Works of Edgar Allan Poe* (New York: Harper and Row, 1970), p. 384.

54 *Red Dragon*, p. 152.

54 *Dr. Johnson on Shakespeare*, ed. W. K. Wimsatt (Harmondsworth: Penguin Books, 1969), p. 126.

54 *The Angolite*, September/October 1990, p. 30.

55 Marshall McLuhan, *The Gutenberg Galaxy* (Toronto: University of Toronto Press, 1966), pp. 15–16.

55-56 Edgar Allan Poe's letter to Thomas W. White, quoted in Lloyd Rose's essay on Poe in *The New Yorker*, April 27, 1992, p. 102.

56 "The Murders in the Rue Morgue," in *Great Short Works of Edgar Allan Poe*, p. 274.

56-57 "The Purloined Letter," in *Great Short Works of Edgar Allan Poe*, pp. 441–442.

57 "The Murders in the Rue Morgue," p. 303.

57 "The Tell-Tale Heart," p. 384.

57-58 "The Black Cat," in *Great Short Works of Edgar Allan Poe*, p. 390.

58-59 "The Murders in the Rue Morgue," pp. 277, 278, 283, 298. For alerting me to the significance of severed heads in this story, I am very grateful to John T. Irwin for his essay "A Clew to a Clue: Locked Rooms and Labyrinths in Poe and Borges," *Raritan* 10, no. 4, Spring 1991, pp. 40–57.

59 "The Murders in the Rue Morgue," p. 313.

59 Bernard Williams, *Ethics and the Limits of Philosophy* (Cambridge: Harvard University Press, 1985), p. 14.

62-64 Paul Bowles, *Let It Come Down* (Santa Barbara: Black Sparrow Press, 1980), pp. 8, 269, 281, 283, 284.

64 "The Black Cat," p. 398.

65n Letter from Paul Bowles, January 12, 1984.

66-67 Patricia Highsmith, *The Mysterious Mr. Ripley: The Talented Mr. Ripley, Ripley Under Ground, Ripley's Game* (London: Penguin Books, 1985), pp. 15, 21, 63, 144, 21.

69 Jim Thompson, *The Killer Inside Me* (New York: Vintage Books, 1991), pp. 185, 160–161.

70-71 Joan Didion, "The White Album," in *The White Album* (New York: Simon and Schuster, 1979), pp. 42, 18, 44–45.

72   *Cronenberg on Cronenberg,* ed. Chris Rodley (London: Faber and Faber, 1992), pp. 86–87.

75-77   *The Killer Inside Me,* pp. 4–5, 160, 92, 179–180.

77-78   *The Stranger Beside Me,* pp. 145, 395.

78-79   Joe McGinniss, *Fatal Vision* (New York: Signet, 1989), pp. 654–655.

80-82   Fyodor Dostoyevsky, *Crime and Punishment,* trans. David Magarshack (Harmondsworth: Penguin Books, 1980), pp. 19, 30, 81, 92, 177.

82-83   Primo Levi, *The Drowned and the Saved,* trans. Raymond Rosenthal (New York: Summit Books, 1988), pp. 48–49.

84   *Crime and Punishment,* p. 90.

84-85   Janet Malcolm, *The Journalist and the Murderer* (New York: Vintage, 1990), pp. 43–44.

89   *Crime and Punishment,* pp. 156–157.

91   *Crime and Punishment,* p. 423.

92   *The Killer Inside Me,* p. 154.

## 4. The Sleaze Factor

95   Anthony Lewis, "'Their Brutal Mirth,'" *New York Times,* May 20, 1991.

95   My information about the *National Police Gazette* comes mainly from Elliott T. Gorn's article "The Wicked World: The *National Police Gazette* and Gilded Age America," published in *Crime Story (Media Studies Journal* 6, no. 1, Winter 1992), pp. 3, 5, 6.

96   Charles Dickens, *Our Mutual Friend* (Harmondsworth: Penguin Books, 1971), p. 246.

96   "The Murders in the Rue Morgue," pp. 282, 291.

96-97   *Crime and Punishment,* p. 180.

100-101   *The Journalist and the Murderer,* pp. 17, 110–111.

102   Margaret Mead, *New Lives for Old* (New York: William Morrow, 1975), p. 343.

108   *Fatal Vision,* pp. 682, 645, 684.

109-110   *The Journalist and the Murderer,* pp. 85, 8, 9, 159–160.

110-111   Norman Mailer, *The Armies of the Night* (New York: Signet, 1968), p. 245.

112-115   Norman Mailer, *The Executioner's Song* (New York: Warner Books, 1979), pp. 820, 612, 628, 582, 546, 584, 587.

115      *The Journalist and the Murderer,* p. 34.
115-117  *Crime and Punishment,* pp. 473–474, 497.
117      *The Executioner's Song,* pp. 778–779.
117      *The Stranger Beside Me,* p. 225.
118-119  *The Executioner's Song,* pp. 645, 807.

## 5. The Trial

122-123  *The Executioner's Song,* pp. 835, 848.
125-126  Walter Goodman, "The Wheels of Justice, Turning Live on Cable," *New York Times,* July 3, 1991.
126      Thom Gunn, "Writing a Poem," in *The Occasions of Poetry* (London: Faber and Faber, 1982), p. 152.
126-127  Larry Rohter, "Solving a Dispute with Fists and Slime as the Nation Watches," *New York Times,* July 3, 1991.
127-128  *The Journalist and the Murderer,* p. 63.
128-131  Elizabeth Hardwick, *The Simple Truth* (London: Virago Press, 1987), pp. 226–227, 108–109, 214, 216, 226.
132-133  Franz Kafka, *The Trial,* trans. Willa and Edwin Muir (New York: Schocken Books, 1970), pp. 213, 214–215.
134      Robert Harbison, *The Built, the Unbuilt, and the Unbuildable* (Cambridge: MIT Press, 1991), p. 162.

## 6. Being There

136      Jerzy Kosinski, *Being There* (New York: Bantam Books, 1988), pp. 26, 5, 95.
138      Robert J. Donovan and Ray Scherer, *Unsilent Revolution: Television News and American Public Life* (New York: Cambridge University Press, 1992); quoted in a review of the book by Richard Wightman Fox in the *New York Times Book Review,* May 3, 1992, p. 7.
144      "The Murders in the Rue Morgue," p. 272.
144-145  Craig Seligman, "Table Talk," *The Threepenny Review* 12, no. 2, Summer 1991, p. 5.
146      *The Killer Inside Me,* p. 60.
146-147  Christopher Ricks, "Racine's *Phèdre:* Lowell's *Phaedra,*" *Arion,* Spring 1991, p. 49.
148      Exerpt from "Herbert White" from *In the Western Night* by Frank Bidart. Copyright © 1990 by Frank Bidart. Reprinted by permission of Farrar, Straus and Giroux,

Inc. Quotation from p. 128. Bidart told me the story about reading the poem aloud during a conversation in September 1991.

## 7. Rendering Reality

*167*  "Killer Dies Shouting," *San Francisco Examiner,* April 12, 1967, p. 1.

*168*  Dave Lamb, "Mitchell Yells, Dies in Gas Cell," *Oakland Tribune,* April 12, 1967, p. 1.

*168-169*  A. D. Hyman, "2 Killers Gassed; Chorus of Protest Arises at Ordeal," *San Francisco Examiner,* December 3, 1938, p. 1.

*170*  Richard Wightman Fox, "The Reality Box," *New York Times Book Review,* May 3, 1992, p. 7.

*173*  Accounts of Kemmler's execution quoted from Arthur Lubow, *The Reporter Who Would Be King* (New York: Scribner's, 1992), pp. 57–64.

*175-176*  Paul Theroux, *Chicago Loop* (New York: Random House, 1990), pp. 45–47, 180.

*177-180*  Weegee, *Naked City* (New York: Da Capo Press, 1985), pp. 78–87.

*182-185*  Ivan Turgenev, *Literary Reminiscences and Autobiographical Fragments,* trans. David Magarshack (New York: Farrar, Straus and Giroux, 1958), pp. 244–270.

*185-186*  Jonathan Eig quoted in *The Angolite,* September/October 1990, p. 42.

*187*  Lord Byron's letter quoted in Leonard Michaels, *I Would Have Saved Them If I Could* (New York: Farrar, Straus and Giroux, 1982), pp. 133–134.

## 8. Enter a Murderer

*188-189*  Aristotle, "On the Art of Poetry," in *Classical Literary Criticism,* trans. T. S. Dorsch (Harmondsworth: Penguin Books, 1974), pp. 38–39, 39–40, 50, 39, 49.

*189*  T. S. Eliot, "'Rhetoric' and Poetic Drama," in *The Sacred Wood* (London: Methuen, 1972), pp. 81, 83.

*189*  Erving Goffman, *The Presentation of Self in Everyday Life* (New York: Anchor/Doubleday, 1959), p. xi.

*189-190*  T. S. Eliot, "The Possibility of a Poetic Drama," in *The Sacred Wood*, p. 68.

*190-191*  *The Simple Truth*, p. 215.

*191*  *The Journalist and the Murderer*, pp. 65–66.

*191-192*  *The Executioner's Song*, pp. 912, 656, 658.

*192*  *The Stranger Beside Me*, pp. 407, 448.

*193*  "Two Prison Pals Get Last Wish," *San Francisco News*, August 29, 1941, p. 1.

*196*  Stanley Cavell, "The Avoidance of Love," in *Must We Mean What We Say?* (Cambridge: Cambridge University Press, 1976), pp. 327–328.

*197*  Bertolt Brecht, *The Messingkauf Dialogues*, trans. John Willett (London: Eyre Methuen, 1974), p. 57.

*197*  "'Rhetoric' and Poetic Drama," p. 82.

*197-198*  *The Messingkauf Dialogues*, pp. 11–12.

*199-201*  William Shakespeare, *Macbeth* (New York: Signet, 1987), I.iii.53–54, I.iii.141–142, V.v.24–26, IV.iii.125–131, IV.iii.211–217, IV.iii.230–233.

*201*  Antonin Artaud, *The Theater and Its Double*, trans. Mary Caroline Richards (New York: Grove Press, 1958), pp. 142–143.

*202*  "'Rhetoric' and Poetic Drama," p. 81.

*203-204*  *The Presentation of Self in Everyday Life*, pp. 211, 97–98, 232, 233.

*205*  Bill Nichols quoted in Anderson and Benson, *Documentary Dilemmas*, p. 38.

*207-208*  *The Theater and Its Double*, pp. 84, 76, 79.

*209*  *The Executioner's Song*, p. 435.

*211*  *Crime and Punishment*, p. 422.

## 9. The Changeling

*213-214*  *The Theater and Its Double*, pp. 25, 76, 77.

*214*  Susan Sontag, *On Photography* (New York: Farrar, Straus and Giroux, 1977), p. 70.

*215-216*  Thomas Middleton and William Rowley, *The Changeling*, in *Five Plays by Thomas Middleton* (London: Penguin Books, 1988), pp. 421, 417.

*217-221*  R. G. Vliet, *Scorpio Rising* (New York: Penguin Books, 1986), pp. 53, 199, 3, 24–25, 50, 22, 191, 169.

222-223   *The Stranger Beside Me*, p. 199.
223-224   Jean Stafford, *A Mother in History* (New York: Pharos Books, 1992), pp. 21, 29.
224-225   William Hazlitt, "On Cant and Hypocrisy," in *Sketches and Essays* (London: George Bell and Sons, 1882), p. 27.
226-227   *A Mother in History*, pp. 9, 30, 77, 58, 59, 49–50.
    228   Mikal Gilmore, "Family Album," *Granta* 37, Autumn 1991, p. 12.
229-230   *The Executioner's Song*, p. 954.
230-231   *The Journalist and the Murderer*, pp. 106, 132, 143–144.

## 10. The Big Clock

    235   Stendhal, *The Red and the Black*, trans. Charles Tergie (Garden City: Dolphin Books, n.d.), p. 459.
239-241   Kenneth Fearing, *The Big Clock*, reissued under the title *No Way Out* (New York: Perennial Library, 1987), pp. 98, 158, 114, 153, 85–86.
    241   *The Executioner's Song*, p. 875.
    243   *The Big Clock*, p. 174.
    245   *The Stranger Beside Me*, p. 414.
249-250   Gerson, Davidson, and Frederick quoted in Jerry Carroll and Alice Kahn, "The Public's Collective Death Watch," *San Francisco Chronicle*, April 23, 1992, D3.
    251   Kevin Leary, "Final Harris Plea—Brain Damage," *San Francisco Chronicle*, April 17, 1992, pp. A1, A19.
252-253   Larry Bensky, "The Killing Fields," *Express*, April 24, 1992, pp. 6–8.
    253   *Oakland Tribune*, April 21, 1992, p. 1.
    254   Larry Hatfield, "Witness' Report: Banal and Macabre," *San Francisco Examiner*, April 21, 1992, pp. A1, A8.
255-256   Kevin Leary, "I Didn't Know It Would Be That Ugly," *San Francisco Chronicle*, April 22, 1992, pp. A1, A8.
    257   Gale Cook, "Real Life Judgment Day: A Memoir," *San Francisco Examiner*, April 19, 1992, pp. B1, B3.
257-258   Magris quoted in Ken Hoover, "Death Penalty Opponents Back in Spotlight," *San Francisco Chronicle*, April 14, 1992.
    260   Corral quoted in William Carlsen and Harriet Chiang, "Harris Death Video Could Be Made Public," *San Francisco Chronicle*, April 23, 1992.
260-261   Hatfield, p. A8.